This innovative social history looks in detail at how the summer solstice celebrations at Stonehenge have brought together different aspects of British counter-culture to make the monument a 'living temple' and an icon of alternative Britain. The history of the celebrants and counter-cultural leaders is interwoven with the viewpoints of the land-owners, custodians and archaeologists who have generally attempted to impose order on the shifting patterns of these modern-day mythologies.

The story of the Stonehenge summer solstice celebrations begins with the Druid revival of the 18th century and the earliest public gatherings of the 19th and early 20th centuries. In the social upheavals of the 1960s and early 70s, these trailblazers were superseded by the Stonehenge Free Festival. This evolved from a small gathering to an anarchic free state the size of a small city, before its brutal suppression at the Battle of the Beanfield in 1985.

In the aftermath of the Beanfield, the author examines how the political and spiritual aspirations of the free festivals evolved into both the rave scene and the road protest movement, and how the prevailing trends in the counter-culture provided a fertile breeding ground for the development of new Druid groups, the growth of paganism in general, and the adoption of other sacred sites, in particular Stonehenge's gargantuan neighbour at Avebury.

The account is brought up to date with the reopening of Stonehenge on the summer solstice in 2000, the unprecedented crowds drawn by the new access arrangements, and the latest source of conflict, centred on a bitterly-contested road improvement scheme.

Andy Worthington is a historian, who specialises in looking at how people in the modern world relate to ancient sacred sites and the wider landscape, particularly through paganism and political dissent. He has written for several magazines in the UK, and has lectured in Britain and Malta. He lives in south London with his wife Dot and their son Tyler. This is his first book.

Reviews of *Stonehenge: Celebration and Subversion*

'This is a fine book in every way, well written, carefully researched and with a remarkable story to tell. It is about the great change in outlook that by-passed conventional politics and directed minds towards idealism and personal transcendence. This phenomenon has rarely been approached by sociologists: their training has not equipped them for it. Worthington's book fills the gap and provides a unique record.'
John Michell, *Fortean Times*

'*Stonehenge: Celebration and Subversion* contains an extraordinary story. Anyone who imagines Stonehenge to be nothing but an old fossil should read this and worry... [This is] the most complete, well-illustrated analysis of Stonehenge's mysterious world of Druids, travellers, pagans and partygoers.'
Mike Pitts, *History Today*

'Andy Worthington has written what is likely to remain the definitive work on the subject, simply because of the depth of coverage and range of viewpoints that it incorporates. If it is impossible to write most political history in such a way that it will achieve universal acceptance, then to write 'contemporary' history about controversial events involving colourful and clashing personalities requires an exceptionally high degree of courage and dedication, and Andy has provided it.'
Ronald Hutton, author of *The Triumph of the Moon*

'The strange events that swirled around Stonehenge in the last couple of decades – the Festival, the Convoy, the annual summer solstice ritual of confrontation between forces of order and disorder – were so bizarre there needs to be a record of them. In his wonderful and often funny book, Andy Worthington tells this, the oddest tale ever told about the most famous ancient place of them all.'
Christopher Chippindale, author of *Stonehenge Complete*

STONEHENGE

Celebration and Subversion

Andy Worthington

STONEHENGE
Celebration and Subversion

Andy Worthington

Front cover photograph: Stonehenge, summer solstice 2001.
Copyright Stuart Henderson.
Background photograph: Stonehenge, VE Day Celebrations 1995.
Copyright Adrian Arbib.

ISBN 1 872883 76 1

Reprinted with minor corrections 2005

Alternative Albion
An imprint of Heart of Albion Press
113 High Street, Avebury
Marlborough, Wiltshire, SN8 1RF

albion@indigogroup.co.uk

Visit our Web site: www.hoap.co.uk

Printed in England by Booksprint

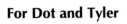

For Dot and Tyler

Contents

Acknowledgements

The creation of this book would not have been possible without the encouragement of two people in particular: Neil Mortimer, of the late, lamented *3rd Stone*, who repeatedly let me write articles, news and book reviews, and Bob Trubshaw, my editor and publisher at Heart of Albion Press, who has been unstinting in his support for the project since accepting the book proposal in autumn 2002.

Heartfelt thanks are also due to my wife Dot and my son Tyler, who have put up with the taxing combination of geographical proximity and mental distraction that tends to afflict those closest to the writing process, and to whom this book is happily dedicated.

In the introduction, I briefly mention several writers whose research and experience provides the bedrock of knowledge about the social history of Stonehenge: Chris Chippindale, Leslie Grinsell, Ronald Hutton, Arthur Pendragon, C.J. Stone and Adam Stout. I would like to thank Chris for accommodating me so cordially in Cambridge, where he furnished me with photos, plied me with red wine and busily engaged in globe-scuttling discussions that ranged freely from the essential unknowability of the Neolithic mind to the burning issues of the conservation of ancient monuments in the present day; Adam for so readily sending me a copy of his excellent thesis 'What's Real, and What is Not'; and Arthur for being so resolutely himself, particularly in the beer garden of the Red Lion in Avebury during the vernal equinox weekend in 2003, when his powers of persuasion were made manifest. As an untried Brother Knight, I hope that this history meets with his approval.

I also wish to thank other writers whose work has illuminated the many themes touched upon in the text: Barbara Bender, Jeremy Burchardt, Aubrey Burl, Paul Devereux, Peter Fowler, George McKay and John Michell. Particular thanks are due to Barbara, who provided me with encouragement and a photo of the 'Stonehenge Belongs to You and Me' exhibition; Paul, who promptly replied to several requests for information; and John, whose multi-faceted mysticism hovers over the whole book like a guardian angel.

As is the way with counter-cultural studies focusing on overlooked or maligned aspects of modern culture, much of the research that has led to the creation of this book took place outside academia and mainstream publishing. The Great White Shark has been a source of constant aid and inspiration, not only presiding over the Festival Zone website, the foremost online resource for information about the festival and free festival scene from the 1960s to the 1980s, but also putting me in contact with many other people who have embraced the project, providing photos and reminiscences. Foremost among these is Roger Hutchinson, the designer of the posters for the Stonehenge Free Festival, who readily made available his archive of photos, posters, flyers and news-sheets of the free festivals of the 1970s.

Particular thanks are also due to Alan Lodge, for the opportunity to show so many photos from his unparalleled archive of the last twenty-five years – over 70,000 images of travellers, free festivals, free parties and protests – and for his astute commentary on the events of this time, both in correspondence and through his website, and to Neil Goodwin, with whom I spent an engrossing afternoon reflecting on the same period in modern history in the Vertigo arts centre in Leytonstone, overlooking the M11 Link Road and the site of Claremont Road. Neil kindly lent me a vast archive of photos, videos, interviews, and a copy of the police report on the Beanfield.

Writers whose campaigning spirit has also proved invaluable to this alternative version of history include Jim Carey (*Squall*), George Firsoff (TRC), Penny Rimbaud (Crass), Alex Rosenberger (*Festival Eye*), the many people who produced campaigning pamphlets in the 1980s and 1990s, including Sheila Craig, Bruce Garrard, Steve Hieronymous, and all those who have worked for the Stonehenge Campaign over the last eighteen years, in meetings, through the newsletter and most recently on the Internet, where a large archive of campaign newsletters and media reports is available.

For their feedback over the last year, I would like to thank Big Steve for the thumbs-up from Gibraltar, Celia and Richie for photos, posters, insight and reminiscences, Andy Hope of the Green Roadshow for his enthusiasm, Tim Malyon for suggestions and permission to reproduce a particularly poignant photo of the Beanfield, and Bev and Del Richardson for keeping alive the long-cherished spirit of 'love and laughter'. I also extend my appreciation to the many people I met through the Stonehenge Solstice Celebration meetings in 2002, among them Steve Bubble, Dice George, Andy Hemingway, Chris Riley, Brian Viziondanz and Willy X. Andy provided me with campaign leaflets and copies of *Festival Eye*, as well as a steady stream of encouragement and anecdotes, and I spent a happy afternoon with Chris in north London, looking at photos and Spiral Tribe posters and discussing the spiritual impulses of the festival scene and of political protestors.

Thank also to the many Druids and representatives of Druid Orders – in addition to Arthur Pendragon – who replied to requests for information: Philip Carr-Gomm for advice, encouragement and permission to reproduce photos; Kreb Dragonrider for his hand-written response from a peace pagoda in Milton Keynes, written as he made his way around the country walking for peace; Veronica Hammond for a phone call full of history and mystery; David Loxley for sending me a long and detailed history of the Ancient Druid Order; Hengist McStone for correspondence and clippings; Liz Murray of the Council of British Druid Orders for facilitating a number of contacts; Emma Restall Orr for the excellent database of articles relating to Stonehenge that she has compiled with Philip Shallcrass, and Tim Sebastian, who keeps inviting me to events that I find myself unable to attend. I would also like to thank Susanna Lafond for invigorating conversations on the 'phone and at the Pagan Federation Conference in November 2003.

Others who have contributed significantly to the development of the book are the photographer Adrian Arbib, who entertained me on several occasions in Oxford and who went out of his way to provide a significant portfolio of photos relating to Stonehenge and the road protest movement; Thalia Campbell of the Greenham

Common Peace Camp, who bombarded me with friendly emails and a package full of postcards from the peace protests; Pete Glastonbury, for all the photos and for an enthusiastic afternoon of anecdotes, astronomy and ancient landscapes; Christina Oakley, for lively conversations about Wicca and modern paganism; Ruth Underwood, daughter of the late Austin Underwood, Amesbury councillor, peace activist and campaigner for the 'lost' village of Imber on Salisbury Plain, who, with her mother Mary, gave me permission to reproduce photos from her father's wonderful archive; and Chris Woodford of Save Stonehenge, who stepped in at the last minute to help me with information about the current road proposals.

May I take this opportunity to thank all the friends with whom I have attended Stonehenge over the past twenty-one years, at festivals, on pilgrimages and at the new open solstices of the twenty-first century: Chris Fenton, Nick Fenton, Ben Graville, Hugo Heppell, Rupert Joy, Sarah Lovett, Tim Morriss, Neil Mortimer, Polly Nash (who also helped with the cover design), Nick Parsons and Dot Young.

And finally, thanks to all those not already mentioned above who provided photos, information and/or general encouragement and enthusiasm: Karin Attwood, Steve Austin, Jo Bradley, Andy Burnham, Shane Collins, Steve Cook, Malcolm Coe, Nick Day, Alan Dearling, Linda Eneix, J.J. Evendon, Polly Farquharson, Paul Gapper, Garry Gibbons, Jeremy Harte, Stuart Henderson, Jeza, Paul Misso, Mogg Morgan, Richard Neville, Andy Norfolk, Ian Oakley, Mark Pilkington, Gerald Ponting, Richard Rudgley, Lionel Sims, Theo Tigger and Weed.

Bob Trubshaw thanks Anne Tarver for preparing the map on page 252.

Contacts for photographers and other contributors

Adrian Arbib is a professional photographer specializing in human rights and the environment. He has documented the struggles of marginalised peoples around the world, and in the UK has covered many of the major political protests and alternative gatherings from the 1980s to the present day.
Website: www.arbib.org
Email: photo@arbib.org

Thalia Campbell and her husband Ian have produced a video, *Greenham: the making of a monument*, which relates the history of the Greenham Common Peace Camp and tells the story of the making of a commemorative statue that now stands in the foyer of Cardiff Town Hall.
Website: www.wfloe.fsnet.co.uk
To order the video email: greenhamsculpture@hotmail.com

J.J. Evendon is an enthusiastic pilot and aerial photographer of ancient sites. Many of his photos are on view in the online galleries at www.megalithic.co.uk
Email: jj@headtorches.com

Paul Gapper is a professional photographer whose work covers a range of topics including travel photography and world religions. His website, which includes a page on the summer solstice celebrations at Stonehenge in 2003, is: www.worldphotos.org
Email: gapper@tiscali.co.uk

Pete Glastonbury lives in Avebury and is a landscape photographer with a passion for Neolithic sites and astronomy. His panoramic CD-ROMs of the Avebury landscape are available online from www.megalithic.co.uk or from the Red Lion in Avebury.
Website: www.users.myisp.co.uk/~gtour
Email: gtour@ic24.net

Neil Goodwin is a documentary film-maker. With Gareth Morris, he co-directed *Operation Solstice*, a documentary on the Battle of the Beanfield, featuring previously unseen footage of police violence, which was described by the author C.J. Stone as 'a film which should be seen by everyone. It should be on the National Curriculum.' A video of the programme, which was originally broadcast on Channel 4 in 1991, is available from Housmans Bookshop, London, or online from Active Distribution or Culture Shop.
Websites: www.activedistribution.org or www.cultureshop.org
Neil Goodwin's email: neilgoodwinuk@hotmail.com

The Great White Shark is the genial overlord of the Festival Zone website, part of a colossal online resource, 'The Archive: UK Rock festivals 1960-75 & UK Free festivals 1965-1985.' Main menus at:
www.festival-zone.0catch.com/free-festivals-menu.html
users.bigpond.net.au/the-archive/
tinpan.fortunecity.com/ebony/546/index.html
Email: archive@bigpond.net.au

Stuart Henderson's photos of the summer solstice celebrations at Stonehenge in 2000 and 2001 are online at: www.spacehopper.org
Email: stu@spacehopper.org

Andy Hope and **Sally Howell** run the Green Roadshow. Powered by wind turbines and solar power, the Roadshow, with its own marquee and circus, keeps the spirit of the free festivals alive through a programme of environmentally-themed entertainment and exhibitions.
Website: www.greenroadshow.co.uk
Email: info@greenroadshow.co.uk

Roger Hutchinson works as a multi-media public artist. Signed copies of his original Stonehenge Free Festival poster, reproduced on A2 acid-free paper from the original artwork, can be ordered directly from Roger.
Email: rogerhutchinson@ntlworld.com
or write: 39 Hazel Street, Leicester, Leicestershire LE2 7JN for details.

Jeza is a professional musician. Website: www.jezaland.com
His extensive gallery of photos from the free festivals of the mid-1970s is online at:
myweb.tiscali.co.uk/jezaland/Festivals/index.htm
Email: mr_jeza@tiscali.co.uk

Alan Lodge is a professional photographer. Samples of his archive of photos from the late 1970s to the present day, as well as numerous articles on free festivals, travellers, free parties and political protest, can be found on his website, 'One Eye on the Road: Tash's Festival, Travellin' & Environmental Archives': www.tash.gn.apc.org
Email: tash@gn.apc.org

Mogg Morgan is a writer, the founder of the Oxford Golden Dawn Society and the proprietor of Mandrake Books in Oxford.
Website: www.mandrake.uk.net

Paul Misso is a professional photographer. His collection of slides of the Glastonbury festival in 1971 is online at: www.alternate-creations.com
Paul's website is: www.healing-spirit.com
Email: paulmisso@ntlworld.com

Gerald Ponting is a writer, publisher, lecturer, photographer and tourist guide.
Website: home.clara.net/gponting
Email: gponting@clara.net

Introduction

On the morning of 21 June 2003, over 30,000 people gathered at Stonehenge to watch the sun rise on the day of the summer solstice, a threshold between worlds and a still point on the central axis of the endless solar year, marking the brief triumph of the sun before it resumes its journey to death and rebirth in midwinter.

It was an extraordinary turnout, almost certainly more than had ever been seen at the temple on a single day in the whole of its history. All had been drawn here for some reason this night, to stand in a field, with no catering or entertainment provided, waiting for a significant summer sunrise to shine into the ruin of an ancient stone temple. It is the story of these people, and how they came to be at Stonehenge on so numinous an occasion, that is told in this book.

Essentially, this is a counter-cultural history of Stonehenge. It looks in detail at two groups of people who have made claims on the temple – for themselves or the wider public – that have often reflected, or even prefigured, counter-cultural changes in society as a whole, and that have done so much to make the monument a 'living temple' rather than a museum. Firstly, the white-robed Druids of the early twentieth century and their modern pagan successors, and secondly those who have long sought to celebrate the summer solstice at Stonehenge with a festival and a tribal gathering. The history of this sometimes riotous and sometimes risible assemblage of celebrants – whose rituals range from silent reverence to subversive irreverence – are shot through with the generally more sober stories of the land-owners, custodians and archaeologists who have attempted to impose order on the shifting patterns of these modern-day mythologies.

Parts of this story have been told before, and I am particularly indebted to Chris Chippindale, Leslie Grinsell and Adam Stout for their research into the early gatherings, to Ronald Hutton for his meticulous studies of modern paganism, and to numerous other writers and contributors – including the Great White Shark and his *Festival Zone* website, C.J. Stone and Arthur Pendragon – for aspects of the temple's recent history. A more detailed list can be found in the acknowledgements.

In a field dominated by archaeological interpretation and a constellation of alternative theories, this book concerns itself less with a search for the true meaning of Stonehenge than with an analysis of its meaning to those who see it as an object of fervent, and sometimes fanatical, devotion. My hope is to have captured something of the impulses – manifested as celebration and subversion – at the heart of the modern-day story of Stonehenge.

Andy Worthington, London, February 2004

Stonehenge from the Heel Stone: the best view of the temple available to the casual visitor today, from behind the fence beside the A344.
Copyright Andy Worthington.

Chapter One

Stonehenge and the summer solstice

The sarsen Stonehenge

All the stories of Stonehenge begin with the monument itself, which is a skilful and beguiling mixture of architecture and astronomy, unique in the archaeological record. Architecturally, the sarsen circle and horseshoe – the part of the monument's long history that most people recognise as Stonehenge – is a one-off marvel of design and engineering.

The sarsen Stonehenge was raised around 2300 BC, after seventy-five of the vast stones – the largest weighing fifty tons – had been dragged twenty miles from the downs around Avebury to the north. Painstakingly shaped by hand into regular pillars, using only the most rudimentary tools – round chunks of sarsen known as mauls, ranging from the size of an orange to the size of a football – thirty were set in a perfect stone circle a hundred feet across, held in place and augmented by the addition of a further circle of flat slabs, known as lintels, which were placed in a continuous ring on top of the uprights. Inside, the ten largest stones, rising in height from seventeen to twenty-one feet above the ground, were raised in pairs in the shape of a horseshoe, forty-five feet in length, whose open end faced the midsummer sunrise. Each of the horseshoe's pairs was also capped with a lintel, making the huge stone doorways known as 'trilithons' (from the Greek for 'three stones').

Everywhere in the sarsen Stonehenge, the attention to detail was astonishing. In a unique application of carpentry techniques to stone, the builders of Stonehenge secured the lintels to the uprights below them by means of mortices and tenons – holes hollowed out of the underside of each lintel fitting snugly over nodules left protruding from the top of each of the uprights. In addition, each lintel in the outer circle was secured to its neighbour by means of a joggle joint, a protruding semi-circle of stone that slotted into a similar-sized hole in its neighbour, the 'tongue and groove' of modern-day carpentry. Each lintel was curved to ensure that the whole ring carefully followed the line of the circle below, running in a perfect circle whose top hovered nearly seventeen feet above the ground. The combination of curves, tongue and groove joints and mortices and tenons ensured that all the fittings acted like ring-beams in a modern building, giving the entire monument a stability that only time, vandalism and the occasional shallow foundations of the standing stones themselves have been able to undermine.

One of the more extraordinary examples of the builders' attention to detail is the fact that, although the circle stands on a gentle slope of land, the stones were erected to compensate for it so that the ring of lintels above it is very nearly horizontal. David

Stonehenge from the Slaughter Stone.
Copyright Andy Worthington.

Souden, who wrote a history of Stonehenge for English Heritage in 1997, noted that 'This would be a great achievement for any building project in history', and the archaeologist Chris Chippindale commented admiringly that the entire inter-locking monument was 'within an inch or so of being precisely circular and completely level.' (Souden 1997: 88; Chippindale 1994: 19)

The solstice alignment at Stonehenge

Arguably, however, admiration would not have turned to devotion were it not for the astronomical alignment to the summer solstice sunrise and the winter solstice sunset, around which the monument was so carefully raised. Alignments to significant celestial events, such as the solstices and equinoxes and even the complex rising and setting positions of the moon's 18.61 year cycle, are not unique in the prehistoric monuments of Europe, but they are generally imprecise, as though symbolism was all that was required. In those that were evidently raised as great statements – be it of temporal power, calendrical certainty, the mystical union of earth and sky, or some other inscrutable purpose – Stonehenge is one of only a select few.

Seven architectural features, sculpted in stone and earth and spread over a distance of nearly half a mile, combined at Stonehenge to create a long, narrow, solar alignment of astonishing accuracy. At dawn on the summer solstice, the first rays of the numinous sunrise were channelled into the heart of the monument through a

An aerial view of Stonehenge from the east, showing the half-ruined temple and its components: the bank and ditch, the sarsens, the bluestones, the outlying stones and the Avenue. The end of the Avenue is visible, along with the fallen Slaughter Stone, at the bottom right of the photo, with the Heel Stone (not visible) just beyond. Copyright J.J. Evendon.

widened gap between two stones of the outer circle and through the opening to the central horseshoe of trilithons. Originally, the dawn light would then have struck the Altar Stone, a solitary stone, geologically distinct from the sarsens that surrounded it, which once stood before the horseshoe's tallest pair but which now lies prone beneath the fallen pillar of the central trilithon.

Funnelling the sunrise into the heart of the monument were two outlying stones and their partners. The first of these, the Heel Stone, a forty-ton hulk of unshaped sarsen, nearly sixteen feet in height, is still standing a hundred feet outside the entrance. The stone-hole of its partner, which stood just eight feet away, was discovered during emergency excavations in 1979. The realisation that the two stones may have been standing at the same time (something that the excavation was unable to prove) caused great excitement in the media and the world of archaeology as they would have straddled the solar alignment perfectly, echoing another pair of outlying stones, which performed a similar function nearer the temple. This pair is the Slaughter Stone, now fallen, and its lost partner, whose stone-hole was discovered during excavations in the 1920s. (Pitts 1981, 1982)

Two additional earthen features completed the long solstice alignment. One is an avenue of chalk-dug ditches and raised banks, which ran up to the entrance from a dip in the land 600 yards away, and the other is the main entrance to the bank and ditch that runs around the circle. Both still survive, although the avenue is severely depleted by centuries of agriculture, and the bank and ditch are often overlooked by visitors whose attention is drawn to the ruins of the sarsen temple instead.

In the generations after the sarsens were first raised, the temple was augmented by up to eighty smaller stones, the enigmatic bluestones from the Preseli Mountains in South Wales, which were brought to Stonehenge by one of two fiercely contested methods: human transportation or glacial action. (For a summary of the bluestone arguments, see Burl 2000a: 364–5; Castleden 1987: 102–6. The debate continued in Burl 2000b; Castleden 2000.)

Over the course of several hundred years, the bluestones – also shaped by hand – were arranged and rearranged in ovals, horseshoes and circles inside the larger building, architectural echoes that did nothing to enhance the aesthetic coherence of the temple, but that were presumably designed to reflect the power of those who decreed the changes. This may have been of prime importance to the chieftains and warriors of the time, who were buried with finely crafted ornaments of gold in huge barrow cemeteries that crowned the ridges around.

Midsummer revels

These are the bare bones of the fascination with Stonehenge, the 'ravaged colossus' described by the archaeologist Aubrey Burl, which 'rests like a cage of sand-scoured ribs on the shores of eternity, its flesh forever lost.' (Burl 2000a: 350) The flesh on these bones, which allows Burl's colossus to come alive, is the meaning that people have brought to this conjunction of ancient place and sacred time.

The celebration of the summer solstice – or its folk equivalent Midsummer – has a long and illustrious history in Europe. Celebrated by William Shakespeare in *A Midsummer Night's Dream*, which has done more to introduce generations of schoolchildren to Classical pagan themes than any other work in the English language, it continues to provide inspiration, even in today's largely secular world. For Midsummer 2003, *The Guardian* included an editorial comment – 'Well met by moonlight: Midsummer is the day for magic' – celebrating the day 'when topsy-turvydom should rule', and encouraging readers to 'Raise your glass to fantasy, moonshine and nightly revels. The real world starts soon enough again tomorrow.' (*The Guardian*, 21 June 2003)

We may not know what those who raised Stonehenge did with their conjunction of stone and sky, but we can recognise, in the echoes of rituals that were widespread in Europe until the nineteenth century, an associative chain that connects us to that time. The Anglo-Saxons may well have known the summer solstice as an auspicious time for sun rituals, similar to the one recorded in the fourth century AD, when the inhabitants of Aquitane, in south western France, 'celebrated a festival by rolling a flaming wheel downhill to a river', later reassembling the charred pieces in the temple of a sky god. (Hutton 1996: 311)

Although the date of the Aquitane festival was not noted, a similar event, involving the rolling of a wheel, was recorded in the Cotswolds in the fourteenth century, on

Midsummer Eve, 'the evening before the Christian Feast of St John the Baptist upon 24 June.' This was the folk version of the summer solstice – Midsummer, rather than the actual astronomical solstice – but it was to prove an enduring festival throughout Europe. The Midsummer wheel was widely recorded in nineteenth century collections of English folklore (and was last seen in Widdecombe in Devon in 1954), but the celebration of Midsummer was even more comprehensively marked by the lighting of festive fires, a tradition which also ran on until modern times. The historian Ronald Hutton noted that the Midsummer fires were first recorded in the thirteenth century in England and the twelfth century in France, adding that 'as appropriate sources before then are so sparse, there is no reason to doubt that the tradition was much older.' (Hutton 1996: 311–2)

The Saxons and Stonehenge

Whether this celebration of Midsummer – whose very name is Anglo-Saxon – ever took place at Stonehenge is something we may never know. The Saxons left no written record of Stonehenge, but it was clearly they who gave the monument the name by which it is still known today, derived from the words for 'hanging stones' – *stan* and *heng/hengen* – meaning that the uprights appeared to be suspended from the lintels above (or, more brutally, that they resembled a Dark Age gallows) or from the words for 'hinged stones' – *stan* and *hencg* – indicating that the observers who named the monument had scrutinised the exceptional methods of construction used by their Neolithic forbears.

On at least one occasion, the Saxons also used Stonehenge as a place of judgement. Sometime in the seventh century AD, when they were reinforcing an uneasy frontier rule – as well as an evidently uneasy transition to Christianity – a man was beheaded at Stonehenge and buried in a rough grave. It is tempting to think that he was no ordinary criminal and that the judgement on his life was made all the more profound by its execution at what was widely regarded as an ancient and terrible place, the work of gods or giants or people from a lost golden age. (Pitts 2001: 300–22)

Bronze Age and Iron Age Stonehenge

We know nothing about the monument during the 1,500 years before the Saxons arrived. Attempts have been made to link the temple with the people of the Iron Age, but at Stonehenge these farmers and warriors settled, for the most part, around the river to the east, and left few traces of their passing around the monument itself. Several commentators have specifically attempted to establish a connection between the temple and the original Druids, the fearsome high priests of the Britons at the time of the Roman invasion. This would explain the destruction of half the monument as an iconoclastic reprisal on the part of the conquerors, prior to the final massacre of the Druids on the Isle of Anglesey in AD 67, but there is no archaeological evidence. (Atkinson 1979: 85–6, 99–100; Michell 1983: 199–200; Walker in Cleal *et al* 1995: 338; Burl 2000: 374)

Neither is it particularly rewarding to look to Celtic-language sources for observations of the summer solstice. The most reputable primary sources are the *Tochmarc Emire*, one of the 'Ulster Cycle' of early medieval Irish tales, and the *Sanas*

Chormaic, an early medieval Irish glossary. Both of these were first recorded between the ninth and eleventh centuries AD and certainly reveal a cycle of seasonal festivals, but one that is based on the quarter days between the solstices and the equinoxes – the first days of February, May, August and November – rather than the solar festivals themselves. The names given to these festivals are Imbolc, 'when the ewes are milked at spring's beginning'; Beltane, the 'lucky fire' lit to protect cattle from disease; Lughnasa, the first fruits festival; and Samhain, the feast at the onset of winter, when the animals were brought in from the fields and those that could not be kept over the cold months were slaughtered. (Hutton 1996: 134, 218, 327, 361)

Maybe a meaning for Stonehenge endured throughout this long period. Or maybe it was sporadically forgotten, as tastes in ritual and religion changed, only to be revived when a new wave of immigrants recognised some significance. However, from the evidence of archaeology and history Stonehenge seems to have been abandoned after 1600 BC, when two circles of pits were dug outside the sarsen structure but never used. Its solar axis lay forgotten for over two thousand years.

The Normans and Stonehenge

When the temple was finally recorded in literature, in the twelfth century, Norman kings were on the throne, the country was officially Christian, and writers were including Stonehenge in lists of ancient wonders and rousing nationalist mythologies.

Around 1130, Henry of Huntingdon, a Lincoln archdeacon, compiled a history of England, in which Stonehenge was judged to be the Second Wonder of Britain, after the Peak Cavern in the Peak District, 'from which', as Aubrey Burl described it, 'swirling winds howled.' Huntingdon described the monument as follows: 'Stanenges, where stones of an amazing size are set up in the manner of doorways, so that one door seems to be set upon another. Nor can anyone guess by what means so many stones were raised so high, or why they were built there.' Around 1138, in a history of British Kings, a mythical, Arthurian history for the temple was concocted by Geoffrey of Monmouth, who suggested that the stones, initially raised by giants, had been magically transported from Ireland by Merlin, and were erected on Salisbury Plain as a cenotaph to British warriors who were treacherously slain by the Saxons.

Between them, these two writers started two lines of inquiry – the scientific and the mystical – that have not ceased to this day. Another 500 years were to pass, however, before two elements vital to the modern counter-cultural history of Stonehenge were introduced: the solstice alignment and the conjuring up of Druids.

All the counter-cultural mythologies that have arisen about Stonehenge – the legends of élite astronomer-priests, of tribal gatherings, and of congregations of earth-worshipping pagans – spring in some way from these roots, when people with curiosity, an eye for detail and active imaginations first began to wonder about the people who raised the temple, to investigate its purpose and, most crucially of all, to suggest that it could have a contemporary resonance.

Chapter Two

Antiquarians and the early solstice gatherings

Romans, Danes and Phoenicians

Despite the increasing fame of Stonehenge in the centuries following Henry of Huntingdon and Geoffrey of Monmouth, it was not until a firm neo-Classical framework for research and inspiration was established in the seventeenth century that more informed attempts were made to explain the monument and its provenance. Even then the plethora of theories was bewildering. In 1620, Inigo Jones, chief architect to King James I, made plans of the temple in which he transformed the unruly horseshoe of trilithons into a Classically-acceptable hexagon, as well as 'some few ingested Notes' proposing that the temple was raised by the Romans, which his assistant John Webb 'moulded off and cast into a Rude forme' as the first full-length book on Stonehenge in 1655, following Jones' death in 1652. In 1624, the historian Edmund Bolton opted for the native Britons at the time of the Roman occupation, deciding 'That Stonage was a worke of the Britanns, the rudenesse it selfe perswades', and concluding that the monument was the tomb of Boudicca. In 1663, Walter Charleton, physician to King Charles II, published *Chorea Gigantum*, which saw the temple 'Restored to the Danes' and

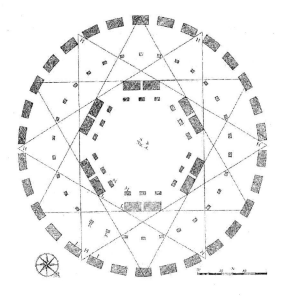

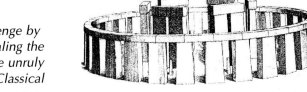

A plan of Stonehenge by Inigo Jones, revealing the transformation of the unruly horseshoe into a Classical hexagon.

included the fanciful proposal that the Danish chieftains stood on top of the trilithons to elect their kings, and in 1676 the self-styled visionary Aylett Sammes even went so far as to ascribe the monument to the Phoenicians. (Jones and Webb 1655; Bolton 1624: 181–2; Charleton 1663; Sammes 1676)

Only a few writers dared to glance into the abyss of pre-Roman British history for clues to the temple's origins. In a criticism of Charleton's theories, one Dr Glisson somehow guessed that it was 'at least 3 or 4 thousand years old', and in 1666 the anonymous author of *A Fool's Bolt soon shott at Stonage* suggested that it was 'an old British triumphal tropicall temple', raised before the first Celts arrived in Britain – although the author somewhat diminished the quality of this insight by proposing that the monument was raised by a tribe of giants from Somerset instead. (Wright 1966: vol.1, lxiii; Legg 1986: 18)

John Aubrey

In the end, it was John Aubrey, a Wiltshire native, who had what Aubrey Burl referred to as 'the imagination and courage to perceive that the stone circles of the British Isles were pre-Roman.' After recognizing that 'all these Monuments are of the same fashion, and antique rudenesse', Aubrey deduced that they had to be prehistoric because they were found in areas including Ireland, Scotland, Wales and parts of England that had nothing in common in either the Roman period or the Dark Ages, and suggested that they were raised by the Druids, the fearsome high priests of the Celts. (Burl 1979: 42; Aubrey 1980a)

Aubrey is known above all as the author of *Brief Lives*, a collection of sharp, witty vignettes of his contemporaries, but he was also a scholar of wide-ranging enthusiasms, and above all a pioneering antiquarian and fieldworker whose eye for the unseen and unknown monuments in the landscape was unparalleled. It was Aubrey who accidentally rediscovered the extraordinary stone circles of Avebury on a hunting trip in 1649, seeing patterns in the megalithic landscape of Stonehenge's near-neighbour that previous chroniclers had regarded as little more than a few 'huge stones' that were 'so rude that they seem rather natural than artificial', and at Stonehenge he discovered a ring of small holes around the perimeter of the monument that are named after him. John Britton, who published a biography of Aubrey in 1845, declared, 'He may be regarded as essentially an *Archaeologist*, and the first person in this country who fairly deserves the name.' It is an opinion that remains pertinent to this day. Aubrey Burl, who has dedicated both of his major surveys of stone circles to his memory, has called him 'without question, the first great English fieldworker and archaeologist.' (Camden 1610; Britton 1845: 3–4; Burl 1976, 2000, 1979: 42)

Sadly, in light of later discoveries that the stone circles date from the Neolithic and the Bronze Age, it has become something of a commonplace amongst archaeologists and historians to lament Aubrey's focus on the Druids. In a study of Aubrey in the 1970s, the historian Michael Hunter declared that 'the effect on English antiquarianism, which he originated, was immense and not entirely salutary', and the archaeologist Stuart Piggott wrote that his 'inferences... were to have unexpectedly far-reaching repercussions on the creation of Druids-as-wished-for which have lasted until today.' (Hunter 1975: 205; Piggott 1975: 130)

We must remember, however, that in the seventeenth century his insight was not only a considerable leap of faith, but was also, at the time, a perfectly understandable conclusion. All that was known of the pre-Roman period was what the Romans and other classical authors had described. No less a source than Julius Caesar had observed, at the time of the first Roman invasion of Britain in 55 BC, that the Druids were 'responsible for all sacrifices, public and private, and they decide all questions of ritual.' (Warner 1960: Book VI, 2, 123)

Although Aubrey first formulated his ideas about stone circles in the 1660s, his plans to publish a full-length book never materialised. When he died in poverty in 1697 the only manifestation of his vision readily available to the public was a passage dealing with stone circles in the updated edition of *Britannia*, William Camden's popular guide to the monuments of Britain. Behind the scenes, however, his manuscripts became essential reading for antiquarians and budding archaeologists. Finally, in 1723, one of his successors rediscovered what was to become a crucial component of the modern-day solstice celebrations at Stonehenge – the temple's long-lost astronomical significance.

William Stukeley

William Stukeley, a doctor from Lincolnshire, was another extraordinary antiquarian and fieldworker. From 1719 to 1724, he visited Avebury on several occasions, witnessing the appalling destruction of the stones over that period, when they were dragged off and broken up in large numbers. His fieldwork was so meticulous that Aubrey Burl has commented that, 'Had it not been for Stukeley, it would be impossible today to write with any accuracy about Avebury.' (Burl 1979: 47)

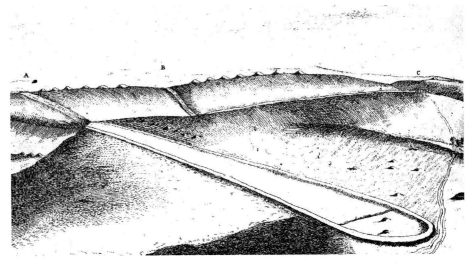

William Stukeley's 'Prospect of the west end of the Cursus of Stonehenge', from Stonehenge, A Temple Restor'd to the British Druids (1740).

William Stukeley: 'Inward view of Stonehenge from the high altar. August 1722',
looking north-east along the solstice alignment, from Stonehenge *(1740).*

In 1723, Stukeley visited Stonehenge for the first time, not only making his
astonishing discovery of the temple's alignment, but also coining the term 'trilithon'
and recognizing two vast and previously unseen landscape features, the Avenue and
a more enigmatic earthwork to the north, a pair of parallel banks and ditches, set
around 600 feet apart and enclosed at either end, which run from east to west across
the landscape for nearly two miles. He interpreted it as a Roman racecourse and
called it the Cursus.

Stukeley described his discovery of the solstice alignment in a hand-written note in
the margin of a manuscript, observing that the temple's builders had set its entrance
'to the N.E. loc. that is the Suns utmost elongation in somer Solstice when they held
a grand festival.' In his book on Stonehenge, published in 1740, he expanded the
theme, writing of the Avenue that it 'answers... to the principal line of the whole
work, the north-east, where abouts the sun rises, when the days are longest', and
stressing that 'The intent of the founders of Stonehenge was to set the entrance full
north east, being the point where the sun rises, or nearly, at the summer solstice.'
(Stukeley 1723: 112; 1740: 35, 56)

He also realised that two outlying stones – the fallen Slaughter Stone and its lost
partner – 'made a grand portal' that straddled the solar axis 'from the altar down thro'
the middle of the Avenue.' This in itself was an extraordinary deduction. Some
obscure sketches made in the Tudor period had shown a partner to the Slaughter
Stone, but the stone itself had disappeared in the following centuries, and, as was
mentioned in the first chapter, its stone-hole was only 'officially' discovered during
excavations in the 1920s. (Stukeley 1723: 57)

William Stukeley: 'A peep into the Sanctum Sanctorum. 6 June 1724', a captivating vision of Stonehenge Restored, from Stonehenge (1740).

The only significant component of the solstice alignment that he missed – probably through a faulty compass – was the position of the Heel Stone. It was left to later writers to grapple with this last piece of the megalithic puzzle. The architect John Wood, who made the first accurate plan of the stones and the henge in 1740, recognised that 'the great Pillar before the Front of Stonehenge is situated North Eastward from that Edifice', although he thought that the stone was 'in a Line to that Quarter of the Heavens where the new Moon first appears on that Day of her Age when the Druids began their Times and Festivals.' (Atkinson 1985; Burl 1999: 136; Wood 1747: 80–1, 95)

In 1770, John Smith, a local inoculator against smallpox, finally surmised the Heel Stone's purpose, writing that 'At the summer solstice... The Arch-Druid standing against his stall, and looking down the right line of the temple, over the stones II and I [the Slaughter Stone and the Heel Stone] his eye is bounded by Durrington Field (a charming horizon about two miles distant), he there sees the sun rise from behind the hill.' Smith's discovery was the one illuminating insight in a book that was otherwise a turgid trawl through the more impenetrable corners of late eighteenth century astronomy, and even then his insistence that it was 'the apex of the stone' that pointed at the sunrise – rather than the gap between the stone and its lost partner – was to prove one of the more enduring misconceptions about the temple's orientation. (Smith 1771)

Fairs and games

Although there is no evidence that Stukeley's discoveries – and Smith's small but significant contribution – immediately encouraged either antiquarians or other interested parties to visit Stonehenge at the summer solstice, there is some slight but intriguing evidence that its folk equivalent, Midsummer, was already being celebrated at Stonehenge.

In 1985, the sports historian John Goulstone found an advertisement in *The Salisbury Journal* of 2 July 1781 for 'a grand two-day festival' called 'Sports at Stonehenge' that was to take place on 4 and 5 of July, featuring a sack race, cricket, wrestling and bowling. Goulstone deduced from the dates that before the great calendar change of 1752, when the Gregorian replaced the Julian and eleven days were lost, this 'festival' would have taken place on 23 and 24 of June, the traditional rather than the astronomical dates of Midsummer. He pointed out that this had happened with three fairs in Amesbury, whose dates had moved forward eleven days – from 6 to 17 May, from 11 to 22 June and from 25 to 26 September to 6 to 7 October – and concluded that 'long before the first influx of Victorian sightseers Stonehenge was already the scene of a genuine midsummer festival.' (Goulstone 1985a; 1985b)

Even though it is tempting to accept John Goulstone's conclusion, no other evidence has so far come to light to justify it, and the confident assertions made by other writers that fairs or festivals took place at Stonehenge at various times from the thirteenth to the nineteenth centuries have, ironically, been demolished by Goulstone himself. Paul Devereux's proposal that 'At Stonehenge... there were 'vile and indecorous games' at the solstice period, as the Bishop of Salisbury described them in 1223', was countered by Goulstone's suggestion that the Bishop was only generally 'denouncing festivals with their "dances of vile and indecorous games which tempt to unseemliness".' The claim that fairs used to be held at Stonehenge from the eighteenth century onwards, which was made by the archaeologist Richard Atkinson, was countered by Goulstone's insistence that three of the fairs in question actually took place in Amesbury (as detailed above) and that a fourth took place 'on Countess Court Downs more than a mile to the east of the monument.' Chris Chippindale also suggested that a long-running solstice fair took place in the eighteenth and nineteenth centuries, adding that the tradition began when 'A royal Warrant of 1680 granted Thomas Hayward, the owner, the right to hold an annual fair at Stonehenge on 25 and 26 September.' This too was countered by Goulstone, who pointed out that 'An attempt to establish a fair at Stonehenge in 1680 was squashed after an objection from Oxford University that it clashed with the Weyhill Fair.' (Devereux 1991: 91; Goulstone 1985a; Atkinson 1979: 611; Chippindale 1994: 156, 43)

The crowds gather

With the claims for Midsummer gatherings at Stonehenge up to the early nineteenth century either in limbo or in tatters, the history of the summer solstice at the monument only comes back to life in the 1850s, when the first observances of

Members of the Devizes Cycling Club at Stonehenge, from a postcard c.1895.

Stukeley's astronomical solstice were noted. Chris Chippindale wrote that by the second half of the nineteenth century, watching the solstice sunrise had become 'the principal annual event at Stonehenge.' (Chippindale 1994: 156)

The first to come were the antiquarians and their aristocratic patrons. In 1858, John Thurnam, the excavator of numerous barrows around Stonehenge and Avebury, witnessed a clear dawn at the stones, and in 1860 the Earl of Carnarvon, accompanied by Henry Long, watched as the sun 'shone out in all his brightness and in full and certain relation to the index-stone, exactly as we had hoped and expected.' Writing in 1885, Carnarvon added, 'since then others have, I believe, watched during the summer solstice in the same place and with similar results.' (Grinsell 1978: 22; Carnarvon 1885)

In 1868, various groups of spectators were recorded at the monument on or near 21 June. In 1872, there were thirty-five spectators, one of whom said he had been present at the solstice several times previously, and by the mid-1870s sunrise on the monument's most auspicious day had begun to attract larger crowds ot the general public, including the Devizes Cycling Club, who made it the object of their annual outing, and who were an early example of a trend towards outdoor leisure pursuits that was to become increasingly prevalent in the first half of the twentieth century. (Winwood 1868; Beck 1872)

In 1875, there were also 'a number of people from all parts of the countryside, principally belonging to the poorer classes', described in *Notes and Queries*, whose

15

reporter observed that 'Inquiries failed to elicit any intelligible reason for this extraordinary early turn out of the population except that tradition that had trickled down through any number of generations told them that at Stonehenge something unusual was to be seen at sunrise on the morning of the summer solstice', a comment that could perhaps be regarded as a garbled folk-memory of the lost Midsummer celebrations of years gone by. ('H.J.' 1875)

In 1878, 300 people attended. Two years later the archaeologist Flinders Petrie, who was surveying the stones at the time, remarked that the custom was by then well established. Up to a hundred people turned up in 1882, when the dawn was obscured by cloud. (*The Wiltshire County Mirror*, 22 June 1878; Petrie 1880: 20; *The Western Gazette*, 23 June 1882)

By the 1890s, the pubs in Amesbury were staying open all night on Midsummer's Eve, taking advantage of 'a loophole in the law that allowed them to sell alcohol to *"bona fide* travellers" at any hour of the day or night.' They evidently did a roaring trade, catering to the large numbers of visitors – 3,000 in 1891 and another 3,000 on a particularly clear night in 1896 – who subsequently made their way to the temple for a radiant dawn. A reporter for *The Devizes Gazette* commented, 'They journeyed from far and near – some in brakes, waggonettes and traps, while the majority travelled on bicycles. The roads leading to the place presented a very animated appearance. People... kept coming in hundreds until nearly sunrise. They heralded their approach by bugle and horn blowing and bell ringing.' There were 'nearly a thousand cyclists, and the sight of the innumerable lamps converging on the stones from different directions was one that impressed the spectators by its novelty and beauty.' (Stout 2003; Brock 1891; *The Devizes Gazette*, 25 June 1896)

Chris Chippindale caught the tone of the gatherings at the stones: 'Some authority, such as the Headmaster of Dauntsey Agricultural School, would discourse from the top of a brake; and there would be three cheers for the lecturer, three for his family, and three for the Royal Family; and *God Save the Queen* would be sung.' The general piousness of the gatherings was also punctuated by outbursts of rowdiness, fuelled by the lengthy boozing sessions of the previous hours. Bottles were broken on the stones and persistent attempts made to climb up onto the lintels of the giant sarsens whenever the police were not looking. These were the first slapstick confrontations in a kind of socio-political farce that, over a century later, still seems destined to run and run. (Chippindale 1994: 156)

As the century came to an end and a regular force of fifteen policemen was deemed necessary to preserve law and order, these tensions provoked one commentator, the writer C.G. Harper, to lament that 'many of the younger people were there for a night out rather than for any more cultured reasons.' Harper's was an early dissenting voice, although he was not the first. As early as 1885, *The Salisbury Journal* published a letter complaining that, 'For some years past the gathering at the grand ruin has been degenerating and... has reached a pass which calls for interference to preserve the peace, and evidently interference of an energetic character.' (Harper 1899: 206-10; *The Salisbury Journal*, 4 July 1885)

The summer solstice, from a postcard c.1910. Note the propped stones and a vehicle and visitors by the roadside in the distance.

The early twentieth century

The impromptu public festivals at Stonehenge that took place in the last half of the nineteenth century were somewhat curtailed after 1901, when two developments took place that were to alter irrevocably both the casual nature of these arrangements and the pre-eminence of the general public.

The first of these was the raising of a perimeter fence around the monument and the imposition of an entrance charge of a shilling. While the ramifications of this financial imposition are discussed below, the background to the raising of the fence – and the disputes that accompanied it – are reserved for a fuller discussion, in Chapter Six, of the campaigns against rapacious landowners that were mounted by a coalition of prominent pressure groups (in particular the Commons Preservation Society and the National Trust) in the last decades of the nineteenth century. These focused on an array of novel concerns: the preservation of ancient monuments and other historic buildings, of historic landscapes and endangered wildlife, and of common land and public access rights.

The second development was the arrival at Stonehenge of the white-robed, modern-day Druids, who are most closely associated – to the general public at least – with the summer solstice at Stonehenge. The Druids are mentioned sporadically through-out the rest of this chapter and the following chapter, particularly at the time of their greatest interaction with the public, during the gatherings of the 1950s and the early 1960s, but their full story, detailing the background to their adoption of Stonehenge, their struggles for access from the start of the twentieth century to the 1930s, and the prominent position that they held in the decades after the Second World War, are discussed at length in Chapter Four.

As a result of the enclosure of Stonehenge in 1901, the archaeologist Leslie Grinsell suggested that the entrance charge 'split the attendance into those within and those outside the enclosure, and in bad weather few bothered to pay for admission to the enclosure.' This was certainly true to some extent. The 'poorer classes' of 1875 were unable to afford a fee that converts to around £5 in today's money, and bad weather contributed to low attendances in 1901 and 1902, when there were just eighty and fifty attendees respectively, compared to the 200 or so who had turned up for a similarly cloud-obscured sunrise in 1900, on the last solstice before the fence was

A charabanc outing to Stonehenge, from a postcard c.1911.

raised. (Grinsell 1978: 22; *The Devizes and Wiltshire Gazette*, 27 June 1901, 24 June 1902; *The Salisbury Journal*, 23 June 1900)

The main influence on the public's attendance, however, seems to have been the strictures of the typical working week. On closer inspection, the only large gatherings of the late nineteenth century took place when the solstice fell on a weekend. The vast gatherings of 1891 and 1896, for example, took place on Saturdays, and it was noticeable that in 1894, when the solstice fell on a Wednesday, only fifty people turned up to watch what Leslie Grinsell described as a 'brilliant sunrise.' (Grinsell 1978: 22)

This was a pattern that persisted throughout the first half of the twentieth century. Although several hundred people saw 'the best midsummer sunrise for several years' in 1903, and similar numbers were frustrated by thick mist in 1904 and cloud cover in 1907, the first great gathering of the twentieth century – a crowd of 2,000 – took place in 1908, when the solstice fell on a Sunday. Significantly, this was also the first year that those enjoying a day out were aided by the tools of a new social mobility, with 'carriages, brakes, motor cars and motor cycles' as well as the traditional pedestrians and cyclists. Similar numbers were evident at the next Sunday solstice, in 1914, when people also arrived in charabancs, the first motorised coaches. (*The Times*, 22 June 1903; *The Salisbury Journal*, 25 June 1904, 22 June 1907; Hudson 1908; *The Daily Mirror*, 23 June 1914)

A new social mobility

In the years following the First World War, as this new social mobility increased, two further developments added to the mass movement of aspirational working people that made the complaints about rowdy crowds of mostly local people in the 1880s and 1890s seem like echoes from an already distant age. The first of these was the growth of the rambling movement, inspired partly by the Romantic poets, who found sublime inspiration through direct contact with nature. The historian Jeremy Burchardt noted of William Wordsworth, 'Only by immersing himself in nature in the most direct way, by walking by the lakes, through the woods and over the fells could Wordsworth obtain the immediacy of experience he sought', and it was estimated that, in search of those experiences, the poet 'walked more than 175,000 miles in the Lake District during his lifetime.' (Burchardt 2002: 121)

As well as being influenced by the promise of Romanticism, the rambling groups were also concerned with the adverse effects of the increasing industrialisation of England. They became particularly prominent in the north-west of England from the late nineteenth century onwards, where an intellectual artisan elite had developed in the early industrial towns, opposed to the scale of urbanisation on which the industrial 'revolution' depended, and identifying strongly with the pre-industrial communities of the past. Jeremy Burchardt observed that 'Northern working-class rambling was a near relative of socialism and non-conformity', and it was the activism of the radical wing of the northern ramblers' movement that led to a celebrated mass trespass – and arrest – on Kinder Scout in the Peak District in 1932. The culmination of a fifty-year struggle for access to the high peaks, the Kinder Scout trespass became a key event in the folk history of the rambling movement, when its leaders were subsequently imprisoned. Although the southern ramblers were generally more quiescent, collectivist rambling was also represented in the south of

An advertisement for an outing to Stonehenge in the 1920s.

England. In the summer of 1932, 16,000 ramblers followed the well-known journalist and writer S.P.B. Mais to Chanctonbury Ring, an Iron Age hill-fort on the South Downs, to watch the sunrise. (Burchardt 2002: 128–9)

The second development was the dawn of a phenomenon that could be called 'event consciousness', a desire to witness 'significant' events that could be considered the innocent precursor to today's globe-trotting cultural tourism. The most spectacular of these was the solar eclipse of 1927, when three million people travelled to the north-west of England for the experience, 'the biggest ever recorded movement of people by train in one day in the UK.' Countless other excursions also took place in these years, with the railway companies in particular taking advantage of the public's appetite for travel and adventure, running 'mystery trains' like the Southern Railway Moonlight Ramble that, in a neat elision of the trends outlined above, took 1,400 people to join the Chanctonbury ramblers in 1932. (Treneman 1998; Walker 1987: 315)

Jazz and motor-cars

At Stonehenge, where there was no direct rail link, the solstice attendees were still dependent on the more limited means of transport established before the war, and large-scale mobility was still confined to the weekends. Record crowds in 1925, when the largest attendance to that date was noted, and 1931, when around 2,500 people were present, again took place on Sundays. Even so, the solstice gatherings of the 1920s and 1930s incorporated elements of these new national movements as well as building upon and augmenting the local festival atmosphere of the late nineteenth century. (*The Times*, 22 June 1925; *The Wiltshire Gazette*, 26 June 1931)

The loophole in the licensing laws was suppressed in 1921, but people brought their own alcohol instead, and with the booze came that other party staple: music. As the archaeologist Adam Stout observed, 'Jazz – the rebel music of the Twenties – was a regular feature, and the sound system made an early debut at Stonehenge.' The crowd in 1929 'passed the hours listening to gramophone selections which were 'broadcast' from a motor van through an amplifier', and in 1930, 'An atmosphere reminiscent of Blackpool beach spread over the roadways leading to the ruin. Girls and boys danced by the lights of motor-cars which lined the roads to the music of gramophones and a complete jazz band.' In 1931, when the new social mobility was most evident, with up to 300 cars, 200 motorbikes and numerous coach parties, the partying was even accompanied by the first impromptu camping: 'Some erected portable tents by the roadside. Music was provided by several gramophones at various points outside the enclosure and minstrels enlivened the vigil with mandolin selections.' (Stout 2003; *The Salisbury Journal*, 23 June 1929; *The Evening Times*, 21 June 1930; *The Salisbury Journal*, 26 June 1931)

Not all commentators were happy with these developments. The reporter in 1930 complained, 'It was eerie, absolutely still, until the silence was broken by an electric gramophone wailing "The Song of the Nile".' For John o'Wiltshire in *The Wiltshire Times*, the charm of the nineteenth century gatherings had been lost, and he lamented of the crowd in 1932, 'They make it a joyous, laughing, almost ribald thing. They spoil it.' What was particularly noticeable about John o'Wiltshire's criticism was that his memory of the gatherings of the century before was already tainted by false nostalgia. Whereas critics of the time had railed against the crowds, he recalled that a handful of people had 'toiled through the night in ones and twos.' A similar snobbery was evident in *The Salisbury Journal*, whose reporter complained that 'Midsummer morning at Stonehenge has become nothing more than a popular festival.' Over forty years before the first free festival took place at Stonehenge, all the components of an establishment-baiting people's gathering were already in place. (*The Wiltshire Times*, 25 June 1932; *The Salisbury Journal*, 24 June 1932)

Chapter Three

The post-war gatherings and the first free festivals

Youth and music

In the years following the Second World War, as tourist numbers at Stonehenge increased (an estimated 20,000 a year in the 1920s increased to 124,000 in 1951 and 337,000 in 1961), so too did the numbers of those joining the Druids on solstice morning. The jazz bands of the pre-war years were replaced in the early 1950s by Morris dancers, stalls and sideshows, including 'Len Buckland's dancing skeleton that bounced in time to a wind-up gramophone.' On Sunday 21 June 1953, a thousand people gathered for dawn at the stones. The only entertainment was provided by the Morris dancers, and no Druids were present until the afternoon. It was, perhaps, the first post-war people's festival, but from then on the crowds began to arrive with the solstice on whichever day of the week it fell, including weekday nights that in the pre-war years had been prohibited to all but a few. Young people in particular, seeking a new thrill, were treating their work and their studies with a flexibility that their parents' generation could only have dreamt about. (Chippindale 1994: 253; *The Salisbury Journal*, 26 June 1953)

Events at Stonehenge were paralleled in the mid-1950s by the first new music festivals. The Sidmouth Folk Festival, which began in 1954 (and is still running

A happy party: dancing in the stones, summer solstice 1956. Copyright Austin Underwood.

Summer solstice 1960: a familiar vantage point.
Copyright Gerald Ponting.

today) was 'part of the Second English Folk Revival, a movement trying to construct a new national tradition of "radical Englishness".' It was followed, in 1956, by the first of Lord Montagu's Beaulieu Jazz Festivals. Although the aristocratic angle was played up (the 1957 festival was advertised as 'a combination of blue blood and the blues'), Beaulieu had an egalitarian feel from the beginning. At the first festival, people camped the night before in the adjourning woods, and the first two-day event in 1958, with its mixture of loud music, overnight camping and lots of young people, has come to be seen as 'the first proper pop festival in Britain.' Noticeably, an explicit attempt was made to link this new festival culture with the gatherings of the past. As the author and cultural commentator George McKay noted, the Beaulieu festivals 'consciously echoed the local Beaulieu fairs of the 1890s, and were seen in some ways as revivals of those lost spring and harvest fairs.' (McKay 2000: 87–8, 2)

In 1960 the high spirits of the Beaulieu festivals tipped over into violence, and there were clashes between, of all things, trad jazzers into Acker Bilk and modernists clamouring for Tubby Hayes and Ronnie Scott. Although the BBC, who were filming, pulled the plug on the 'Battle of Beaulieu' and Lord Montagu promised to hold no further events, the festival – and the conflict – returned the following year. As well as discovering their own space, listening to loud music, drinking alcohol and exploring the borders of sexual mores, many young people were also increasingly unafraid to voice their opinion – either over their tribal rivalries or in a wider socio-political context.

'Rowdies' and riotousness

The ensuing riotousness is discernible at Stonehenge from as early as 1955, when one participant recalled 'a howling mass of people, old, young, children jumping the prostrate stones, teenagers running madly chasing each other and shouting, others lying on the ground wrapped in rugs, picnic parties, litter and bottles lying around.' In 1956, the year of the first Beaulieu festival, the numbers at Stonehenge swelled to 2,000 and there were reports of conflict between the Druids and the general public:

The Druids and the crowd, summer solstice 1960. Copyright Gerald Ponting.

'just as the Druids had formed in procession to walk along the ancient trackway south-west to the disc barrows on Normanton Down... the mob broke into the most unruly behaviour – including fireworks – in living memory at Stonehenge, and 15 military police were called from Bulford Camp to restore order.' (Helen O'Neill in Chippindale 1994: 253; Grinsell 1978: 16)

Ironically, much of the trouble in the 1950s came not from the general public but from off-duty military personnel based in the same camps that were charged with supplying reinforcements to the police. In 1952, a local resident complained to *The Salisbury Journal* that the Morris dancers at the solstice ceremony were 'frustrated by the disgusting carryings-on of some 20 Air Force officers who were completely drunk and a disgrace to all around them', and although 'a suspected undergraduate in a duffle coat' and representatives of another unlikely anti-establishment group – the Young Conservatives – were blamed for the rowdiness of 1956, the majority opinion was that the fault lay squarely with 'a group of young soldiers from one of the camps on the Plain, much the worse for wear.' (*The Salisbury Journal*, 27 June 1952; *The Daily Telegraph*, 22 June 1956)

By 1957, a new 'rebel music' – skiffle – revived the youth-based musical contributions to the solstice gatherings that jazz had performed in the pre-war years, with 'two rival skiffle groups, each with its own band of supporters, trying to drown each others' efforts from opposite sides of the circle.' In 1959, a Mrs Prideaux-Brune of Gosport was so appalled that she wrote to *The Daily Telegraph* to complain, 'we suffered from 'skiffle groups' yelling vulgar songs with vulgar voices (about four songs which they repeated over and over again with ghastly monotony).' (*The Salisbury Journal*, 28 June 1957; *The Daily Telegraph*, 14 July 1959)

That year, around 1,400 people assembled for their own solstice ceremony on the Sunday. The Druids waited until the Monday, reckoning this to be the longest day, but there was trouble again, when another 1,600 people turned up, 'some very drunk.' As thirteen Druids and Druidesses – including the Grand Druid of Brittany – arrived to conduct their ceremony, they were 'accompanied by a good deal of jeering and barracking from younger members of the public.' (Grinsell 1978: 16)

Conflict is always newsworthy, of course, and for the most part the solstice gatherings of the time seem to have been innocently exuberant affairs. In 1960, when 3,000 people were present, the writer Gerald Ponting, who was then a student at Southampton University, visited with a friend on his Lambretta scooter, meeting up with other student friends, including college jazz band Group One, who 'had announced their intention of playing at the stones on midsummer morning and had booked a coach for their supporters.' Gerald's recollections certainly suggest a light-hearted gathering, and his diary entries reveal nothing of the conflict between the crowd and the Druids that provided such a focus for the press. Although he derided the dawn ceremony as 'farcical', he was free to join the Druids for a midnight ceremony at the barrows, where 'all joined hands for a blessing of the coming year.' (*The Salisbury Journal*, 24 June 1960; Ponting 2003)

Throughout these years the youth cults continued to mutate and attract participants from further afield. In 1961, *The Salisbury Journal* noted that the 'trouble-hunting teddy-boys and their girl friends in bizarre dress' left early, but that many other sections of the crowd were 'weirdly garbed... slightly embarrassed spectators eyed each others' clothes – many of which bore witness to their wearers' imagination. One youthful Beau Brummel wore a long, bright blue blanket over his head, decorated with a pheasant tail-feather. The rest of his outfit consisted of dark corduroy trousers, no socks, 'peep-toe' sandals, and sunglasses.' (*The Salisbury Journal*, 23 June 1961)

A 'concentration camp atmosphere'

Despite the sartorial developments, outbursts of 'rowdiness' persisted. *The Times'* report for 1961 noted that 'As on previous occasions, unruly elements sought to lessen the dignity of the proceedings by their behaviour.' Eight wheelbarrows of broken bottles were collected afterwards, 'groups of jeering louts perched on top of the stones' and a 'strong force of military police was also on duty.' Such was the perceived threat from the solstice gatherings that in its annual report to the Ministry of Works for 1960, the Ancient Monuments Board declared, 'While we see no objection to you allowing a ceremony to be held, we deprecate the behaviour of some of the large crowd of onlookers and fear the possible harm to the monument. Last summer spectators forced their way through the boundary fence and a large crowd assembled in the centre of the monument. Many individuals climbed the stones to use them as vantage points.' (*The Times*, 22 June 1961; Daniel 1992: 24)

The following year, the civil servants responsible for the monument gave prominence to the views of the Chief Constable of Wiltshire: 'so long as there were Druids about, there would be a substantial body of weirdies making a thundering nuisance of themselves. It was clear that he did not hold the Druids responsible... but he was quite sure that the mere presence of Druids would attract undesirables to the neighbourhood and that the latter would then proceed to make the night hideous.' (Public Record Office 1962)

In 1962 and 1963, temporary barbed-wire fences were installed in an attempt to keep the crowds at bay, although it was to little avail. In the daylight hours of the

The crush at the last summer solstice before the clampdown.
Copyright Austin Underwood.

1963 solstice, for example, the central enclosure was filled with a mass of people, through which the Druids were forced to press their passage, watched over by two dozen sharply-dressed Mods sitting or standing on the surviving arc of lintels at the north east of the circle, facing the sunrise.

The clampdown came the following year, when access was restricted to 'certain types of Druids only' from 9.30pm to 3.30am. The exclusion zone was certainly observed – in 1965 the first clear solstice sunrise for fourteen years was witnessed by a group of just twenty-five Druids while 300 other people were kept out behind the fence, and in 1966, following an official analysis of the solstice arrangements in which a 'concentration camp atmosphere' was deemed necessary if 'organized parties of hooligans' were to be kept under control, a newspaper report confirmed the desolate success of the new policy: 'Military police were everywhere. Both civilian and military police dog-handlers patrolled the five-foot Dammert wire perimeter... the whole of the monument and its concentration-camp barbed-wire entanglements were floodlit throughout the night.' (Wiltshire Record Office 1966; *The Salisbury Journal*, 23 June 1966)

The new exclusion zone was so successful that in 1966, when the Druids arrived late, no one at all was within the circle to witness the sunrise. It was noticeable, however, that the hard-core party-goers turned up anyway. A police report described how 'people came and strummed guitars in the field next to the monument, perhaps joined by a crowd from the officers' mess of the nearby army camp.' In the opinion of the police, 'It was generally a pretty happy event, with no policing problems. Everybody had gone by 6 a.m.', although it was also obvious that the policy of exclusion was only adding to the temple's growing role as a counter-cultural icon. Those who were studying youth movements closely could see that for young people the rules laid down by the older generation were there to be broken. It was only a matter of time before Stonehenge succumbed to this new wave of people power. (Weird Wiltshire 2003; Wiltshire Police 1981)

These developments were most readily apparent at the music festivals. Although Lord Montagu held no further festivals at Beaulieu after 1961, the National Jazz Festival took over his pioneering work that year, under the leadership of Harold Pendleton of the National Jazz Federation. Pendleton, who had helped organise the Beaulieu festivals, ran the Marquee Club in London, and saw which way the wind was blowing more clearly than either Lord Montagu or the Ministry of Works. Musical and social innovations followed in swift succession. In 1963, the Rolling Stones were added to the bill, and they were so successful that the following year the festival was renamed the National Jazz and Blues Festival and the Stones returned in triumph as the headline act. By 1965, according to the official handout, 'the pure jazz-men [were] outnumbered by beat and rhythm-and-blues groups who [were] no strangers to the hit parade.' On the social front, the festival's organisers began promoting public indecency in 1964 with the provision of a unisex crash tent on site. For two years, the authorities failed to notice, but by 1966 the police began to complain about the 'immorality of young people being allowed to sleep together in the overnight marquee.' (McKay 2000: 90)

Swinging London and the Summer of Love

As the demands of the young grew more apparent, the focus for the social, sexual, political and spiritual revolution that was to manifest itself in the free festival scene was the London of the swinging sixties, where the familiar superstars of music, fashion and photography – the Beatles, the Rolling Stones, David Bailey – were joined by more subversive underground elements.

From Australia came Richard Neville and his influential London edition of *Oz*, the taboo-busting underground magazine that had been offending sensibilities in Sydney since the early 1960s. Neville knew London's premier black activist, Michael X, who owned a building in Notting Hill's Powis Terrace that was to become the epicentre of the free festival spirit in Britain. It was in the basement of this building that the revolutionary communism of west London's squatters and activists manifested itself in the creation of the Notting Hill Free School, an organisation that was founded by, amongst others, Pete Jenner, the manager of Pink Floyd, and John 'Hoppy' Hopkins of *IT*, the other great underground magazine of the time, which was launched in 1966 as *International Times* until a certain long-running British newspaper took offence.

All of the above were involved with Release, an organisation dedicated to the protection of people busted by the police in drug cases, which was to remain

*Oz 13 invites its readers to a
'Legalise Pot' rally.
Poster by Martin Sharp, image
supplied by Weed, thanks to
Richard Neville for permission.*

prominent into the 1980s. In September 1966, along with Rhaunie Laslett who was running the then-radical Notting Hill Housing Trust, they came together to promote an event that was to become 'the most dynamic multi-cultural street festival in Europe' – the Notting Hill Carnival. Although a Caribbean Carnival had begun in the area in 1959, it was the 1966 event – consciously reviving an annual fair that had been held in the area until the start of the twentieth century – that united the black and white locals (including the area's many hippies) in a vibrant mix of celebration and protest. (Neville 1995: 91; Moody 2002; McKay 2000: 90)

By 1967, the existing youth cults – Mods, beats, folkies – had mutated into hippies. In April, the 'Summer of Love' announced its presence at 'The 14-Hour Technicolour Dream' in Alexandra Palace, a multi-media extravaganza featuring Pink Floyd and '5,000 stoned, tripping, mad, friendly, festive hippies.' By the time of the hippies' ascendancy, however, the floaty vibes of peace and love were regularly supplemented by muscular politics. In March, the first student occupation took place, when over 2,000 students occupied the London School of Economics. (McKay 2000: 90)

In June, when the Summer of Love reached Stonehenge for the summer solstice, the euphoria of the hippies' cultural ascendancy was somewhat overshadowed by the arrest of Mick Jagger and Keith Richards on drug charges. Protests began immediately. From the hippies' psychedelic nerve centre, the UFO Club on Tottenham Court Road, hundreds of protestors made their way to Piccadilly Circus, where they held an all-night vigil by the statue of Eros. Others took the fight to Fleet

Street, to protest outside the offices of *The News of the World*, which was widely believed to have set the Stones up. Mick Farren, musician and prominent counter-cultural activist, recalled other suggestions that had followed the Fleet Street proposal, ranging 'from Hyde Park (that was impractical) to Stonehenge (that was implausible)', an aside that reveals the monument as an established counter-cultural icon. (Neville 1995: 82; Farren 2001: 130)

As the furore over the arrest of Mick Jagger and Keith Richards reached a crescendo, the political rhetoric was stepped up. *IT* was confident enough to proclaim in an editorial, 'No matter how many arrests the police make, there can be no final bust, because the revolution has taken place in the minds of the young.' On the morning of the verdict, *The Times* published a famous editorial advocating leniency – 'Who Crushes a Butterfly on a Wheel?' –and a 'Love-In' planned for Hyde Park on 16 July became a 'Legalise Pot' rally instead. Richard Neville recalled that '*The Times'* metaphoric butterflies, so far from being broken, had metamorphosed into a field of fluorescent flower children, dancing, hugging and swapping colossal joints. Allan Ginsberg sat cross-legged on the grass playing a Tibetan squeeze box and chanting *Om Mane Padme Hum, Om Mane Padme Hum.*' (Neville 1995: 83, 86)

By August the transformation was complete. Jeremy Sandford, playwright and social commentator, wrote of the 1967 National Jazz and Blues Festival, 'This was the year of flower power. Hippies completely replaced the familiar beatniks of yesteryear. Beads and bells ousted duffle coats and cider jugs.' In September, over 2,000 hippies attended the Notting Hill Carnival, whose social and political context was highlighted in a performance called *England This England*, described by *Kensington News* as a 'musical parody of the housing problem.' (Sandford and Reid 1974; McKay 2000: 91)

The first free festivals

The first free festivals took place in the UK the year after, at Parliament Hill Fields on Hampstead Heath and in Hyde Park. Although they were, strictly speaking, one-day free concerts, they were to prove enormously successful, and they clearly provided a template for the more extended gatherings of the 1970s. On 5 May, Jefferson Airplane headlined in Hampstead, as part of the Camden Festival, and from June to September a series of four concerts took place in Hyde Park, organised by Pete Jenner of the Free School and his colleague Andrew King. With respectable family backgrounds and a wealth of connections in the London arts scene, Jenner and King were able to bridge the gap between the underground and the establishment, taking advantage of a certain tolerance towards hippie ideals (a typical press report cited a 'flourishing cult of love, equality and denial of material wealth in favour of community benefits') and getting support from a number of MPs, including Hampstead's Ben Whittaker. (Shark 2003a)

The first free concert in Hyde Park, with Pink Floyd headlining, took place on 29 June, the week after the solstice at Stonehenge, and is widely regarded as one of the most blissful collective events of the decade. John Peel recalled the Floyd's music as being 'like a religious experience' and concluded, 'I think it was the nicest concert

I've ever been to.' Around 15,000 people turned up, and similar numbers attended the other free concerts that summer, with Traffic headlining on 28 July, Family on 24 August and the Move on 28 September. As with the first concert, the general opinion seems to have been that these were 'intimate, relaxed, comfy, laid-back parties.' (Shark 2003a)

Post-war politics

While the first one-day free festivals were taking place in a kind of blissful otherworld, the counter-culture's radical political edge was sharpening. In addition to the developments discussed above – the liberating social influence of the festivals, with their communality and their casting off of sexual and societal restraints, and the various strands of revolutionary Marxism, with its struggle over the ownership of property and land – the counter-culture was also committed to large-scale political protest, the development of which paralleled that of the music festivals and the solstice gatherings at Stonehenge.

In 1958, the year that the 'first proper pop festival' took place at Beaulieu, the Campaign for Nuclear Disarmament was formed and the first large-scale political protest took place in post-war Britain. Over the four days of Easter, a community of 10,000 protestors marched fifty-three miles from London to the Aldermaston Weapons Research Establishment in Berkshire. The following year, the route of the CND march was reversed. From Aldermaston a travelling festival, with 'jazz bands and guitars, songs and slogans, banners, placards and pamphlets' made its way to London, where over 15,000 people gathered in Trafalgar Square. At Beaulieu, the press remarked for the first time on the 'weirdies' in attendance, foreshadowing the complaints of the police and civil servants at Stonehenge in 1961. The post-war generation was already evolving its own rituals, mingling celebration and protest, as the jazz musician George Melly recognised at the time, when he commented that 'Beaulieu, like Aldermaston, has become one of the secular festivals of the atheist's year.' (Minnion and Bolsover 1983; McKay 2000: 88)

Melly's reference to atheism was not simply a personal confession. He was also pointing out the existence of a largely youth-based, anti-establishment position – against the tyranny of church and state – that would be pursued throughout the following decade, when this revolutionary atheism developed into anarchy, psychedelia, free love and violent political protest. In turn, with a crushing irony for atheists like George Melly, this also evolved into a multitude of searches for a viable new religion.

The escalation of large-scale political protest began as early as 1961, when 32,000 CND marchers were joined by 100,000 supporters in Trafalgar Square, and acts of widespread civil disobedience were undertaken by various local CND groups throughout the year. Even more gathered in Hyde Park in 1962, where they were addressed by survivors of the bombing of Hiroshima. As the Bay of Pigs gave way to Vietnam, the focus of the anti-war protestors diversified. Although 150,000 people gathered for the Trafalgar Square rally at the end of CND's Easter march in 1965, it was the banners opposing the Vietnam War that were beginning to dominate the event. (McKay 2000: 88–9)

By 1968, the anger that fuelled the protestors became explosive. On 17 March, there was violence at a demonstration outside the American Embassy in Grosvenor Square. Nigel Fountain recalled that 'It was the antithesis of the CND marches...[The] issue wasn't peace, it was war: victorious war for Vietnam's National Liberation Front, and class war on the bourgeoisie.' In May, Paris erupted in riots between students and the police. Schoolchildren joined in, marching through the streets chanting, 'Power is in the street, not in Parliament', workers held a general strike, and the university was occupied. Jean-Jacques Lebel, a prominent activist, declared, 'We want everyone to use the university for whatever they want. Not only for education, but also to eat, sleep, fuck and get high... We want to demolish the consumer society.' In August, police in Chicago mounted the first ferocious assault on the counter-culture, gassing and clubbing an assembly of peaceful protestors, and in October another massive demonstration against the Vietnam War took place in London. 70,000 people marched through London to a rally in Hyde Park, while another 3,000 went to Grosvenor Square to protest outside the US embassy again and to burn the American flag. In a milder version of the events of Chicago, but one that was indicative of what was to come, the Grosvenor Square protest 'ended in a hail of truncheons.' (Fountain 1988; Neville 1995: 110–1, 150–1)

1969: protest and confrontation

By 1969, protest and confrontation had become synonymous. On May Day, another demonstration against the Vietnam War took place in London. With Grosvenor Square off-limits, many activists joined a group of Australian ex-pats, who ended up outside Australia House, where Germaine Greer, declaiming the popular anti-war cry, 'We are all Vietcong! We are all Vietcong!' set fire to the Australian flag instead. (Neville 1995: 150–1)

In Hyde Park, the one-day free festivals continued, although the intimacy of the year before was over. On 5 June 1969, 120,000 people turned up for the disappointing debut of Blind Faith, a supergroup featuring Eric Clapton and Steve Winwood, and over 250,000 (with 2,000 camping the night before) for the celebrated but largely inaudible Rolling Stones concert on 5 July that turned into a wake for the band's recently sacked guitarist Brian Jones, who had drowned in his swimming pool a few days before. Mick Jagger flounced around in a white dress and stumbled his way through a poem by Shelley, a cloud of butterflies was released, and the event was later issued as a film, *The Stones in the Park*.

More significant in the long run, however, were some of the other events of that summer, when the free festival spirit began to overwhelm the aims of the more commercial promoters. Over the August Bank Holiday weekend, the second Isle of Wight festival drew a crowd of 200,000 to watch Richie Havens play songs from his latest album, *Stonehenge*, and in particular to witness the return of Bob Dylan after three years as a recluse. Unprepared for such a massive influx of people (just 10,000 had attended the first Isle of Wight festival, set up merely to raise money for a local swimming pool), the organisation was stretched to breaking point. Richard Neville recalled, 'the nights were freezing, all the blankets sold, the food ran out and the latrines stank.' By the final day, large sections of the fence had been torn down by the crowd, piled onto vast bonfires of rubbish that blazed across the site. (Neville 1995: 164)

The breakdown of central authority at the Isle of Wight set the tone for the decade to come, but its direction was signposted even earlier. That June at Stonehenge, when the solstice fell on a Saturday, 2,000 revellers had lost their patience with the restrictions, crashing through the fence and drowning out the Druids with their own spontaneous ceremony. (Chippindale 1994: 253)

Stonehenge 1970

By 1970, the fences – real and metaphorical – were coming down everywhere. At Stonehenge, where the authorities had proposed reinforcing the defences and remonstrating with the crowd through a loudspeaker, officials from the Ministry of Works declared instead that 'It is our view that appeals to a crowd consisting largely of drunks and hippies (as was the case this year) are likely to be entirely wasted, and would not justify the expense of a PA system. The small minority of normal individuals are not in need [of] exhortations about their behaviour.' With a precedent so forcefully established the year before, up to 3,000 hippies again joined the Druids for the celebration of the summer solstice, and a gigantic party took place around the perimeter of the monument. (Wiltshire Record Office 1970)

Doug Burnett from Michigan, on his first trip to Europe, had planned a solstice visit as the culmination of his travels. After paying to visit the stones in the daytime, he found a spot to camp overnight and met up with other like-minded people: 'As the sky darkened and the lights came on, the serious partying began. Bottles and joints were passed around our group and to others near us. Inside the fence, in the stone circle, I saw figures in white robes – Druids, I was informed – performing some kind of ceremony. And right behind them was a man with a movie camera filming their every action. Outside we continued to party: campfires were lit, songs sung and toasts given – everybody was everybody's friend. No telling how long this went on. Finally exhausted, I fell into a fitful sleep… I woke in the pre-dawn gloom to discover that the sky was cloudy – no chance to view a sunrise today. Inside the stones the Druids and the camera were still doing their dance. Outside it looked like a refugee camp: campfires smouldered, trash covered the ground and there were sleeping bodies everywhere.' (Burnett 1998)

Revolutionary fervour: Phun City and the Isle of Wight

Elsewhere, the gatherings grew even more unruly. The week after Stonehenge, on 26–27 June, the second Bath Festival of Blues and Progressive Music, held at Shepton Mallet in Somerset, burst at the seams. The year before, 30,000 people had turned up; this time it was closer to 150,000. While the paying crowd was entertained by the likes of Led Zeppelin and Frank Zappa, the most riotous band of the time, the Pink Fairies, played off the back of a lorry to a free festival that had spontaneously erupted outside.

A month later, on 24–26 July, Phun City, which took place on a common in Worthing, created its own accidental vision of the alternatives that would be pursued

The Isle of Wight festival, 1970, with 'Desolation Hill' in the distance.
Copyright Steve Cook.

throughout the 1970s and beyond. Conceived as a commercial festival by Mick Farren and *IT*, the event raised conservative heckles with its promotional invitation – 'Get your end away at Phun City' – and was stymied by an injunction that was lifted too late to prevent it being anything other than an organisational disaster with no effective infrastructure whatsoever. Fortunately, all the bands, including the MC5 and the Pink Fairies, played for free, and up to 10,000 people turned up, camping in the woods in the most feral display of the counter-culture to date. As Mick Farren described it, 'At night the whole site was bathed in lightshows, free food operations sprung up, the Angels stole beer wholesale and distributed it to the kids, dealers stopped selling dope and gave it away, collections were made to keep the generators going. The thing had become a model of the alternative society, it was nothing like our original concept, but it worked.' (Farren and Barker 1972)

The final transforming event of the summer was the third (and last) Isle of Wight festival, which again took place over the August Bank Holiday weekend, with a line-up of global superstars including The Doors and Miles Davis. Richard Neville described it as 'an attempt at a Grand Festival, a state-of-the-art fling', adding that, 'From the start, the mood of the crowd kept the promoters on the defensive and profits in doubt.' As had happened at Shepton Mallet in June, a spontaneous free festival grew up outside the festival proper, with Hawkwind joining the Pink Fairies on the back of a lorry on a mound renamed Desolation Hill, surrounded by a refugee-like encampment dubbed Canvas City. *Oz, IT* and *Frendz* (another radical magazine) got together to produce *FREEk*, a daily news-sheet full of gossip, sloganeering and a tally of drug busts. Italian and French protestors were prominent (including Jean-Jacques Lebel, the spokesman of the 1968 student occupation in Paris) and Mick Farren, now a self-styled White Panther (inspired by the Black Panther movement in the US), stormed around demanding that the on-site representatives of the global food and drink corporations donate all their products to

A bucolic moment at the Trentishoe Whole Earth Fayre in 1976. Copyright Roger Hutchinson.

the masses. By the second day, the more agitated members of the free festival began to pull down the perimeter fence, and on the final day, when Jimi Hendrix gave his last major performance before his death three weeks later, the organisers gave up the struggle and the festival was declared free. (Neville 1995: 218–9)

The festivals of the early 1970s: 'exercises in communal living'

As the 1970s progressed, the first small, deliberately free festivals began to take place, where the various tribes of the counter-culture began to meet and mingle, unsupervised. Penny Mellor, who worked for Festival Welfare Services – a government-funded umbrella organisation for all the welfare groups that provided invaluable assistance at the free festivals from 1976 until its funding was finally withdrawn in 1995 – recalled that 'Some of these early festivals were less pop concerts, more exercises in communal living, an attempt to create a blueprint for a better world.' (Stone 1996: 84)

These exercises varied considerably in their approach, taking in themes as varied as urban decadence, whole earth idealism and radical politics. Free events took place at numerous venues in Bath from 1972 until the end of the decade, although it was difficult for organisers to top the first year, when property millionaire Charlie Ware lent the hippies a sixty-bedroom hotel in one of the town's most upmarket streets. Trentishoe Whole Earth Fayre, which began in June 1972 on cliffs in Devon overlooking the Bristol Channel, and which continued (in some form or another) in 1973, 1975 and 1976, offered free food, a full environmental agenda and water from a truck supplied by the self-styled Pot Dealers of the South West. Radical politics were provided at Windsor, the so-called People's Free Festival, which first set up camp in the Queen's backyard – Windsor Great Park – over the August Bank Holiday weekend in 1972, and which will be discussed at length in Chapter Five. (Shark 2003b; 2003c)

John Michell and Glastonbury

What set the Stonehenge Free Festival apart was its focus on a sacred space at a sacred time, something that was only shared by the 1971 Glastonbury Fayre, which took place over the solstice weekend at Worthy Farm in Pilton, a few miles from Glastonbury but with an outstanding view of the Tor and the Vale of Avalon. A small festival had been held there the year before – on 19–20 September, organised by dairy farmers Michael and Jean Eavis, who had been inspired by the Bath Festival that June – but it is the 1971 festival, of all the early free festivals, that is remembered as 'the legendary one.' (McKay 2000: 96)

The organisers, Arabella Churchill and Andrew Kerr, like the organisers of the Hyde Park festivals, were well-heeled and well-connected. Arabella Churchill was Winston Churchill's granddaughter, and Andrew Kerr had been Randolph Churchill's P.A. for many years. Both felt that all the other festivals of the time were over-commercialised, and redressed the balance with a privately funded event that not only drew some of the star players of the time – David Bowie and Joan Baez, for example, as well as free festival stalwarts Hawkwind and the Pink Fairies – but that also maintained high ideals. According to George McKay, Andrew Kerr 'had been

John Michell at Stonehenge,
summer solstice 1986.
Copyright Chris Chippindale.

35

Glastonbury 1971: the pyramid stage and the crowd. Copyright Paul Misso.

reading the Bible about redistribution and decided to practise what it preached.' In addition, no alcohol was for sale on the site and all the food was vegetarian, but most of all it was the festival's spiritual angle that echoed down the years. (McKay 2000: 68)

Kerr in particular was inspired by John Michell's *The View Over Atlantis*, published in 1969, which introduced themes of earth energies, spiritual engineering and sacred geometry that were to resonate through the following decades, and which revived, as centres of mystical power, not only Glastonbury but also Stonehenge and Avebury. Ronald Hutton suggested that *The View Over Atlantis* was 'almost the founding document of the earth mysteries movement', and Adam Stout called it 'a blunderbuss of a book, firing in all directions at once. Every last shibboleth of the archaeological establishment was systematically disinterred and reified. Michell, the self-styled "cosmological switchman", was deliberately turning the world upside down.' (Hutton 1991: 121; Stout 2001; Nicholson 1987: 27)

Michell revived the concept of ley-lines, straight lines across the countryside, connecting sites of ancient sanctity, which had first been proposed by the Herefordshire businessman and photographer Alfred Watkins in the 1920s, and which were interpreted by Michell as 'connected with a former code of mystical science which acknowledged the existence of energy streams across the earth and the part they play in the renewal of all life on this planet.' A ley-line joined Glastonbury to Stonehenge; another, which Michell called the St Michael Line, ran from Cornwall to East Anglia, joining Glastonbury with Avebury along the way. From China came lines of dragon power (*lung-mei*), to create an international matrix of energy lines, and from all corners of the world came a complex system of numerology that united these global threads even more closely. One of the more startling conclusions of his numerological studies was that 'The New Jerusalem was built on earth to the patterns and numbers whose origin lay in divine revelation, and which we find at the Great Pyramid, at Stonehenge, at Glastonbury Abbey and everywhere in the great monuments of the former world.' (Michell 1983: 8, 211)

According to George McKay, 'Andrew Kerr had actually wanted to hold his free festival at Stonehenge, with a circular stage, to celebrate the summer solstice there', but when he met Michael Eavis the plans shifted to Glastonbury. Kerr took from John Michell the correspondence between the pyramids and the sacred sites of England, and set about erecting a pyramid stage as the centrepiece of the festival. He planned it as a scaled-down model of the Great Pyramid, and even sought advice from John Michell, who suggested that the proportions of the pyramid should be based on the dimensions of Stonehenge. With a final nod to his mentor, Kerr raised the stage on the ley-line joining Glastonbury to Stonehenge, locating the exact spot over a 'blind spring' revealed by dowsing, another lost art reawakened by the posthumous publication of Guy Underwood's *The Pattern of the Past*, in which the author 'claimed to have found a "blind spring" of water welling up from deep in the earth, concealed under the centre of every stone circle which he tested.' (McKay 2000: 69; Hutton 1991: 122)

In addition to all the connections between Stonehenge and Glastonbury outlined above, the focus on the summer solstice at Glastonbury in 1971 complemented the events that had been taking place at Stonehenge over the preceding few years. In 1972, a small, informal free festival took place at Worthy Farm, lasting for five days and beginning the day *after* the solstice, when the festival-goers had once more joined the Druids at Stonehenge. Arabella Churchill recalled: 'Throughout the seventies, I'd get calls from Michael [Eavis] most Junes: "Bella, I'm not actually having a festival but lots of people seem to be arriving – come and give us a hand". Some very nice, small, unstructured events took place.' (McKay 2000: 97)

Phil Russell and Stonehenge

A similar overlap of interests between Stonehenge and Glastonbury took place in 1973, and it is in this context that the organiser of the first Stonehenge Free Festival, a charismatic young man called Phil Russell, enters the picture. Despite the obvious counter-cultural influences provided by the Glastonbury festivals and John Michell, apparently Phil came to Stonehenge as part of his own unique trajectory.

An orphan from a wealthy background, he was due to inherit land and property in Hertfordshire on his thirtieth birthday, but in the meantime was funded by a private allowance that left him free to pursue his own interests. In many ways, Phil was typical of the free festival agitators of the time – part acid prankster and part well-heeled dandy. In London, he fell in with a group called the Dwarves, 'a kind of Notting Hill version of the Yippies in America: a joke-prankster group', and adopted the name by which he became better known: Wally Hope. He took the name Wally from a popular festival cry (a kind of 'Everyman' joke that arose when the crowd began echoing the name of a lost dog being summoned by his owner at the last Isle of Wight festival) and he had the word 'Hope' embroidered on a shirt that 'became his trademark: a riot of spectacular colour with the eye of Horus in the middle banked by a rainbow.' (Stone 1996: 82, 84)

Phil's allowance also left him free to travel. He regularly visited America, where he sympathised with the plight of the Native Americans; Cyprus (his birthplace); and Ibiza, where he became entranced by the mythology of the sun. According to his friend Jeremy Ratter, who took the name Penny Rimbaud and who later co-founded the anarcho-punk collective Crass, it was at a well-known hippie café on the White Island that Phil first came up with the idea of a free festival at Stonehenge. He 'wanted to claim back Stonehenge (a place that he regarded as sacred to the people and stolen by the government) and make it a site for free festivals, free music, free space, free mind.' (Rimbaud 1981)

The two had met in the early 1970s. Phil's guardians lived near Jeremy's commune in Essex, and one day Phil just turned up. Here the festival developed from its Mediterranean origins, filtered through his exposure to other cultures, his interest in the legends of King Arthur, and his central fascination with sun worship. At the commune, moreover, he revealed aspects of himself that were significantly different from the other privileged individuals who had set up the festivals in Hyde Park and Glastonbury.

According to Jeremy, during the preparations for the first Stonehenge Free Festival Phil performed miracles: 'One day in our garden, it was early summer, he conjured up a snowstorm, huge white flakes falling amongst the daisies on the lawn. Another time he created a multi-rainbowed sky – it was as if he had cut up a rainbow and thrown the pieces into the air where they hung in strange random patterns. Looking back on it now it seems unbelievable but, all the same, I can remember both occasions vividly.' On another occasion, beating out rhythms with sticks on the dying embers of a fire, Jeremy was convinced that he and Phil were 'speaking to each other ritually by ESP in an acid-religious ceremony without drugs.' It was after this experience that he allowed Phil to use the facilities of the commune to organise the first festival at Stonehenge. (Rimbaud 1981; Stone 1996: 80)

1974: the first Stonehenge Free Festival

The first Stonehenge Free Festival duly took place at the summer solstice in 1974, alongside a by-way just a few hundred yards to the west of the stones. Despite a leafleting campaign and promotion by Radio Caroline, it was a small gathering, numbering about 500 people at the most. The only music was provided by early

FREE STONED HENGE ROCKS OFF
EVERY SUN DAY FOR EVER

Wally Hope: the 'Free Stoned Henge' flyer produced by Phil Russell in 1974. Russell himself is at the centre in the photo at the bottom. Image provided by Roger Hutchinson.

synth pioneers Zorch, who set up stage facing the stones, and who had to compete with a wonky PA system. (Shark 2003d)

It was obviously a slightly surreal affair. Tim Abbott, a friend of Russell's and later a councillor in Wilton, recalled that 'Rhonan O'Rhailly of Radio Caroline sat in his limousine suffering badly from hayfever and muttering about private television coverage of the proceedings being broadcast to Europe from an aircraft above the North Sea.' Nik Turner of Hawkwind, who stopped by for a few hours on the way back from Wales to London, seems to have been at a different event: 'There were no bands, no PA, no stage. It was just a gathering of people to celebrate the solstice.' (Abbott 1990; Stone 1996: 219)

Phil Russell's fence-hopping antics may have had little impact if the festival had stopped soon after the solstice was over, but by this time he had persuaded thirty people to stay on in the field beside the stone circle. They styled themselves 'The Wallies of Wessex' and lived a makeshift, communal lifestyle in tents, a rickety polythene-covered geodesic dome and a small fluorescent tipi. Nigel Ayers, who visited at the time, said, 'It was an open camp, inspired by a diversity of wild ideas, but with the common purpose of discovering the relevance of this ancient mysterious place by the physical experience of spending a lot of time there.' (Ayers 1996)

A ceremony at the 1974 festival.
Copyright Austin Underwood.

The Wallies went to court in August, in the newspapers' silly season, and the story was widely reported. They included in their number Sir Wally Raleigh and Wally Woof the Dog, they gave their address as 'Fort Wally, c/o God, Jesus and Buddha, Garden of Allah, Stonehenge Monument, Salisbury, Wiltshire', and they had a snappy motto: 'Every Body is Wally, Every Day is Sun Day.' The fancy dress went down well too, with Phil appearing in the uniform of an officer of the Cypriot National Guard. When they lost the case, Phil told the press: 'These legal arguments are like a cannon ball bouncing backwards and forwards in blancmange. We won, because we hold Stonehenge in our hearts. We are not squatters, we are men of God. We want to plant a Garden of Eden with apricots and cherries, where there will be guitars instead of guns and the sun will be our nuclear bomb.' (*The Times*, 13 August 1974)

The case over, they returned to Stonehenge, where they resurrected Fort Wally just yards away from its previous incarnation, on the by-way on the other side of the fence from the land that 'belonged' to the monument. Visitors at the time had mixed feelings about the enterprise. Roger Hutchinson, the artist responsible for the early festival posters, suggested, 'it appeared that Phil was depressed by the lack of support for the tasks that needed to be done to keep the encampment viable.' Nigel Ayers, who bluntly suggested that Phil 'cut a rather more healthy and clean-cut image than the other scruffs at Fort Wally', painted a slightly different picture, proposing that Phil 'saw himself as the leader and was not afraid to march round issuing orders, not that anyone paid much attention to him.' (Shark 2003d; Ayers 1996)

Fort Wally lasted until after the winter solstice, when some of the group moved into a squat in Amesbury, and Phil went to Cyprus for the rest of the winter. Returning in

*Roger Hutchinson's poster for the 1975 festival,
planned with Phil Russell at Fort Wally in 1974.
Copyright Roger Hutchinson.*

Freedom festival: frolics in the River Avon during the free festival in 1976.
Copyright Roger Hutchinson.

the spring, he resumed preparations for the coming festival, but in May, after stopping at the squat in Amesbury en route to Cornwall, he was arrested for possession of a small amount of LSD by policemen who raided the squat unexpectedly and who claimed, somewhat improbably, that they were looking for an army deserter. The second Stonehenge Free Festival took place without him.

1975: the ineffable solstice

For the 1975 festival, the site was moved to the east of the stones, by the King Barrows. The weather was hot and sunny, attracting a crowd of up to 3,000 on Midsummer's Eve. Two bands – Hawkwind plus Here and Now – both began what were to become legendary associations with the festival that year, and there was good food, with Jeremy doing bread runs and the Hare Krishnas providing a free food tent (as they had the year before), demonstrating an awareness of the principles of freedom and the importance of sacred sites, whatever their denomination, that continues to this day.

Paul Aitken, a Stonehenge regular, recalled the 1975 festival as 'very much linked with the stones. Partly because of its position in King Barrow woods, on the line of the Avenue, there was this continuous umbilical cord of people going to and from the stones.' The festival and Stonehenge were 'actually linked in a living way, and although it was ostensibly a music festival, there was a lot going on that was quite different.' (Aitken 1998: 201)

Some of these differences were highlighted in a rhapsodic, utopian recollection of the 1975 festival by Jeremy Ratter and other members of the Crass Collective: 'Wood-fires, tents and tipis, free food stalls, stages and bands, music and magic. Flags flew and kites soared. Naked children played in the woodlands, miniature Robin Hoods celebrating their material poverty. Dogs formed woofing packs that excitedly stole sticks from the innumerable wood piles and then scrapped over them in tumbling, rolling bundles of fur. Two gentle horses were tethered to a tree and silently watched the festivities through the dappled light that danced across their bodies. Old bearded men squatted on tree stumps muttering prayers to their personal gods. Small groups of people tended puffing fires upon which saucepans bubbled and bread baked, the many rich smells blending across the warm air. Parties of muscular people set out in search of wood and water, accompanied always by a line of laughing, mimicking children. Everywhere there was singing and dancing. Indian flutes wove strange patterns of sound around the ever-present bird song. The beat of drums echoed the hollow thud of axe on wood. Old friends met new, hands touched, bodies entwined, minds expanded and, in one tiny spot on our earth, love and peace had become a reality.' (Rimbaud 1981)

Most remarkable of all were the experiences of the solstice. One festival-goer, Martin Williams, recalled that 'Tolkien-esque wanderings through woods led slowly to the dawn, and one of the most amazing sights I've ever seen. We had wandered quite a way from the festival site and as the holy dawn broke we looked back over the sloping hills to see literally hundreds of people, sitting cross-legged in meditation, as the sun came up over the horizon.' Another commentator 'experienced an epiphany in front of the Heel Stone' at dawn: 'As the sun rose I felt its power flowing into me transforming me from an old wrinkled party balloon into a thrusting airship! I strode back, reborn, along the ancient processional path that led across the fields with a mission to get things moving in the right direction and I worked all that day clearing the site of litter and helping in the free food kitchen.' (Shark 2003d)

The following comes from a dialogue between Paul Aitken and the archaeologist Barbara Bender. BB: 'Were you allowed into the stones?' PA: 'Well, in the sense that we allowed ourselves in. At the solstice we went down there in the afternoon rather than the sunrise – the real experience was the indescribable ceremony that took place in the afternoon. You were with the same people that you'd been living with, and everybody was suddenly completely different and the whole atmosphere was completely different. The stones were completely different and there was really no turning back from there.' The key word here, I think, is 'indescribable.' For Paul, as for many others, the communal solstice at Stonehenge was a numinous and life-changing experience, but one that remains ineffable, a modern-day mixture of the social and the spiritual for which no definition exists. (Aitken 1998: 202)

After ten days or so, the festival came to an end. A collection was made for the farmer whose land the festival was occupying, a substantial amount of money was raised to his evident satisfaction, and the site was thoroughly tidied after the event. According to C.J. Stone, 'Everything was done properly, with the best will and organisation imaginable – Phil's vision brought to life.' Ironically, the only trouble – apart from one band that was so out of it that the members started fighting on stage

Tipis, with Stonehenge in the background.
Copyright Roger Hutchinson.

– came not from the festival itself, but from groups of young locals and off-duty military personnel from the nearby army camps (the same camps that had provided so much of the antagonism evident at the gatherings of the 1950s). The Festival Zone website commented bluntly that 'Freaked-out squaddies, most out of their faces on a cocktail of chemicals, stumbled about, getting into grief with the pissed local youth.' (Stone 1996: 91; Shark 2003d)

The lonesome death of Phil Russell

Only after the festival had dispersed did the truth about Phil Russell's incarceration begin to emerge. After his arrest, he had almost immediately been placed in psychiatric care. He was released two days after the last vehicle left the site of the festival that he had inspired, but he was by now a broken man, bloated, scared, 'a sun-worshipping warrior afraid of the sun.' Large doses of anti-psychotic drugs – administered without any legal approval – had destroyed him in less than two months. (Stone 1996: 89)

He died soon after, although even after his death the full details of what had happened to him never emerged. Two coroners' inquests were adjourned, and by the time of the third all the evidence had conveniently disappeared. Phil Russell was whitewashed out of history, the official view being similar to that of the policeman who said at the inquest, 'Well, he thought he was Jesus Christ, didn't he?' (Stone 1996: 92)

To this day, the circumstances surrounding Phil's death remain obscure. Jeremy Ratter and his friends were convinced that his life was deliberately destroyed, and they set about marshalling evidence, which included the obvious suspicions – the convenient dates of his arrest and discharge, the disappearance of all the evidence – with more worrying indications that something larger was amiss than the casual destruction of an eccentric individual who was unlucky enough to be sectioned in a psychiatric hospital. In the course of an investigation that took a year and a half, Jeremy discovered that there had been a second death – another of the Wallies was found 'tied to a tree in Epping Forest with a joint in his hand' – and he also apparently uncovered 'links between the Essex police and the Brighton underworld, a whole network of murky dealings and unpleasant goings-on.' (Stone 1996: 93)

In the end, however, Jeremy aborted his investigation, convinced that he was under permanent surveillance and that his life was perhaps in danger. When two policemen turned up at the commune to mention that they knew he was writing a book, he burned the manuscript and all the evidence. This could well have been the end of the story, but when C.J. Stone contacted Trevor Helm, a solicitor who had worked on Phil's case, Helm told him that he had written to the psychiatric hospital where Phil had been sectioned and that 'they'd as good as admitted that Phil had been overdosed on psychiatric drugs', that on visiting Jeremy at the commune he'd 'seen some people literally crawling around in ditches, keeping an eye on the house', and that although the firm that he worked for kept 'meticulous records', all the files relating to the case had disappeared from his office. (Stone 1996: 95)

Not everyone remains convinced, however. When C.J. Stone interviewed Chris, one of the original Wallies, for *Fierce Dancing*, he 'thought it was no wonder that Phil had been certified back then.' Endorsing the establishment view, Chris suggested that 'He must have sounded mad with all his strange declarations', and concluded that 'His death was brought on as much by his own intransigence – and by their failure to understand what he was trying to say – as by any dark machinations.' Tim Abbott put forward a similar – though more sensitively considered – opinion: 'His vision had a surreal clarity but his grasp of the necessities and realities of life was too fragile for him to challenge the establishment head-on and survive.' The truth will perhaps never be known, but the shadows obscuring Phil's death were to provide the basis for a potent modern-day mythology. (Stone 1996: 112; Abbott 1990)

1976: heat and dust

In 1976, perhaps in honour of Phil, the festival moved to the west of the stones again, where the first embryonic gathering had taken place. It was blistering hot weather for the fortnight, 5,000 people attended, and there were six stages and a large number of tepees. For C.J. Stone, 'Phil's vision had become enshrined in the national consciousness', and there were favourable reports in the media. One reporter talked to a Londoner who told him that for many people the festival was 'their chance to practice their own lifestyle away from the prejudice of the cities. He pointed out the workers' co-operative bakery, where wholemeal bread was being baked, and the tiny stalls selling tea, fruit and home-made candles, all at rock bottom prices. Food supplies were being bought locally and a farmer in the area had agreed to supply

Nudity and ritual at the 1976 ceremony.

daily churns of milk.' Even the locals seemed not to mind: 'One middle-aged man said, "I only came to laugh but now I'm here I think it's great," and many of the leaders in the town [Amesbury] agreed that the festival had "not been detrimental".' Relations between the festival-goers and the authorities were so amicable that 'the fire brigade sprayed water for the hippies to dance and play in around the stones' and even the police joined in, using their car headlights to illuminate the stage when the power from the generators failed. (Stone 1996: 95; Shark 2003d; McKay 2000: 24)

At the solstice, Druids and festival-goers were at the circle together. Instead of waiting until the afternoon to hold their ceremonies, hundreds of the festival-goers were determined to honour Phil's memory at the most numinous time, staging what the pagan commentator George Firsoff referred to as an 'invasion' of the temple, which 'led directly to the festival people acquiring a right of religious access to the stones.' Jeremy Ratter brought Phil's ashes in a small wooden box on which was inscribed 'Wally Hope, died 1975, aged 28: a victim of ignorance' and the crowd scattered them over the megaliths. Sid Rawle, the self-styled 'King of the Hippies', chanted a mantric requiem, someone read out a poem, a military helicopter flew low, and a cameraman making a film of the proceedings saw 'an ethereal body dancing in and out of the stones.' It was the last sighting of Phil Russell. (Firsoff 2002b; Stone 1996: 96)

Chapter Four

The Druids

Running parallel to the stories of public access to Stonehenge in the previous chapters is the persistent presence, on or around the summer solstice, of the modern-day Druids. Although their association with Stonehenge can only confidently be traced back to the end of the nineteenth century, a survey of their earlier history is vital in establishing a context for their adoption of Stonehenge as a sacred site.

John Toland

According to much of the modern-day Druids' own literature (e.g. Nichols 1992: 99), the refounding of Druidry in Britain began at the end of the seventeenth century, when John Toland, variously described by modern writers as 'an alarming religious theorist', an 'Irish revolutionary' and a 'dangerous free-thinker', met John Aubrey in Oxford. (Chippindale 1994: 85; Shallcrass 1999: 6; Piggott 1975: 136)

Historians and Druids alike agree that this meeting took place. Toland himself wrote of his time at Oxford that Aubrey was 'the only person I ever then met, who had a right notion of the temples of the Druids, or indeed any notion that the Circles so often mention'd were such Temples at all.' In the Druids' history, Toland was then elected as the first chosen Chief of the modern Druid Order at a meeting in the Apple Tree Tavern in Covent Garden in September 1717, 'by delegates from the Druid centres of York, London, Oxford, the Isles of Man and Anglesey, Cornwall, Scotland, Ireland, Wales and Brittany', and the Order was officially inaugurated on Primrose Hill at the autumn equinox. (Toland 1747: vol. 1, 112; Bonewits 2002)

Although this is the founding legend of the modern Orders, its authenticity has been widely challenged not only by historians but also by other Druids. Chris Chippindale and Philip Carr-Gomm, the Chosen Chief of one of the modern Druid Orders – the Order of Bards, Ovates and Druids (OBOD) – have both pointed out that Toland himself took a cynical view of the historical Druids. In letters to his patron Lord Molesworth, Toland railed against their deviousness, calling them 'masters of the art of managing the mob, which is vulgarly called leading the people by the nose' and declaring that 'no Heathen Priesthood ever came up to the perfection of the Druidical, which was far more exquisite than any other system; as having been much better calculated to beget ignorance, and an implicit disposition in the people, no less than to procure power and profits to the priests, which is one grand difference between the true worship and the false.' (Chippindale 1994: 85; Carr-Gomm 1991: 24–6; Toland 1726)

—A British Druid

William Stukeley's fanciful image of a Druid, from Stonehenge *(1740), based on similar depictions in Aylett Sammes'* Britannia Antiqua Illustrata *(1676) and Henry Rowland's* Mona Antiqua Restaurata *(1723).*

Aubrey as a Druid

Similarly, although historians and Druids alike agree that Aubrey's research into stone circles and Druids facilitated a revival of interest in Druidry, opinions differ over his role in the rebirth of Druidry as an active force. Ross Nichols, the founder of OBOD and its Chief Druid from 1964 until his death in 1975, suggested that Aubrey was not only aware of the Classical sources regarding Druidry, but also that he was a practicing Druid himself. Taking as his starting point the older Druid legend that a group of Druids was in existence in 1245 – the Mount Haemus Grove, based in Oxford – and that there had been an even earlier grove at the same location, Nichols suggested that Aubrey 'determined to revive Mount Haemus, and a group began to wear the robes and to carry out some of the ceremonies. This would have been in 1694 or soon after. We do not know which ceremonies – probably the equinoxes.' (Nichols 1992: 97)

Those who knew Aubrey paint a different picture, of an inconstant enthusiast, prone to obsessions, of which Druidry was one. John Batteley, a keen antiquary and a contemporary, recalled him exclaiming, 'Behold, the golden sickle with which the Druids used to cut mistletoe!' on being shown a perfectly ordinary Roman strigil – a

A portrait of John Aubrey intended as the frontispiece to Monumenta Brittanica, *from J. Britton's* Memoir of John Aubrey *(1845).*

kind of back-scratcher, and, moreover, one made of gilt not gold – and concluded that Aubrey, 'in other respects a man of learning, was apt superstitiously and idly to wrest almost everything to the religion and worship of the Druids.' (Batteley 1774: 116)

Modern scholars have been no less sceptical. Michael Hunter concluded his study of Aubrey with the observation that he 'often seems bafflingly inconsistent as an intellectual figure', but the most pertinent reasons for suspecting that Aubrey was not a Druid are revealed in the scholarly reservations and more personal doubts expressed in his work. Writing of his discovery that the stone circles pre-dated the Romans, Aubrey was sure that he had presented 'a clear evidence that these monuments were Pagan-Temples: which was not made out before', but conceded that it was only a '*probability*, that they were *Temples* of the *Druids.*' In addition, Hunter noted that 'his faith in his theory that the Druids built stone circles was easily shattered when someone told him that so erudite a scholar as Sir Robert Sibbald backed the Danes.' Sibbald, the author of *Scotia Illustrata*, had not even made such a claim, and in any case, as Aubrey's friend James Garden pointed out in a letter, 'supposing he had said so that were not enough to overturn your opinion concerning these monuments.' (Hunter 1975: 209, 224; Aubrey 1980b)

Stukeley as a Druid

Other reputed Druid leaders of this early period – William Stukeley and William Blake – are beset by similar problems. Stukeley, the successor to John Toland in the approved list of Chosen Chiefs, certainly did more than any other writer of the time to propagate the connection between the ancient Druids and the temples of Stonehenge and Avebury that had been proposed by John Aubrey, although nothing

Stukeley's self- portrait as Chyndonax, from the frontispiece to Stonehenge *(1740).*

in his writing proves that he was the Chosen Chief of a revived Druid Order covering the British Isles and Brittany. There is no mention, for example, of the Druids under Stukeley attending Stonehenge for the summer solstice, which might be expected if the man who brought together the solstice and the Druids were the chief of an active group of Druid revivalists.

Stukeley's fascination with the Druids was, however, a theme that ran throughout his entire adult life. In his early years, when he became a Fellow of the Royal Society and founded the Society of Antiquaries, he undertook some of his extraordinary fieldwork accompanied by fellow members of the Society of Roman Knights, an organisation of close friends and antiquarians, formed to record and preserve Britain's Roman remains, in which all the members took Celtic or Roman names. Lord Winchelsea, his patron, became the Belgic prince Cingetorix, and his good friend Roger Gale was Venutius, the ruler of the Brigantes. Interestingly, only Stukeley took a specifically Druidic name – Chyndonax the Arch-Druid. Although this confirms his obsession with Druids, it does nothing to prove that his adoption of the name was anything more than a typical affectation of the time. The verdict of Philip Shallcrass of the British Druid Order (another modern order) was that 'Stukeley at least claimed to be a Druid, through probably more as a romantic flourish than a meaningful statement of fact.' (Piggott 1950: 44, 53–7; Shallcrass 1999: 6)

Nevertheless, a change came over Stukeley after he returned to Lincolnshire in 1726 to become an ordained minister in the Church of England. Perhaps through 'some kind of revelation or born-again conversion', as John Michell suggested, he was seized by 'the idea that the Druids had first proclaimed in Britain the very same principles of true, patriarchal religion as were now upheld by the Church of England', and that if this truth were once more revealed, 'here was to be open'd the glory of Christ's kingdom on earth.' These investigations led to the theories expounded in his books on Stonehenge and Avebury, published in 1740 and 1743. They have earned him the scorn of archaeologists over the last fifty years or so – Stuart Piggott, for example, called his work a 'mass of absurdity' and Chris Chippindale referred to his 'fantastical Druidic vapourings' – but at the time they were neither unusual nor badly received. (Michell 1982: 10–11; Piggott 1985; Chippindale 1994: 81)

Druidic theories were abundant in the literature of the time. John Wood, the supposedly sober architect who accurately surveyed Stonehenge in 1740, filled his subsequent book with outlandish proposals that Stanton Drew, the megalithic complex near Bristol, was a Druid university, and that colleges were established for Druids at Stonehenge, philosophers at Avebury, prophets on Exmoor and bards at the fortuitously named Harptree in the Mendips. Although Stukeley was subject to criticism in his lifetime, the most representative comments on his theories came from the 'meticulous antiquary' Richard Gough. In 1768, in a survey of commentators on Stonehenge, Gough concluded that, 'The most accurate examiner and describer of this stupendous pile, which could have been nothing but a religious, and consequently a druidical, monument, is Dr Stukeley in *Stonehenge.'* (Wood 1747; Haycock 2003; Gough 1768)

William Blake

Opinion is just as divided over the role of William Blake. Like Stukeley, Blake actually claimed to be a Druid, giving it as his reason for refusing to take the oath when he was on trial in Chichester, but Philip Shallcrass described him as 'the unlikeliest of Druid chiefs, since he viewed Druidic beliefs and practices as exemplary of everything that is worst in human nature. He loathed the concept of measurement and geometry, which he saw as stifling true vision, creativity and freedom.' The apologists for Blake, on the other hand, exploit the dualism and ambiguity in his work to suggest that the opposite is true. Ross Nichols found 'Blake's clearest setting forth of shapes and meanings... in the 'Four Zoas', which hold the heart of his mysticism' and in which are 'embedded' the 'basic ideas of the Druidic rituals.' (Carr-Gomm 1991: 26; Shallcrass 1999: 6; Nichols 1992: 104)

Perhaps the most subtle analysis of the roles of both Blake and Stukeley in the revival of Druidry was put forward by John Michell, who suggested that Blake was Stukeley's 'prophet', but that the differences between them were 'those between poet and priest.' For Michell, 'Blake's golden age was a state of inspired anarchy while Stukeley's was one of sacred order.' Blake's Druids, with law and science, 'brought to an end the innocent, poetically inspired golden age of Jerusalem in Britain', and the corruption, which spread around the world, could only be reformed at its source,

A vast, visionary trilithon in William Blake's
Jerusalem: The Emanation of the Giant Albion *(1804).*

'by invoking again the spirit that reigned in the Jerusalem of primal antiquity.'
Michell concluded that although Blake and Stukeley were at odds politically, 'as
prophets they were united by their common vision of the New Jerusalem on earth,
first to be revealed in England.' (Michell 1982: 15, 24)

What is particularly satisfying about Michell's conclusion is not only that it feeds so
successfully into the undercurrents of mystical Romanticism that he himself was so
influential in re-establishing in the 1960s, but also that it sidesteps the whole issue of
whether they were 'real' Druids or not. From the moment that the historical Druids
had been reintroduced through Classical sources, writers had struggled to reconcile
the conflicting reports of their sophistication, in their role as native philosopher-
priests, and their savagery, which was particularly prominent in the tales of human
sacrifice reported by Tacitus, who described how 'this inhuman people were
accustom'd to shed the Blood of their Prisoners on their Altars, and consult their
Gods over the reeking Bowels of Men.' (Leland 1709: 46)

The supposed Druid leaders discussed above were not immune to these misgivings.
Aubrey thought the pre-Roman natives 'almost as salvage [savage] as the Beasts,
whose Skins were their only rayment.' Stukeley could only cope with the reports of
sacrifice by describing them as 'deriv'd from some extraordinary notice they had of

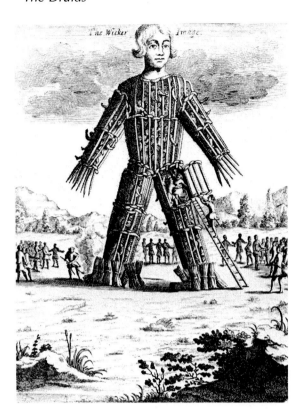

The Wicker Man, from Aylett Sammes' Britannia Antiqua Illustrata *(1676).*

mankind's redemption; and perhaps from *Abraham*'s example misunderstood', and Blake's apocalyptic visions, in which the temples 'Resound with the cries of Victims, shouts and songs and dying groans' seem to have been inspired by Aylett Sammes, who introduced the notion that the Druids 'burn[ed] criminals alive in great wickerwork effigies.' Given these reservations, it's not surprising that in the end the prophetic and poetic gifts of Stukeley and Blake have provided a more resonant legacy than the shadowy origins of the modern-day Druids. (John Aubrey, 'An essay towards the description of the north division of Wiltshire', quoted in Hunter 1975: 176; Stukeley 1740: 54; Michell 1982: 15)

The Druid revival: Henry Hurle and Edward Williams

For historians, the revival or rebirth of Druidry can only be traced as far back as 1781, when Henry Hurle, a carpenter and builder, established the Ancient Order of Druids in London. Like other organisations created at the time – the Ancient Order of Foresters, the Ancient Order of Royal Shepherds and the Society of Oddfellows – these Druids took their inspiration from Freemasonry, itself a development of the 'lodges' of the original 'masons', the medieval traders and artisans who established themselves in associations with mythical histories, secret signs and initiation rites. The earliest secret societies of Freemasons seem to have originated in Scotland at the end of the seventeenth century, expanding rapidly throughout England in the decades that followed. Like the medieval 'crafts', they established themselves in lodges. Some, like the Druids, chose to dress in loose white robes. Most adopted

The 'Grand Conventional Festival of the Britons', an extraordinary fantasy from Samuel Rush Meyrick and Charles Hamilton Smith's The Costume of the Original Inhabitants of the British Isles *(1815).*

initiation ceremonies involving the esoteric significance of ritual objects: a death's head, two pillars, a square and a compass, for example. However, in common with the majority of Masons and the other secret societies they inspired, mysticism was not high on the Ancient Order's agenda. Behind the obscurantism of its initiations and ceremonies was nothing more sinister than an élite Christian brotherhood, 'a friendly society, devoted largely to charitable work and the mutual benefit of members.' (Hutton 1999: 52–6; Shallcrass 1999: 8)

Crucially, the new secret societies invested themselves with a deeper significance by taking from Freemasonry the tradition of claiming an immemorial antiquity. The Oddfellows claimed to have been founded by Roman soldiers, the Foresters counted Alfred the Great and William Rufus as early members, and the Druids went so far as to name Noah as their founder. As fables establishing a legitimising authority, these tales were superb, but as truth they were sadly lacking. Ronald Hutton concluded, 'None, in reality, sprang from an earlier provenance than the last quarter of the eighteenth century', and the historian Mark Carnes stated, 'no idea was more commonplace, nor more palpably untrue, than the fraternalists' claims of ancient and venerable origins.' (Hutton 1999: 59; Carnes 1989: 28–62)

Even so, the illusions continued. At the end of the eighteenth century, a Welsh Druidic tradition was successfully conjured up by Edward Williams, better known as Iolo Morgannwg. Williams was a stonemason and an accomplished scholar and poet, but he was also, as Ronald Hutton put it, 'a reckless romantic, imprudent in his attitude to the truth as he was in his politics, his financial habits and his consumption of laudanum.' When he discovered that the existing Welsh manuscripts constituted an insufficient history, he forged a new one. Using scraps of the old manuscripts, he created ceremonies, costumes, regalia and hierarchy which, he claimed, had been known by the Order in Druidical times, and he held his first Gorsedd (Assembly of Bards) on Primrose Hill at the autumn equinox in 1792, conducted within a small stone circle made of stones that he had brought along in his pocket. (Hutton 1991: 140)

Fortuitously for Williams, his 'revival' of Welsh Druidry coincided with a more general revival of Welsh patriotism. With his inspiration, the London-based Welsh community revived the Eisteddfod (a medieval competition of the Bardic arts), and in 1819, when an Eisteddfod was held in Glamorgan, Williams' entire Gorsedd ceremony was included for the first time. Today, long after the extent of his forgery has come to light, the Bardic tradition that he created still effectively constitutes the Welsh cultural elite. Even the Queen, initiated as part of her regal duties, adds to the ongoing process of myth-making on a national scale. Compared to this, Williams' contributions to the ritual awakening of Stonehenge would seem to pale into insignificance. However, his Gorsedd of 1792 was the first recognisable combination of three factors – a sacred place, a stone circle and the quarters of the solar year – that are at the heart of the modern-day story of Stonehenge.

Mystical Druidry and the Ancient Druid Order

Despite the forgeries and the façade of mysticism, it is clear that by the late eighteenth century some branches of the Masonic tradition began to develop genuine esoteric concerns alongside the generous dose of patriarchal Christianity that sustained the majority. The four cardinal points of the compass, which were to retain a significance that runs up to the present day for the majority of Druids and other pagans, were invested with esoteric meaning: the east stood for wisdom, the west for strength, and the south for beauty. The north, as Ronald Hutton described it, 'was regarded as the place of darkness, and shunned, following a tradition given biblical authority in the book of Jeremiah and embedded in English folk culture.' Throughout the nineteenth century, the tools and rituals of the secret societies were refined. The pentagram, present from the earliest days, was fixed as the symbol of the most sacred principles, along with the hexagram (also known as the Seal of Solomon) and the triangle, the square and the compasses, which were fixed as symbols of the first three degrees of initiation. (Hutton 1999: 56)

Offshoots of the original Ancient Order also became prevalent at this time. For the most part they were subtle variations on the familiar theme of the friendly society – the United Ancient Order of Druids (1833) and the Order of Druids (1858). However, this was also the time that a more radical group emerged, an organisation that would come to be known variously as the Druid Church of the Universal Bond, the Circle of the Universal Bond or, more commonly, as the Ancient Druid Order.

Like the other Druid groups, the Ancient Druid Order claimed a long history, as it does to this day – 'a continuation of the Mount Haemus Grove founded in Oxford in 1245', that was 'reconstituted in 1717 from Druid groups existing in various parts of the British Isles and Brittany.' David Loxley, the current Chief of the Order, includes the Elizabethan magician John Dee and Thomas Paine, author of *The Rights of Man*, as members, along with other, more familiar names – Aubrey, Stukeley, Blake – and refers to the Order as a more or less constant revolutionary force. According to Loxley, the Druids allied themselves with dissidents after the English Civil War – Gerrard Winstanley's Diggers, who will be discussed at length in Chapter Five, and the Levellers, the dispossessed of Cromwell's New Model Army, who sought to prevent enclosure by 'levelling the land', and whose socialist rhetoric was so persuasive that entire regiments subscribed to the cause. Loxley also claims that Druids were transported to the colonies without trial at the end of the eighteenth century, and that they endeavoured to establish a true Commonwealth and Republic from the nineteenth century onwards. (Loxley 2002, 2003)

Alongside its alleged revolutionary tendencies, the Druid Order was also involved in a spiritual quest. By the second half of the nineteenth century, they had become 'the most active and prominent practitioners of mystical Druidry in the country', immersed in the growth of occultism and spiritualism that was prevalent at the time and heavily influenced by the teachings of the Theosophical Society, founded by the Russian medium and mystic Madame Blavatsky. Theosophy, which brought eastern influences to the fore, taught that 'all the main religious and mystical traditions of the globe reflected the same primal wisdom, and encouraged a syncretization of them to enhance human knowledge and ability.' (Hutton 1999: 224, 79)

Many of the Theosophists were also active in the revival of interest in ritual magic that arrived in Britain in the mid-nineteenth century via the French mystic Eliphas Lévi, who 'provided both a conceptual framework and a set of practical manuals for a new generation of magicians.' Prominent amongst the new organisations was the Hermetic Order of the Golden Dawn, one of whose members, Samuel Liddell Mathers, went further than anyone before in reintroducing elements of genuine ceremonial magic to the working tools of Freemasonry. Mathers was also responsible for a significant change in the interpretation of the cardinal points, reclaiming the north from the Freemasons' Biblical fear and establishing it as 'a place of divinity and elemental power.' In another move away from the restrictive worldview of the Masonic tradition, the Golden Dawn added figures from Christian and Hebrew mythology to the traditional Classical imagery of the secret societies, reflecting its roots in the magical tradition and creating 'a divine kaleidoscope, which could be adjusted to meet the differing spiritual needs and instincts of the various members.' (Hutton 1999: 70, 236, 80)

As well as Lévi's influence on magic, his myth-making, linking the Egyptians with the Knights Templars and the Holy Grail and blending the European magical traditions of the cabbala and the tarot, created 'a powerful implicit criticism of orthodox Christianity and an alternative history of Western culture which could be taken up by radicals on both the left and the right.' A case in point would seem to be the Ancient Druid Order which, according to David Loxley, 'has never believed in the historical validity of the Bible or the social structure of Britain', as this, 'from its monarchy to its social justice system with its moralistic rules', is 'based on an interpretation of an imagined past which is just an illusion.' (Hutton 1999: 72; Loxley 2003)

The Ancient Druid Order and Stonehenge

Under the influence of Theosophy and occultism, the Druid Order finally adopted the summer solstice at Stonehenge, bringing together Stukeley's rediscovery of the astronomical alignment of Stonehenge and Edward Williams' skilful combination of stone circle, solar festival and Druidic ritual. Even so, despite the interest in the temple's summer solstice alignment that had been shown by both antiquarians and local people from at least the middle of the nineteenth century onwards, public records of the solstice gatherings make no mention of the Druids at Stonehenge until the start of the twentieth century, although the Druid Order seems to have been involved in solstice celebrations at the temple for some time before it was fenced off in 1901.

The historian Miranda Green commented that 'By the late nineteenth century, latter-day Druid groups were using Stonehenge on ceremonial occasions, particularly at the summer and winter solstices.' Stuart Piggott conceded that 'Druid bodies of some sort were certainly holding ceremonies there by the end of the last century', and Chris Chippindale credited their involvement 'for some years' before 1905. The Order's own records apparently contain a reference to a 'Midnight meeting and morning service at sunrise at Stonehenge' in 1898, when Edwin Arnold and other members of the Order were joined by Druid representatives from France and Belgium. However, no outside commentator has been able to confirm other claims in the Order's records that its association with Stonehenge began nearly a century before. In the 1940s, Robert MacGregor Reid (Chief Druid from 1946–64) wrote, 'I have personally been at Stonehenge at dawn since 1909 and my father George MacGregor Reid (Chief Druid) who is now 98 has attended way back to 1867 and speaks of others in those days that took the celebration back to 1810.' (Green 1997: 172; Piggott 1975: 181; Chippindale 1994: 174; Loxley 2003)

References to the Druid Order in the early part of the twentieth century are certainly both more numerous and more easily substantiated. Philip Shallcrass suggested that Gerald Massey, who was Chief Druid from 1880–1906, was 'blocked out from the sacred place' in 1903. Miranda Green wrote that in 1901 'the police ejected the Chief Druid, who then soundly and publicly cursed' the owner, and several commentators have remarked on conflict every year from 1903 to 1906, when the Druids were discovered burying the ashes of their deceased brethren inside the circle. (Shallcrass 1999: 8; Green 1997: 172–5; Grinsell 1978; Sebastian 1990: 103–4; Chippindale 1994: 174)

The Ancient Order of Druids

The Druid Order was not the only Druid organisation to take an interest in Stonehenge at the start of the twentieth century. On 24 August 1905, 700 Brothers of the Grand Lodge of the Ancient Order of Druids finally convened at the temple for a mass initiation of 256 members, including Stonehenge's owner, Sir Edmund Antrobus. Following bizarre ceremonies involving hundreds of grown men in white robes, wearing false white beards and brandishing sickles, the rest of the day was a dignified affair, as befitted these pillars of the establishment. There was a banquet in

Ancient Order of Druids ceremony, August 1905, from a contemporary postcard.

a marquee, and the music, provided by a military band, included an original composition entitled 'The March of the Druids.' (Chippindale 1994: 173)

Druids of the Ancient Order may have sporadically attended solstices at Stonehenge throughout the rest of the century, but they only returned *en masse* for a couple of other high-profile events. On the occasion of their 150th Anniversary, in June 1931, an International Druid Conference was held in Southampton, preceded by a pilgrimage to Stonehenge on 17 June, when the Druids were addressed by their President, Brother Hugo Reise of Hamburg. And at the 1956 solstice, accompanied by a portable harmonium, they performed a ceremony that was witnessed by Richard Atkinson, who was excavating at the time. (Grinsell 1978: 13)

George MacGregor Reid

The Ancient Druid Order, on the other hand, was to become the group most closely associated with the summer solstice at Stonehenge, although their story only really came to life in 1909, when George MacGregor Reid became Chief Druid. The inventor of the tonic drink Sanatogen and the author of numerous books including *The Natural Basis of Civilisation*, *Rational Dietetics* and *Women's Place and Importance*, MacGregor Reid was 'a fine orator' and 'a tallish man who could dominate crowds.' He added his own eastern influences to Druidry, having travelled extensively in Afghanistan and India, where he had been initiated as a Buddhist and had taken the name by which he was known as a Druid – Ayu Subhadra Savvanus. According to Ross Nichols, one of his most popular sayings was that 'God is too big and too great for any church.' (Nichols 1992: 107–8)

George MacGregor Reid.

'On or about' Monday 21 June 1909, MacGregor Reid officiated at a ceremony at which his son Robert was present. No record has been found for 1910, but a ceremony took place in 1911, and another on Sunday 23 June 1912, conducted by the Universal Bond of the Sons of Men, one of several aliases. Present at this latter ceremony was John Soul, otherwise known as 'The Shepherd of Stonehenge.' Described by Chris Chippindale as 'the leading Stonehenge eccentric of his generation, who had abandoned the mundane business of his grocer's shop to live out a Druidical fantasy-life in a long white beard and a longer white robe', Soul was held in higher esteem by the Druids. According to Ross Nichols, 'He was constantly at Stonehenge... always ready to expound as much of the truth as he judged his listeners equal to understanding', and he became prominent in the Druid Order, for whom 'He was naturally regarded as the monument's guardian; he understood its structures and interpreted its shape with intuitive correctness long before any recent studies.' (Grinsell 1978: 14; Chippindale 1994: 190; Nichols 1992: 108)

A.G. Bradley, a writer who toured Wiltshire in these years, captured something of the flavour of these early Druidic solstices: 'Midsummer morning has of late become quite a function at Stonehenge. Large gatherings of the enthusiastic and the curious meet here in the grey dawn, and go out, some of them, to greet the rising sun in garments of daring design, and of a pattern which would, in all likelihood strike terror into the shades of the original Druidic worthies they are supposed to personate.'

More significant in the long run was Bradley's analysis of the visitors – Druidic or otherwise – who were increasingly drawn to the monument at solstice: 'Stonehenge, always from earliest times a point of intelligent pilgrimage, widens its sphere of interest as the years go by: a process inevitable to the advance in population, in enlightenment, and, above all, in facilities for travel.' (Bradley 1907: 268)

The first confrontations

From 1913–15, there was conflict, heralded in 1912 when discussions between the Druids and Sir Edmund shifted from access to the more thorny issue of money. According to a Druid journal of 1929, 'The real trouble in 1912 was that a demand was made upon our Chosen Chief to provide £2,500 for underpinning and refixing some of the stones. The Chosen Chief offered to raise this sum sobeit the landlord gave him a document in writing guaranteeing the members of [the Order] the right to worship without let or hindrance at all times within Stonehenge. The promise was given by word of mouth, but the Chosen Chief insisted upon having it in writing. This the landlord refused, and thus the Chosen Chief in turn refused to supply the £2,500 until the written document was produced giving value in return for the money raised.' (*New Life and Druid Journal* 1929, quoted in Loxley 2003)

The events of 1913 were described by Philip Shallcrass: 'Failing to gain access to Stonehenge at the summer solstice in 1913, MacGregor Reid cursed Sir Edmund Antrobus after an angry confrontation with police at the tollgate. Reid's lengthy oration began, 'In grief and sorrow I call down the curse of Almighty God, and of his Spirit Messengers, that the weak may be liberated from the molestation of the tyrannical', and ended with a chant of 'Om Mane Padme Om'.' (Shallcrass 1999: 8)

The following year, MacGregor Reid and nine companions, 'some of whom claimed descent from the ancient so-called fire-worshippers of India', paid for admission whilst protesting against it. At 3.19 a.m., MacGregor Reid 'began to recite the prayers of the sun-worshippers at the altar, but he had not proceeded very far before Supt. Buchanan of the Wiltshire Constabulary called his attention to the notice posted within Stonehenge prohibiting the holding of any form of meeting or service within the circle, and requested him to desist. Dr Reid disregarded the warning and continued the recital in a louder voice than before, whereupon Supt. Buchanan informed him that he would have to leave the enclosure. Dr Reid declined to leave, and he was then forcibly ejected.' He returned, with his colleague George Catchlove, both 'wearing white robes, purple cassocks and stoles etc.' at 11 a.m. and 6 p.m., when they conducted services outside the enclosure. (*The Salisbury Journal*, 27 June 1914)

In 1915 there were further unsightly tussles, with the Druids refusing to pay and one of their number being forcibly removed from behind the Altar Stone. When Antrobus died soon after, relations between the Druids and the temple's owner had deteriorated to such an extent that the Druids took pride in claiming that his demise was the direct result of the curses of the previous three summers. (Chippindale 1994: 156)

Cecil Chubb

Fortunately for the Druids, the next owner, Cecil Chubb, a local landowner who allegedly bought the stones on a whim, allowed them free access on or around the solstice for the next three years. In October 1918, when he unexpectedly gave the monument and the land around it to the Commissioners of Works 'for the benefit of the Nation', there were high hopes that access would be made even easier. Chubb, who, according to George Firsoff, was a Druid himself, included three conditions with the Deed of Gift that accompanied his donation: 'that the premises shall as far as possible be maintained in their present condition', 'that no building or erection other than a pay box similar to the Pay Box now standing in the premises shall be erected... within 400 yards of the Milestone' and 'that the public shall have free access to the premises' on payment of no more than one shilling per head. (Michell 1986: 9; Firsoff 2002a)

There were reasons for the Druids to feel upbeat. At the time, George MacGregor Reid expressed the belief that 'there would be no obstacle in future to his co-religionists performing their worship on the site on Midsummer day.' Tim Sebastian of the Secular Order of Druids (another modern order) pointed out that 'The Druids were asked to legitimise spiritually the handing-over, and it was the Arch-Druid who actually handed over the title-deed to national representatives', and Leslie Grinsell commented, 'It is believed that the Inspectorate of Ancient Monuments of the (then) Office of Works formally granted permission for the modern Druid ceremonies to be continued.' (*The Times*, 2 October 1918; Sebastian 1990: 105; Grinsell 1978: 15)

Wrangles with the Ministry of Works

From the beginning, however, the temple's new administrators seem to have taken a dim view of the Druids' rituals. In 1919, when they sought access on 21 and 22 June, the custodian, Mr Smith, was obliged to enlist the aid of four policemen to restrain them. The following year, they retaliated by demanding four days' access on and around the solstice, prompting a refusal from an exasperated official who declared, 'some limit must be set to this absurd and degrading nonsense.' In the end, they celebrated on Sunday 20 June, and were not present on the day of the solstice. Other people – curious members of the general public – may well have been at Stonehenge instead, similar to the gathering reported in the press the following year, 1921, when no Druids were mentioned. (Chippindale 1994: 190; *The Times*, 22 June 1921)

The Druids certainly held a ceremony that year (probably on the nearest Sunday), although as late as 16 June they had been threatening to stay away. A letter to the Ministry from Thomas Ireland, the Druids' 'corresponding Councillor', railed against the entrance charge as an 'abuse of the Holy Place of our most Ancient Faith on behalf of selfish interests.' Ireland declared that 'The government have conferred upon it the status of a Circus or Museum, instead of its right due as The Cradle of

George MacGregor Reid conducting a Druid ceremony, from a 1920s postcard.
Note the aerodrome in the distance.

Religion in this our land', and concluded that 'until the state calls upon its officials to withdraw the showman spirit from this sacred circle, our feet will stand no more where Druidhs [sic] have stood praying for Universal Peace and Brotherhood.' (quoted in Loxley 2003)

Despite Ireland's bombastic pronouncements, the main conflict of the time centred on the Ministry's plan to divert the last right of way running through the temple, and on this issue at least the Druids met with some success. Local opposition was led by John Soul, and at a meeting with officials in Amesbury in July 1921 a compromise was reached and an agreement made 'to admit ratepayers and their friends to Stonehenge free of charge in lieu of rights of way.' (John Soul, Druid Order records, 11 July 1921, quoted in Loxley 2003)

On Wednesday 21 June 1922, 'much amusement was caused by a party of military officers who, in garments of white sheeting, and with false beards, held a mock Druidical ceremony.' The Druids withdrew to a disc-barrow on Normanton Down for their ceremony, although they returned to Stonehenge for a ritual on 24 June. Legal rights to use the barrow, referred to by David Loxley as 'the double circle' or 'the double mound nearby which was linked with Stonehenge by a pathway through the centre of the temple', were provided by Lady Grey of Normanton Farm, a

The Druids reveal their eastern influences in a 1920s postcard.

sympathetic local landowner, and it became a regular haven for the Druids' ceremonies whenever there were 'disruptive influences' at Stonehenge. (*The Salisbury Journal*, 23 June 1922; Loxley 2003)

In 1923, non-Druidic visitors – by now a regular feature – were handed leaflets notifying them that the Druids would be conducting their own service on Sunday 24 June, but they were back at the solstice the following year, amongst several hundred people present. In 1925, when the solstice fell on a Sunday and the largest attendance on record was reported, conflict between the Druids and the authorities seemed to have come to an end. MacGregor Reid 'explained that the Office of Works had given permission for the Druid Order to hold their service.' (Grinsell 1978: 15)

So it was surprising, at the 1926 summer solstice, to find the Druids storming the fences to gain entry. They had been banned from the solstice for again trying to inter the ashes of one of their dead, an action which until then had apparently been a fairly regular occurrence, despite the conflict it caused from 1903 to 1906. In 1924, the same year that the Commissioner of Works declared that 'under no circumstances can any burials be permitted within the precincts of Stonehenge in the future', one Druid claimed that parts of the ashes of fifteen deceased Druids had been buried at the monument up to 1919. (Chippindale 1994: 190; *The Times*, 12 September 1924)

In the wake of the ban – and, it should be noted, the first officially recorded 'invasion' of Stonehenge – Chris Chippindale suggested that the Druid Order withdrew from the solstice for a number of years to the disc-barrow on Normanton Down, but Druids were certainly present throughout this period. Editions of an official publication, *The Druid's Journal*, were published for the solstice ceremony on 26 June 1927, 24 June 1928, 23 June 1929, 22 June 1930 and 21 June 1931. (Chippindale 1994: 190; Grinsell 1978: 15, 28)

This latter date was another big public celebration, with around 2,500 people attending. Again it was a Sunday (in common with the dates for *The Druid's Journal* above), and what emerges clearly from a study of the solstice celebrations in this period is that the Druids, like the general public, were only able to congregate in large numbers on a Sunday. Also apparent is the fact that ordinary people were only prepared to gather in large numbers if the Sunday was the actual day of the solstice. Like the antiquarians and locals of the nineteenth century, ordinary people were fascinated by Stukeley's astronomical solstice, whereas the Druids were prepared – however reluctantly – to treat their rituals as a kind of moveable feast.

Certainly, tensions remained between the Druids and the authorities. In 1932, the Ministry of Works banned the sale of *The Druid's Journal*, prompting MacGregor Reid to pledge to 'hold no further meetings at Stonehenge.' Typically, it seems to have been an empty promise. Although the Druids shunned the actual solstice, they conducted ceremonies every year, as Patricia Drummond and C. Burke of the Ancient Monuments Inspectorate of the Department of the Environment discovered in 1978, when they searched their records at Leslie Grinsell's request. The dates Drummond and Burke winkled out of the archives varied considerably, but the chain was unbroken. Ceremonies took place on 16 June 1933, 15 July 1934, 23 June 1935, 25 July 1936, 25 July 1937 and 24 July 1938. No date was specified for 1939, although David Loxley suggested that the ceremony took place on 20 June, with another ceremony on 23 June at Parliament Hill on Hampstead Heath. (Grinsell 1978: 15; Robert MacGregor Reid's diary, quoted in Loxley 2003)

The 1940s and 1950s

Although most commentators have presumed that the activities of the Stonehenge Druids were suspended throughout the war years, David Loxley provided details of their attendance from 1940–5, seemingly reinforcing his suggestion that, 'We have attended Stonehenge, sometimes in very small numbers, every year including the two world wars.' For the most part, the records mention two or three delegates, rarely present at Stonehenge on the solstice itself but often on the days around, and often conducting other ceremonies at the 'double circle.' The only surprising references are to a crowd of 400 at the 1941 solstice, when John Soul held the ceremony for the Druids, and a crowd of 200 on 21 June 1942, reported by the secretary of the Order and evidently unconnected with the Druids. (Loxley 2003)

After the war, the Druid Order returned in larger numbers, celebrating the 1946 summer solstice at the disc barrows west of Bush Barrow on Normanton Down with a 'Peace Reunion of the Companions of the Summer Solstice' at Stonehenge itself the week after. On 22 June 1947, a memorial service was held for the recently deceased George MacGregor Reid, and access continued into the 1950s under the guidance of his son Robert. Records exist for Druid ceremonies in 1948, 19 June 1949 and 18 June 1950. In 1951, the year of the Festival of Britain, the Druid Order issued a Festival Souvenir brochure, and around 900 people attended a ceremony on 24 June entitled 'The Ritual of Light.' (Grinsell 1978: 16)

A newspaper report from 1952 gives some examples of the Druids' rituals at the time: 'About 100 people, including American tourists, braved heavy rain in the early hours of Sunday to travel from neighbouring towns and villages to witness the Midsummer service of the Druid Universal Bond at dawn. In front of the Altar Stone the ritual was led by the General Council of the Order, wearing white robes, purple cassocks and golden girdles. On the altar were the elements for the communion – a golden chalice, a red rose, fire and bread; and in the centre of these was the Pentagram. As the sun rose behind a bank of dark cloud at 4.43 a.m., Druids crowned their leader with oak leaves, sang the Song of Dawn, uttered their secret invocation to the High Intelligence, recited the Benediction of the Blessed Awen [literally, 'flowing spirit'] and at the end of the service celebrated communion in the four elements of air, fire, water and earth. Across Salisbury Plain swept a piercing wind, and the spectators, most of whom wore winter clothing, kept to the shelter of the huge trilithons.' (Stonehenge Campaign 2002)

In 1953, the Druids celebrated in early July, allowing members of the general public to occupy centre-stage on the actual day of the solstice. With no Druids and only a few Morris dancers for entertainment, this was the day that a thousand people held their own dawn celebration (the event that I have already considered as the first modern-day people's festival), although the Druid Order visited in the afternoon to hold a requiem for Companion Alice Lucy Smith (Aithne), who had 'not missed a Stonehenge festival since 1921.' (Grinsell 1978: 16)

Throughout the rest of the 1950s, as illustrated in the previous chapter, the crowds accompanying the Druids in their ceremonies became a regular feature, although arguably the most important development in Druidry during this post-war period was not the attendance at Stonehenge for the summer solstice, but what was happening behind the scenes.

Gerald Gardner and Wicca

1946 was the first year that one particularly influential individual, Gerald Gardner, was recorded as a member of the Circle of the Universal Bond. By December he sat on its governing council. That same year he also took a seat on the council of the Folk-Lore Society, which he had joined in 1939, just before war broke out. (Hutton 1999: 224)

Gerald Gardner (right) with Monique Wilson, who established covens in Scotland in the 1950s and who also knew Bev Richardson (see Chapter Five). Copyright Raymond Buckland (courtesy of Fortean Picture Library)

It was a fruitful period for Gardner. Over the next few years, he put together most of the background and materials required to launch a new religion – Wicca – in the 1950s. Presented, typically, as a surviving strand of an ancient tradition – in this case a surviving coven of witches in the New Forest – Wicca was in fact the first manifestation of a modern form of paganism that was to prove enormously successful, and that was also to affect the future of Druidry. Its main influences, above and beyond Gardner's own extensive research and experience as a retired colonial administrator with a life-long interest in antiquarianism and the supernatural, were the works of four particular writers, prominent in the first half of the twentieth century – the archaeologist Margaret Murray, the mystics and occultists Aleister Crowley and Dion Fortune, and the poet Robert Graves.

Murray, who worked primarily as a diligent Egyptologist, achieved widespread fame through her investigations of the long-held theory that paganism was exterminated in Europe during the Great Witch Hunt of the seventeenth and eighteenth centuries. In *The Witch Cult in Western Europe* (1921), she presented the witch religion as an ancient fertility cult that had survived in a fairly uniform manner across Western Europe until its deliberate and systematic suppression. The witchcraft presented by Murray was a fertility cult focused on a horned god representing the regenerative power of nature, and her witches met in covens of thirteen, holding 'sabbats' four times a year on the quarter days at the opening of the seasons – Candlemas, May Day, Lammas and All Hallows – when there was feasting, dancing, magic, sacrifice and ritualised sexual intercourse.

Murray's thesis was presented with a suitable veneer of academic rigour, although she generalised wildly and distorted the primary source material about the witch trials to her own ends. The entire basis of the four sabbats, for example, was a solitary source from Forfar in 1661. Much of her inspiration came from two works of dubious veracity: Jules Michelet's *La Sorciere* (1866), a poetic evocation of the witch

The Druids at Stonehenge, 1951. Gerald Gardner is third from the left, with bagpipes. From Stonehenge and the Druids, *a 'Festival Souvenir Brochure' produced for the Festival of Britain in 1951.*

tradition that was written over a two month period as a cynical – and successful – attempt to produce a best-seller and that consequently owed virtually nothing to primary research, and *Aradia* (1899) by Charles Leland, 'an unusually unreliable scholar', who claimed that his book reproduced a manuscript handed down by a surviving group of Italian witches. (Hutton 1999: 196, 147)

Other sources were the Romantic poets of England. Her goat god, for example, was clearly the same classical figure of Pan who had developed as the guardian and the personification of the English countryside in the previous century, associated, in the poetry of Wordsworth, Keats and Shelley, with 'instinct, unreason and the natural self', and radically reappraised by the poets as more relevant than the 'moderation, balance and self-knowledge through reason' offered by Pan's classical rival, Apollo. (Hutton 1999: 46)

Although Murray's methods and conclusions were immediately called into question by colleagues, her mass-market follow-up, *The God of the Witches* (1931), was so successful that it created an illusion that no amount of academic criticism could dislodge. She had succeeded in presenting witches as 'joyous and life-affirming... contrasted with the gloom of Christianity', and in laying out a structure and a history for Gerald Gardner to adopt. (Hutton 1999: 192)

Gardner also needed a goddess to balance his god, to create the sexual polarity and gender equality that provided such a definitive break from the traditional all-male élites and which remains central to most forms of modern paganism today. Again, there were obvious influences. Like Pan, the pagan goddess had been revived by the Romantic poets. From a solitary Classical source – Apuleius' *Metamorphoses* – Keats and Shelley had created a universal goddess associated with both nature and the moon. Significantly, both the goddess and Pan were embraced by the Golden Dawn – which also broke new ground by treating female and male members as equals – but it is clear that Gardner was additionally influenced by the goddess' ongoing evolution. (Keats 1818; Shelley 1820)

By 1880, the goddess of the poets had become a composite figure, both the creator of the world and the redeemer of mankind who had fallen from grace with nature. In 1903 Jane Harrison, a classicist at Cambridge, took the attributes of the goddess one step further, proposing that she had a three-fold aspect like the Fates or the Graces of Classical antiquity. Harrison only specified two of her roles – maiden and mother – and it was left to Aleister Crowley, in 1929's *Moonchild*, to add his interpretation that the third aspect was that of the crone. (Harrison 1903: 257–322; Crowley 1929: 187–8)

Both the god and the goddess were further promoted in the 1930s by Dion Fortune, whose Christian leanings were almost entirely submerged in two novels that promoted Pan and the Great Goddess – *The Goat Foot God* (1936) and *The Sea Goddess* (1938). The three-fold goddess was subsequently embraced by Robert Graves in *The White Goddess* (1948), an influential work of non-fiction prose, in which the poet, stressing the purported historical accuracy of his vision, embraced the concepts of ancient matriarchal religion and the Great Goddess. Maintaining throughout that her reign would begin in earnest when people started to believe in her in large numbers, he duly delivered the fully-formed Triple Goddess to Wicca just when she was needed.

Despite this roll-call of obvious antecedents and the familiar whiff of false antiquity, Gardner's new religion was genuinely radical. Wicca championed feminism by reclaiming the image of the witch and by elevating priestesses above priests. It defiantly replaced Christianity – rather than seeking to incorporate it – with its counter-cultural deities and its veneration of Nature. It broke social taboos by performing rituals naked (an innovation apparently inspired by Leland's *Aradia* and Gardner's own fascination with naturism), reclaiming the human body and its sexuality as sacred along the way. Although it differed from Druidry in its general disregard for ancient monuments, its focus on the moon and its emphasis on working in private, Wicca was also clearly influenced by Gardner's recent involvement in the Ancient Druid Order, and in particular his friendship with another significant figure in the development of modern paganism, Ross Nichols, the Druid Order's Scribe.

Ross Nichols

Nichols, a teacher, historian, poet and painter, aided Gardner in the writing of his first book about the new religion, *Witchcraft Today*, which was published in 1954. One of the more far-reaching results of his influence on Wicca, Druidry and paganism in general was the creation of the eight-fold year of festivals, combining

Ross Nichols.
Copyright Philip Carr-Gomm.

the solstices and the equinoxes with the quarter days at the start of February, May, August and November – Margaret Murray's witch festivals – which by the 1950s had started to become known by their Celtic names: Imbolc, Beltane, Lughnasa and Samhain.

Nichols had first embraced the concept of the eight-fold year in the 1940s, primarily through research into the folklore of the British Isles. At the time, the Druid Order celebrated only two seasonal festivals – the summer solstice at Stonehenge and the autumn equinox at Primrose Hill – but in 1956, influenced by Nichols and the 'independent' Druid James Duncan ('a kind of successor to John Soul' according to Nichols, and apparently one of several hundred such 'hereditary' Druids), Robert MacGregor Reid was persuaded to hold a spring equinox ceremony near Tower Hill, 'a traditional site of one of the places of free speech in Britain.' Prevented by the authorities from using Tower Green, the Order settled for a paved area near the church of All-Hallows-by-the-Tower. This immediately became a regular ceremony, although Nichols' attempts to persuade the Order to adopt the other five festivals (the winter solstice and the quarters of the Celtic year) were frustrated, and it was left to Gardner's Wiccans to take them up instead. (Shallcrass 2001; Nichols 1992: 111–2)

The solstices and the equinoxes were seized upon with particular enthusiasm by Doreen Valiente, Gardner's high priestess, who composed an invocation for Yule (Midwinter) shortly after her initiation in 1953. This was soon followed by other poetry for ceremonies at midsummer and the equinoxes, and it was chiefly through her influence that the Druids' festivals began to take their place alongside the Celtic quarter days. (Hutton 1999: 246–7)

By 1958, the eight-fold year was fully established, when a coven in Hertfordshire 'objected to the fact that whereas the main sabbats, at the quarter days, were celebrated on the actual dates, the festivals at the solstices and equinoxes were held at the nearest monthly meeting, which was pegged by the full moon, as a sign of their lesser status.' The coven 'asked Gardner if they could accord them equal importance, and hold them on the calendar dates. He agreed at once, and this created the standard, eightfold, pattern of Wiccan seasonal festivals', which has subsequently 'become ubiquitous in modern paganism.' (Hutton 1999: 248)

The Order of Bards, Ovates and Druids

Significantly, Ross Nichols took the eight-fold year with him when he split from the Ancient Druid Order and set up a new Order, the Order of Bards, Ovates and Druids, in 1964. The impetus for Nichols' departure was a dispute over the leadership of the Order following the death of Robert MacGregor Reid, although its genesis can be traced back to the latter years of his father's tenure, when the elderly Chief had 'discovered and adopted a certain Universalist Church, announcing that it and Druidry were in effect united', and had put forward a man called Smith as his successor, in preference to his son, whom he considered 'to lack both philosophic depth and leadership.' On George MacGregor Reid's death, the Order was divided. Some bowed to the late Chief's wishes, while the majority, having no wish to pursue the alliance with the Universalist Church, prevailed upon Robert to become their new Chief. (Nichols 1992: 109)

Robert MacGregor Reid's tenure seems to have been generally satisfactory. Pursuing a policy established by his father in the 1940s, he established links with other organisations around the world, and with the help of Lewis Spence, a folklorist and incurable Celtic Romantic, who continued to promote Edward Williams' fantasies as 'the central text of the 'Celtic mysteries', connections with Celtic organisations were particularly encouraged. Representatives from forty different countries – including Finland, Italy, Russia and Hungary, as well as the more obvious locations of Brittany, Cornwall and Wales – subsequently became involved in the gatherings at Stonehenge, although as Ross Nichols pointed out, it was necessary for the definition of Druidry to be 'fairly loosely applied.' (Hutton 1991: 141; Nichols 1992: 110)

As has been noted, however, throughout this period both Gerald Gardner and Ross Nichols had aims that were not being adequately addressed by the existing Order, and on Robert MacGregor Reid's death, after a 'paper-thin majority' had voted for the homeopath Thomas Maughan as the new Chief, 'a number of senior members voted against his leadership', and a second split occurred. Nichols wasted no time in establishing his new Order, breaking with tradition by establishing three grades of initiation – Bard, Ovate and Druid – based on 'old documents specifying a hierarchy', and bringing to life his long-cherished dream of a seasonal round of ceremonies based on the eight-fold year. (Nichols 1992: 112)

On a point of principle that should be heartening to all those concerned with open access to Stonehenge, Nichols' new offshoot promptly abandoned the summer solstice ceremonies at the great temple on Salisbury Plain, choosing instead to conduct their midsummer rituals at Hunsbury, an Iron Age hill-fort near Northampton. Nichols' exodus was precipitated by the restrictions first imposed between 1962 and 1964, when the temple was fenced off with electrified wire and access was restricted to 'certain types of Druids only' between 9.30 pm and 3.30 am. In Nichols' own words, 'After experience of this, the main Order refused to function under circumstances whereby the people – unruly or not – were kept away from the publicly-owned oldest national shrine on the day of the year designed for its cult.' He added, 'The answer should of course have been a few more police, not barbed wire.' (Nichols 1992: 113, 202)

Subsequently, the Order transferred its summer solstice ceremonies (and its observations of the equinoxes) to Parliament Hill in Highgate, 'where great cooperation was found and where the people of England's capital could easily reach what may have been their old centre... one of the unfencible places, like Hyde Park

The Ancient Druid Order ceremony in 1966.
Copyright Austin Underwood.

The Druids in the long hot summer of 1976.
Copyright Jeza.

Corner, a place of free speech.' The seasonal cycle of ceremonies was completed with a Beltane celebration on Glastonbury Tor (around the time that John Michell envisioned the St Michael Line) and an observation of Lughnasa in a private wood in the Chilterns, with the other festivals (the winter solstice, Imbolc and Samhain) taking place in the comfort of private rooms in London. (Nichols 1992: 113)

The Ancient Druid Order and the 1960s counter-culture

The remaining members of the Ancient Druid Order continued to celebrate the summer solstice at Stonehenge throughout the 1960s and into the 1970s, although in failing to hold to OBOD's principles the rump of the freedom fighters who had fought for access in the first half of the century began to look more and more like an opportunistic élite.

David Loxley, whose first summer solstice with the Order was in 1967, maintains otherwise. Pursuing his claims that the Druid Order represents a tradition of historical radicalism, he has drawn specific parallels with the counter-culture of the time, pointing out not only that he knew both Sid Rawle and John Michell when they all lived off Portobello Road in the 1960s, but also that 'the power of the subconscious history of Stonehenge' is such that 'The hippies took on some of the ideals of Gerrard Winstanley and Thomas Paine, without knowing they were members of our group.' Loxley's conclusion, that 'The Free Festival is a 20th century rejected people's version of what we have been doing for centuries, and if we cease to exist as a group, the idea will live on', certainly suggests a contemporary radicalism, and also helps to explain why, during the time of the free festival at least, the Druids and the festival-goers were at the stones together during the summer solstice on several occasions, including the scattering of Phil Russell's ashes in 1976. (Loxley 2003)

Chapter Five

Pagans and politics

With Phil Russell's death, the organisation of the Stonehenge Free Festival devolved to various individuals who had been involved in its founding, those who had subsequently been involved in the festivals of 1975 and 1976, or who had claims on its administration from their involvement in other projects. For the most part the leadership of the festival seemingly evolved naturally, in response to its collective needs, and those who reflected Phil's ambitions for Stonehenge stepped forward to contribute what they could. Three people in particular were to remain prominent throughout the festival years and beyond: Bev Richardson, a man central to the festival's connection with the stones, now living in Ireland; the late John Pendragon, another spiritual leader remembered with widespread affection; and Sid Rawle, the 'King of the Hippies', briefly introduced in the preceding two chapters.

Bev Richardson

Bev Richardson, born on the Isle of Man in 1947, has recounted three formative experiences that influenced his own mixture of mysticism and politics. These he has described as a combination of 'magic, environmentalism and civil disobedience.' The first was standing on the cliffs outside his home at the age of ten, watching the Sellafield Nuclear Reactor burning, sixty miles away. The next was guarding a railway station car park in Wales as 'a 16 year old boy-soldier' during the Cuban missile crisis of 1963. And, most crucially, 'as a lonely 13 year old', being 'drawn by coincidence and circumstance into the gentle influence of an old gentleman of powerful magic and magical mirth.' The old gentleman in question was Gerald Gardner, and Bev has written that he found his path in life through Gardner's example. (Richardson 1998, 1996)

After Gardner's death in 1964, Bev maintained contact with other Wiccans throughout the rest of the 1960s, working in the Witches Mill, which was owned by Scotty and Nikki (Monique) Wilson, 'the Lady Olwen from whom the American Gardnerian tradition springs.' In 1968, he met and married a young woman called Del, who had dropped out of school the year before to hitch-hike the length and breadth of Britain. After settling down for six years to raise a family, they subsequently returned to the mainland in the mid-1970s, to resume life on the road – with wagons and horses – and to bring the most explicitly pagan credentials to the free festival scene and to Stonehenge in particular. Bev wrote of the festival at Stonehenge that 'there was an important spiritual journey that was going alongside

Bev Richardson with the box that contained Phil Russell's ashes, summer solstice 1981. Copyright Alan Lodge.

the daily life', and added 'this it was that gave such power to the Midsummer celebration at the stones.' (Richardson 1996; Richardson in Shark 2003d)

Most noticeable was the stamp of his own interpretation of Wicca, which stood out most forcefully, providing invaluable inspiration to the embryonic pagan leanings of the festival-goers. Eschewing 'the framework of any organized tradition', his idiosyncratic approach, akin to a kind of personal revelation, remains intact to this day. As recently as 1996, he wrote, 'I get strange questions from Gardnerians even now, who want to know the words and forms of rituals from "source" as 't were, who get quite miffed when I tell them I haven't a clue, wasn't interested, never learnt them, didn't even consider them important. They were after all only the clothes that people put on magic to make it recognisable.' (Richardson 1996)

John Pendragon

John Pendragon (1946–98) gained his distinctive surname in 1977, when he, Bev and Sid Rawle were at South Cadbury hill-fort in Somerset (widely regarded as the site of King Arthur's Camelot), hoping to establish a fund to buy a permanent festival site. According to Bev, 'the idea of an Arthurian Camelot festival was the main topic of our conversation that day, and John offered the idea of a warband of spiritual

*John Pendragon,
summer solstice 1982.
Copyright Alan Lodge.*

warriors, so we with loving humour appointed him as Pendragon and so it stuck to him.' (Richardson 2003)

Described as 'the archetypal hippie' by C.J. Stone, 'fluffy and idealistic, with a cosmic turn of phrase', John has also been described by others who knew him as 'A beacon for Truth, Justice and the freedom to choose the way you want to live', as someone who 'freely gave of his energies in support of a better, more caring, sharing world' and as a campaigner for ecological and political issues whose efforts 'struck a chord in the hearts of many devoting their lives to leaving the earth a better place than they found it.' Alan Lodge (also known as Tash), a photographer, free-festival regular and welfare volunteer, recalled him as 'an inspirational character who believed that the core of the 'peace and love' ethic of the sixties contained practical ideals fundamental to the survival of a sustainable counter-culture', and stressed in particular his notable contributions to 'the magical solstice ceremonies in the Stones.' (Stone 1999: 221; John De Atma, Raefn and Crystal Jane in Dice George 2001; Lodge 1998)

John's own catch-all appreciation of the significance of the festivals at Stonehenge was summed up in a piece that he wrote in his newsletter, *Tribal Messenger*: 'The Stonehenge Free Festival, for myself and thousands of other people, was about the opposite to commercialism and war. It was about love, peace, sharing, happiness, ecology, beauty, brotherhood and sisterhood, Yin and Yang, meditation and celebration, physical and spiritual awareness, rock and roll, music and theatre, sunshine and sun-bathing, alternative lifestyles and cosmic energy.' (quoted in Shark 2003d)

Sid Rawle

The 'showman' of the three – and the more overtly subversive – was Sid Rawle. In the mid-1960s, Sid was already a colourful figure in the London's counter-cultural scene, where he gave the youthful squatting movement some historical ballast by establishing the Hyde Park Diggers, inspired by the example of the original seventeenth century Diggers, founded by Gerrard Winstanley.

A wool trader whose business was ruined in the early years of the Civil War, Winstanley moved to Surrey where he became an agricultural labourer and an avid pamphleteer with a visionary agenda of radical land reform. In *The New Law of Righteousness*, published in January 1649, he identified private property as 'the curse and burden the creation groans under', and urged the poor to rise up – with spades rather than weapons – and take back the land that had been violently taken from them by the ruling classes, who had kept it through repressive legislation backed up by the corruption of the church. By May 1649, when the execution of Charles I seemed only to have replaced one tyrant with another and the new regime was busy

Sid Rawle blessing a baby,
summer solstice 1982.
Copyright Alan Lodge.

enclosing commons and raising taxes, Winstanley put his newly conceived radicalism into practice. Gathering like-minded people around him, Winstanley and his Diggers dug up common land on St George's Hill 'to sow Corn, and to eat our bread together by the sweat of our brows.' (For further details see Monbiot 2000.)

The Digger movement expanded rapidly, inspiring communes in seven other counties, and although it was crushed by Cromwell's forces within a year, Winstanley's legacy lived on, reinterpreted during the revolutionary upheaval of the Romantic era by Thomas Spence (who proposed that 'private ownership of the land was the root of all social evil'); Robert Owen (who set up co-operative agrarian communities in the 1820s and 1830s) and Feargus O'Connor's Chartists. The Chartists 'tried all the political strategies in the repertoire of radicalism, from constitutional lobbying to alternative assemblies, general strikes and armed uprisings' and their Land Plan, unveiled in the 1840s, was 'the most impressive manifestation of working class commitment to radical agrarianism.' Significantly, they added a historical dimension to their land claims by holding 'occasional meetings at the mounds and hill-top enclosures which ancient custom had appointed as places of festival and public gathering.' (Burchardt 2002: 37, 39; Michell 1982: 154)

After the failure of the Chartists to effect change by either violent or non-violent means, land reform reached Sid Rawle via the radical undercurrents of three other movements. These were the preservation societies of the late nineteenth century (which will be discussed in the next chapter), the rambling groups who occupied Kinder Scout in 1932, and the more contemporary example of the San Francisco Diggers, also inspired by Winstanley, who set up communes and ran celebrated free food kitchens at the many free festivals that took place in California's hippie heyday.

The history of radical agrarianism was not all that Sid Rawle brought to the counter-culture of the 1960s. As was pointed out in the last chapter, he also knew both John Michell – who was beginning to formulate the views that would emerge in *The View over Atlantis* – and the Druid David Loxley, who had his own specific historical claim on the Levellers and the Diggers.

The Diggers on Dorinish Island

By 1970, John Lennon was so impressed by Sid Rawle's revolutionary rhetoric that he summoned him to the offices of Apple, the Beatles' short-lived and ill-conceived utopian business offshoot, and offered him custodianship of Dorinish Island – a small, uninhabited island off the coast of County Mayo that Lennon had bought in 1967 – for use as a Digger commune, 'for the common good.' After a brief recruitment drive amongst the hippies of London, twenty-five adults and a baby duly set off for the west coast of Ireland. Rawle described their initial experience as follows: 'We decided we would hold a six-week summer camp on the island. Then we would see what came out of that and decide if we wanted to extend our stay. It was heaven and it was hell. We lived in tents because there were no stone buildings on the island at all', although he concluded that, 'Most of the time it was really good.'

In the end, the Diggers stayed for two years, growing their own vegetables, which they stored in specially dug hollows, and cadging lifts off the local oyster fishermen every fortnight or so for supplementary shopping trips to Westport on the mainland. There was a certain amount of conflict – in March 1971 *The Connaught Telegraph* declared, 'After a year of seething anger, Westport has finally declared war on the "Republic of Dorinish"' – but the commune finally closed down of its own volition the year after, when a fire destroyed the main tent used to store supplies. (Clarke 2002)

Rawle had made sporadic visits to England throughout the duration of the commune. At the Glastonbury Fayre in June 1971, for example, free food had been provided by two groups – the wittily named Communal Knead, and Sid's Diggers, now known as the Digger Action Movement. On his return to London in the spring of 1972, he took the Diggers' message on from Dorinish and Glastonbury to a new and more politically explosive location. Along with members of the Free City of Camden, 'a loose street-by-street network of squatters, revolutionaries and artists' and the ubiquitous White Panthers, he was involved in setting up the first People's Free Festival in Windsor Great Park over the August Bank Holiday weekend, under the leadership of Bill 'Ubi' Dwyer, a well-known anarchist activist, 'on the basis of an acid vision he'd had.' (McKay 2000: 95; Krystof 1989; Stone 1999: 157)

The Windsor Free Festival

Windsor was the most direct affront to the land rights of the establishment yet seen. By squatting the Queen's own backyard, the festival's organisers were joining the Diggers in taking on unfinished historical business. Windsor's park had been common land before it was enclosed by King George III to provide himself with an exclusive hunting ground. The hippies were simply taking back land that had been stolen from the people for 200 years.

Bill Dwyer's professed aspirations for the festival were enormous, as befitted an experienced acid prankster with an eye for publicity. He claimed to expect that a million people would turn up, suggested that 'the festival will finish when those attending it so decide', and set himself up as the Church of Aphrodite Pandemos, promising 'sacrificial cakes, sex rites, athletic competitions and all those things pleasing to gods and men.' In the end, only around 700 people turned up, to find that they were almost outnumbered by a police presence estimated at 600 officers. In almost every way, the event (which only lasted three days) was a shambles, with the organisers forced to play an endless game of cat-and-mouse with the police, the infrastructure almost non-existent, and electricity so scarce that Hawkwind's set was powered by an ice cream van's generator and lit by its headlights. (McKay 2000: 97)

Nevertheless, a precedent had been set, important lessons had been learned, and the following year the second People's Free Festival drew up to 8,000 people over a period of ten days. Following the example of the last Isle of Wight festival, a daily news-sheet, *Windsor Freep*, was produced. As well as providing gossip and other, more essential information (guidelines for on-site responsibility, detailed descriptions of the risible hippie disguises used by undercover police), the news-sheet also

Sunset at the Windsor Free Festival, 1973.
Copyright Roger Hutchinson.

outlined the festival's aims – 'communal living, living close to the land, living by sharing, and getting high' – and subscribed to John Lennon and Yoko Ono's notion of 'nutopia', a 'state of the brotherhood of man, recognising no national boundaries or artificially imposed lines over our beautiful planet.' (Shark 2003e)

By the summer of 1974, the momentum of the third People's Free Festival seemed unstoppable. 300,000 leaflets were distributed, British Rail provided extra train services, and 300 bands volunteered to play, spread over six stages. In fact, Thames Valley police were gearing up for a clampdown, but in the meantime the first Stonehenge Free Festival took place. Significantly, the two events were not entirely unrelated.

Phil Russell revisited

In truth, whatever Phil Russell's spiritual aspirations for the Stonehenge Free Festival, the Wallies' six-month occupation of the land adjoining the temple was a confrontational political gesture and an affront to the establishment. This was clear from his more serious moments both before and after the diversionary buffoonery that took place in the courtroom in the summer of 1974, on those occasions when he was more shaman than showman. According to Jeremy Ratter, Phil despised the outbursts of police violence that had marred the Windsor Free Festival in 1973, when, either naked or dressed in faded jeans and his 'Hope' shirt, he had 'danced amongst the rows of police asking, 'What kind of gentle-men are you?' or mocking, 'What kind and gentle men you are'.' (Rimbaud 1981)

A victim of the police violence,
Windsor 1974.
Copyright Steve Austin.

In August 1974, on a sabbatical from Fort Wally, Phil and his companions witnessed the unprecedented police violence that closed down the third and last Windsor Free Festival, after nine days during which over 10,000 people had been drawn to the festivities. In an early morning raid on 29 August, hundreds of police officers gave the crowd little time to disperse before laying into them with truncheons. In Phil's own words, 'I saw a pregnant woman being kicked in the belly, and a little boy being punched in the face. All around, the police were just laying into people. I went to one policeman who had just knocked out a woman's teeth and asked him why he'd done it. He told me to fuck off or I'd get the same. Later on, I did.' After Windsor, the Wallies attended a protest that was held in Hyde Park, and on both occasions Phil extolled the virtues of Fort Wally, attracting more people to the experimental camp. (Rimbaud 1981)

There is an insight into Phil's motivation in the closing lines of an article he wrote for *Maya*, the magazine of the Windsor Free Festival, in the summer of 1974: 'Sons of the Sun, the Wallys, are letting the mysteries of Stonehenge work through them, despite the barbed wire that surrounds it, despite the army bases, and despite the stale nets of secular legalisms. Freedom is a career.' Phil worked steadily towards his vision. He had written about communal living and the ideals of 'nutopia' in *Windsor Freep* the year before, and his land claims found an echo in the Albion Free State manifesto, published the year of the first festival at Stonehenge: 'The dispossessed people of this country need *Land* – for diverse needs, permanent free festival sites, collectives, and cities of Life and Love, maybe one every fifty miles or so, manned and womaned by people freed from dead-end jobs and from slavery in factories mass-producing non-essential consumer items.' He was perhaps inspired by examples of communal living from the United States, where Wavy Gravy and General Waste-more-land, part of Hog Farm, a travelling, clownish commune, had written that 'The hankering for material things, physical comforts, the emphasis on

The back of Phil Russell's 'Free Stoned Henge' leaflet, printed at Fort Wally in 1974, revealing more of his kaleidoscope of religious beliefs. Image supplied by Roger Hutchinson.

status is from the old order, which is collapsing. He who lives by the will of God moves into the New Age.' (Shark 2003d; McKay 2000: 16; Neville 1995: 223–4)

Phil was certainly part of the New Age, including Christianity in his mix of sun worship and radical land claims. In spring 1974, in a letter to a farmer near Stonehenge advising him of the coming festival, he wrote, 'Our Lord God and his son Jesus Christ, have ordained a spiritual Pilgrimage to Stonehenge on 20th June, 21st etc to fulfil the Two Commandments – Love God, Love your neighbour.' In addition, Nigel Ayers noted that Phil talked regularly about 'his belief that he had met the reincarnated Jesus Christ in Cyprus', a visionary experience that seems to have happened in his youth and that manifested itself in his writing in the otherwise inexplicable description of himself as 'Son of the Sun, born Cyprus 1960.' (Abbott 1990; Ayers 1996; Russell 1974)

A particularly intriguing aspect of Phil's apparent Christianity is the way it combined with his mysticism – his central preoccupation with sun worship that has already been touched upon in Chapter Three – to create a kind of mystical monotheism for which a precedent can be found in the works of Aleister Crowley, whose works were read avidly by many of those immersed in the counter-culture of the 1960s and early 1970s (Led Zeppelin's Jimmy Page being perhaps the most prominent example). In *Windsor Freep*, Phil wrote, 'Let us open ourselves to the light, we are all brothers and sisters under our father the sun. Sun power the indestructible', a solar paean whose intensity recalls the central rite of Crowley's short-lived commune in Sicily, where a prayer was made to the sun four times daily using the names of various Egyptian gods, and that is most evident in Crowley's writings for the Ordo Templi Orientis, in which he declared that 'In the macrocosm is one sole God, the Sun', and his Gnostic Mass, in which he described himself as part of a single entity, the 'centre and secret of the Sun' and the 'hidden spring of all things known.' (Russell 1973; Symonds 1971: 235; King 1973: 172; Suster 1988: 57–8)

Jeremy Ratter's conclusion about his friend was that 'Wally was an English shaman. He was an animist and, like all those involved in magical processes, his life was characterised by massive self-discipline. The only drug he took was acid, which he saw as a sacrament.' He added, 'Everything in Wally's world had life. There wasn't anything that wasn't something. He moved through a symbolic universe where things had inherent meaning, moving in constant tension from one set of meanings to another.' (Stone 1996: 82)

In the end, whether Phil was a shamanic animist with a penchant for magic or a mystical monotheist at the dawn of the New Age, clearly he alone made the vital connections between the impulse of the 1971 Glastonbury free festival and the existing solstice celebrations at Stonehenge that created a genuinely radical mix of the mystical and the political. By combining the political occupation of the land around Stonehenge with the spiritual occupation of the temple itself, he brought to life a distinctive counter-cultural agenda that remains vibrant to this day.

The Watchfield Free Festival

By the time of Phil Russell's death in September 1975, his spiritual succession was more or less secure. If no one could match what Tim Abbott called the 'surreal clarity' of his vision, Bev Richardson, John Pendragon and Sid Rawle were all capable of blending libertarianism, ecological awareness and pagan spirituality in such a way that the heart of the free festival scene began to look less like an ad-hoc collective of 'freaks' (the hippies' chosen definition of themselves from the 1960s to the early 1970s) and more like a legitimate – if unruly – sibling of the pagan revival.

It remained for the festival's political edge to be redefined, and here Sid Rawle stepped in. Imprisoned after the last Windsor festival along with Bill Dwyer, Sid came to Stonehenge as one of the chief organisers of the fourth People's Free Festival, which took place in August 1975 at Watchfield, a disused airfield in Oxfordshire. Set up as a one-off replacement for the bitterly contested Windsor site, Watchfield was an extraordinary event – the only instance in British history of the government providing a free festival site. Although no inquest had taken place after the brutal suppression of Windsor the year before, Home Secretary Roy Jenkins clearly felt that the hippies were due some kind of compensation. Independent reports suggested that the police's instructions for people to leave the site had not been clearly heard, that the Drug Squad broke the law in searching suspects for drugs, that excessive force had been used in the eviction of the site, and in particular that the 220 people arrested had been treated with unnecessary harshness. Taken to

*A light-hearted moment at the Watchfield festival, 1975.
Copyright Nick Day, with thanks to Garry Gibbons.*

a nearby army barracks, suspects were made to undress completely, and were subjected to anal and vaginal searches, according to one of the doctors present. (Shark 2003e)

Watchfield duly cemented the success of the second Stonehenge Free Festival, running for nine days, attracting over 5,000 people, and providing the clearest working example to date of the free festival as a self-regulating alternative community, despite a persistent police presence that led to ninety-five arrests, and sporadic violence from the Windsor chapter of the Hell's Angels. Festival regular Convoy Steve 'especially liked the daily site meetings where everyone sat around and said their piece. Policy was made, site matters were discussed and it felt like real democracy in action.' The organisers were upbeat about future prospects for a permanent festival site, and there was even a cautious endorsement of their views from the local Tory MP Airey Neave, who 'thought a new site should be provided so long as it was self-financing and not an imposition on local villagers, ratepayers or taxpayers.' Another Tory MP, Philip Goodhart, 'felt it reasonable that people should have somewhere to go: a national centre.' (Shark 2003f; *The Times*, 26 August 1975)

In the end, however, the most significant aspect of the trade-off between the festival-goers and the government that led to the provision of Watchfield was that it also included the Stonehenge Free Festival in its ambit. According to Sid Rawle, 'the

MP Airey Neave (right) chats to festival-goers at Watchfield.
Copyright Nick Day, with thanks to Garry Gibbons.

representatives stated that if they [the festival-goers] kept away from Windsor Great Park, they would be left alone at Stonehenge.' (Firsoff 2002b)

The infrastructure of the Stonehenge festival

On a day-to-day, year-to-year basis, the Stonehenge Free Festival also required the steady commitment of a large number of other volunteers to support an infrastructure that was flexible enough to allow its spontaneity to thrive but that was strong enough to prevent its descent into unprincipled chaos. These included coordinators, technicians and people to provide materials and services, above and beyond the vital support work that was provided by Festival Welfare Services, Release, BIT (an all-round underground information service that was also set up in the 1960s), the St John's Ambulance teams and the Samaritans.

Particularly notable amongst the festival faithful was Nik Turner, a member of Hawkwind at the time of the first few Stonehenge festivals, who subsequently established himself at the helm of a number of other regular free festival bands including Sphynx and Inner City Unit, and who lent his pyramid stage to the festival each year. Also notable was the Polytantric Commune, partly drawn from the ranks

Tribal Messenger: *the front cover of John Pendragon's magazine,
showing Nik Turner's pyramid stage.*

of the White Panthers but consisting mainly of teenagers at the time of the first festival, who had been drawn into Phil Russell's orbit at Fort Wally and who grew up with a passionate belief in the festival's existence as something akin to a birthright.

The only noticeable absence from the early days was Jeremy Ratter, who felt alienated from the new regime, arguing that 'They were into political confrontation, whereas Phil was into peace.' He became involved in a wrangle with Sid Rawle over the box that had contained Phil's ashes. Jeremy wanted it burned, but discovered that Sid had kept it as a memento. It was the start of a process in which Phil Russell became an icon. The box – the symbol of his martyrdom, his elevation from Phil Russell the man to Wally Hope the saint – was to become something of a Holy Grail amongst the festival crowd in the years to come, while Jeremy, as we shall see in Chapter Seven, was to contribute to the iconography of Phil's life in an altogether more startling manner. (Stone 1996: 96)

Meigan Fayre and Seasalter

The final contributory factor in the establishment of a pool of willing volunteers to run the festival at Stonehenge was the growth of the free festival scene in general from 1976 onwards. That summer – one of the hottest in living memory – a whole season of free festivals was established. It began with the Rhayader festival in the mountains of mid-Wales in July, and was followed in August by the North Country Fair in the Pennines and Meigan Fayre in Pembrokeshire's Preseli Mountains, the supposed source of Stonehenge's bluestones. Meigan Fayre had begun as a typical small-scale festival in 1974, growing the following year as word spread, and attracting over 4,000 people in August 1976 for what one attendee described as 'the most beautiful and wonderful of all the UK free festivals', with astonishing views over the Preselis, and phenomenal sunsets over the Irish Sea. Although George McKay suggested that the festival was 'kept deliberately low-key to make a local rather than a national festival', the focus on Wales was on the increase, augmented by the establishment of Tipi Valley earlier in the year, a self-sufficient alternative community in which both Sid Rawle and various members of the Wallies were involved, and by the realisation that both Wales and the North of England were more amenable to free festivals than the increasingly hostile south of England, where, with the exception of Stonehenge, the optimism of the organisers of the Watchfield festival was beginning to appear misplaced. (Chris Church in Shark 2003g; McKay 2000: 99)

Despite the continuing involvement of the government advisory committee that had helped to establish the Watchfield site, attempts to secure a venue for the fifth People's Free Festival ran up against persistent opposition. The aptly named Thames Valley Festival Intelligence and Discouragement Group scuppered plans for the first proposed site, Tangmere (a disused Battle of Britain fighter base in West Sussex) by informing the locals, who swiftly put together an injunction. Other problems beset plans for venues in Plumpton and Lewes, and when another site was finally found, at Broad Oak valley in Kent, the injunctions began once more. Police set up roadblocks, festival-goers and government advisors alike were told to keep away, and only when a vanguard of the festival's organisers occupied a marshy field beside

Parade at Meigan Fayre, 1976, with Sid Rawle and John Pendragon.
Copyright Jeza.

the village of Seasalter, near Whitstable, was the event reluctantly allowed to proceed. Even then, the police turned up in force, and the ensuing nine-day festival, attended by around a thousand people, ended up costing £20,000 to police, an amount that even some of those opposed to it conceded would have been better spent on securing a permanent site. (Shark 2003h)

1977: The Lord of Misrule

In 1977, under the collective umbrella of its new leadership, the Stonehenge Free Festival moved further away from the stones, to the north-west of the car park, near Fargo Plantation and the western end of the Cursus, where it more or less settled in for the duration of its existence. There were about 6,000 people overall, mostly enduring indifferent weather, but by now the festival clearly had its own momentum. Roger Hutchinson's poster for that year, in cut-up letters like a ransom note, declared, 'Yes, it's yet more alternative society propaganda. A stoned love-in of free thinking people, celebrating the midsummer solstice, is going to take place at Stonedhenge this summer accompanied by lotsa rock'n'roll and all the other paraphernalia of the usual free freak festival. Da date is 17th June 1977 for at least 10 daze.' It ended with the message 'Wally Lives', although possibly the festival was beginning to outgrow even the wildest dreams of its founder. (Hutchinson 1977)

For a fortnight every year, it was an independent state, a police no-go area that revealed on occasion an almost primal pleasure in confronting authority. One festival-goer recalled that when a police van drove onto the site to arrest someone, it

Tribal gathering at the Stonehenge Free Festival, 1977. The meeting tent, raised by the tipi tribe, where site meetings (and jam sessions) took place every morning. Copyright Roger Hutchinson.

was 'surrounded by about 50 hippies, who rocked it from side to side and threw policemen's helmets in the air. The plods beat a less than dignified retreat while everyone who saw it hooted with laughter.' (Steve in Shark 2003d)

In most respects, however, the charms of the festival were less to do with confrontation than inspiration. A sign over the entrance declared, 'It's never too late to have a happy childhood', and alongside the drugs, the music and the classless sociability, the festival was a kind of giant playground for the inner child, a chance to do pointlessly exhilarating things like driving slowly down the main drag in a Mini loaded up with dozens of passengers. Festival Welfare Services, in its first report, noted the festival's inclusiveness, pointing out that 'there were many people who had not been to a festival before' and that it was 'quite a revelation for them', and adding that 'The festival was also attended by people from abroad, and many local people were seen on the site during the evening, enjoying the music and meeting people with different lifestyles.' (Douglas 1977)

Perhaps the most fundamental rationale for the festival's existence was provided by John Michell, who suggested that its free-form subversion 'fulfilled a human need which had been repressed by the Reformation: the need for a period of respite, when the restrictions of law and morality, necessary in every settled society, are relaxed and for a short season the Lord of Misrule holds sway. This need was once generally recognised by rulers, who indulged it for the sake of peace and order throughout the rest of the year.' As ever, Michell's pronouncements maintained a continuity with the undercurrents of Romantic and radical history, in this case the author Harold Massingham, who spent the inter-war years encouraging his countrymen to awaken themselves to the beauty of nature and of natural living, reviving the spirit of the land so that the 'Lord of Misrule will be proclaimed, and all the blessed sons and

Revellers relaxing during a sunny interlude at the Stonehenge Free Festival, 1978.
Copyright Roger Hutchinson.

daughters of men will gather to the Feast of Fools.' (Michell 1986: 10; Massingham 1932: 171)

For a large number of those attending the Stonehenge festival throughout these years, the celebration of the solstice at the stones retained the central significance it had during the sweltering hot summers of 1975 and 1976. On the morning of the solstice in 1977, two-thirds of the festival-goers joined the Druids, who were led on this occasion by the actor William Roache (*Coronation Street*'s Ken Barlow), although all parties were disappointed by the weather. Under a grey and cloudy sky, they waited in vain for sunrise, and one newspaper reported that 'the only lights to appear in the East were a couple of shells fired on an artillery range.' (Bev Richardson in Shark 2003d; Weird Wiltshire 2003)

1978: the return of Glastonbury

In 1978, there was more of the same – up to 6,000 people and generally atrocious weather – but the festival held up well. Festival Welfare Services described it as 'a model free festival.' Lord Pembroke, a local landlord, provided firewood. The Department of the Environment took a non-confrontational approach to the solstice and 'opened the monument to all comers on Solstice Day.' Even the local Conservative MP wrote to *The Times* to declare: 'Either the festival must be stopped – and I question whether it could or should be – or better arrangements must be made.' (McKay 2000: 100; Daniel 1992: 129)

The other face of Stonehenge: the little-known Glastonbury festival of 1977.
Copyright Roger Hutchinson.

Almost more significant than the festival, however, was what happened afterwards. Around 500 people in trucks and buses (the first manifestation of what would soon come to be known as a convoy of New Age Travellers) made their way to Glastonbury in an attempt to hold another free festival at Cinnamon Lane, where a small alternative community of caravans and tipis had been in existence for a number of years. According to Glastonbury resident and festival-goer Alister Sieghart, 'It was the early days of making the vision of festivals being a summer-long nomadic culture real.'

When the convoy arrived, the local police had been forewarned and blocked off access, but after radioing around they came up with an alternative venue – Worthy Farm, the site of the 1971 Glastonbury Fayre, which, as previously noted, had been drawing small numbers of free festival regulars after the solstice at Stonehenge on a regular basis ever since. The free festival that took place at Worthy Farm from 28 June to 8 July was a turning point for the farm's owner, Michael Eavis, and others close to him. As Alister Sieghart put it, 'I remember seeing Andrew Kerr there, and him saying, 'This is better than '71.' I think it was this free festival that rekindled Michael's interest in holding another festival... Actually it was Rebecca, Michael's daughter, and Andrew Kerr – it was *their* interest that was rekindled.' The following year, Michael Eavis set up an official Glastonbury festival, a commercial event, but one with a fund-raising ethos that has, of course, gone on to become the largest and most influential commercial festival in Britain today. (McKay 2000: 20)

Significantly, however, Stonehenge and Glastonbury were not the only free festivals to take place in 1978. Overall, there was a marked increase in festival activity throughout the whole period from March to September, effectively constituting the dawn of the summer-long nomadic culture referred to by Alister Sieghart above. In March, the first free festival took place at Cissbury Ring, a vast Iron Age hill-fort – and the site of significant Neolithic flint mines – on the South Downs, overlooking

Worthing. Cissbury had been a favoured site for Wiccans and other pagan groups for a number of years, and, despite regular opposition from the authorities, has maintained its appeal to the present day.

In May, the first free festival took place at May Hill in Gloucestershire, and there was similar activity in East Anglia, where, from June to August, the Albion Fairs presented what George McKay described as 'The first summer of a moveable feast across the countryside, from fair to nomadic fair.' That summer, the northern festivals also took off. Up to 20,000 people turned up for the third free festival at Deeply Vale, and the momentum continued at Rivington Pike in September, where a smaller crowd of free festival devotees, described by Festival Welfare Services as 'very together people', enjoyed 'beautiful weather on a beautiful site.' Even the negative elements – a group of Hell's Angels with a shotgun – were dealt with, escorted off-site by the local police. (McKay 2000: 100; Shark 2003i; Shark 2003j)

The only real difficulties in a wet but militant summer took place, yet again, in the south. The last People's Free Festival – at Caesar's Camp in Bracknell – was limited to acoustic music only and drew a maximum of 300 people, and at Stonehenge, despite the success of the festival, the political battle against its very existence began in earnest, with senior policemen, prominent archaeologists and the National Trust all airing their criticisms in public.

Chapter Six

Fences and archaeologists

Nemesis: Glyn Daniel, the police and the National Trust

In 1978 the political wrangle against the very existence of the Stonehenge Free Festival began in earnest. The Chief Constable of Wiltshire called the festival-goers and the Druids 'nothing more than a bunch of sordid mystics.' T-shirts proclaiming 'I'm a sordid mystic', and 'Got pissed and mystic' appeared overnight, but behind the levity a more serious problem was growing. In *The Times*, the Director-General of the National Trust lamented, 'Once again the National Trust, the police and the local authority have been powerless to prevent the heavy loss suffered each June by the Trust's public-spirited farm tenant.' This was not strictly true. The journalist Tim Malyon 'had alerted the Trust to the new, live interest in Stonehenge… when the Festival was small and the farmer on whose land it took place, a Trust tenant, would have been willing to lease it', but it was the Trust's version of events that was to prevail over the altruism of its tenants and of other local land-owners like Lord Pembroke. (Sebastian 1990: 111; *The Times*, 22 June 1978; Fowler 1990a: 147)

As the furore over the festival grew, *The Times* at least allowed Sid Rawle to respond to the National Trust's complaints, which he did by emphasising the festival's religious diversity and its mystical heart: 'What has happened at Stonehenge for the last five years is that for the week of midsummer thousands of pilgrims from many religious persuasions have come here… We come to Stonehenge because in an unstable world it is proper that the people should look for stability to the past in order to learn for the future. The evidence is indisputable that Stonehenge and the surrounding area is one of the most powerful centres in Europe. It is right that we should meekly stand in the presence of God, but it is proper that we should sing and dance and shout for joy for the love and mercy that He shows us. We would not run a road through Stonehenge and given our way it would soon be removed. A very important part of the monument is now a tarmac car park, ugly to behold. We would not surround it with barbed wire and arc lamps. Holy land is holy land and our right to be upon it cannot be denied ' (*The Times*, 28 June 1978)

'The only possible comment is Christ Almighty!' was Glyn Daniel's blunt rejoinder in *Antiquity*. Every few years, since he took over the editorship of the flagship archaeological journal in 1958, Professor Daniel had railed against the occupation of Stonehenge at the summer solstice by 'horrid bogus Druids' and 'hooligans'. The surprise, in 1978, was that after writing, 'It seems simple to urge the Department of the Environment and everyone else to ban Stonehenge and its environs for the octave of midsummer', he proceeded to ask, 'But what if these characters are really using Stonehenge as a cult-symbol, and in all sincerity?' (Daniel 1992: 127, 51)

It was a question not asked again for a number of years. By the time the next issue of *Antiquity* was published, Daniel was apoplectic once more, enraged by a piece of 'bullshit bureaucracy' that had been written by some hapless assistant secretary in the Department of the Environment in response to a letter querying the Druids' right to gather at Stonehenge for the summer solstice. The civil servant had written that 'The Druids have been allowed to perform their Solstice rites at least since just after the First World War. If they were forbidden entry they would allege religious persecution and force their way in unless physically stopped by the police. The latter would not welcome the job especially under the eye of the TV cameras. Do you really expect Ministers to agree in these circumstances to stop what has been a traditional event, no matter how dubious the historical connexion?' In response, Daniel fumed, 'When we reread those bland phrases 'religious persecution', 'traditional event', 'the eye of the TV cameras', we boil with such rage that the platen of the typewriter is endangered.' He went on to lament that 'Traditions can easily be fabricated, and so we shall find Salisbury Plain at the Summer Solstice full of rival bands – Druids, Moonies, Loonies, Boobies, Straight Trackers, Bent Trackers, Geomantics, Pyramidiots, Atlanteans – the lot.' (Daniel 1992: 129–30)

1978: the third enclosure

The second great change of 1978 was not explicitly concerned with the festival, although it was to have an impact on every potential visitor that was at least as far-reaching as the raising of the first fence in 1901. As early as 1975, when the annual number of visitors had regularly begun to exceed two-thirds of a million, the monument's curators, the Department of the Environment, had set up a working party to discuss the problems of the management of the site and to propose possible solutions. It was a labyrinthine process, and by 1978 they had come to the conclusion that the public would finally have to be prohibited from approaching the monument directly. The turf between the stones, which had been replaced by orange gravel in 1963, was restored, but visitors now had to view the monument from a distance. The festival, with its assumed right of access, was now the only potential opportunity for any member of the general public, outside of the rarefied worlds of archaeology and the government, to walk amongst the stones.

Significantly, senior archaeologists were consulted over the plans to prevent almost all access to the stones. It had, of course, long been a wish of Glyn Daniel's to ban 'all special entry for religious, social and secret societies' and to close the monument 'in perpetuity' to all but the occasional educational party. These sentiments were echoed, more moderately, by Richard Atkinson, who conceded that 'The present policy of excluding all but educational parties from the stones is a compromise, certainly, but one which seems to me the only solution in the circumstances.' In the pages of *Antiquity* in which these opinions were expressed, it was only Aubrey Burl – after conceding that 'Damage to the monument will persist so long as people are allowed to visit it' – who proposed an alternative solution: 'to increase the entrance fee and create a good long walk to the site, perhaps from the Winterbourne Stoke cross-roads where the visitor could start in a prehistoric context with the prospect of a mile and a half ramble across the Plain.' (Daniel 1992: 129–30)

The preservationists

The archaeologists and those responsible for looking after Stonehenge had not always been so implacably opposed towards the public at Stonehenge. In the nineteenth century, the conflicting interests of today's curators – the maintenance of Stonehenge and the maintenance of access rights to it – were both championed by representatives of an extraordinary alliance of influential, Liberal land-owners who set up societies and campaigned in parliament for the preservation of common land and public access rights, of ancient monuments and other historic buildings, and of historic landscapes and endangered wildlife.

The prime movers in the preservationist movement were: Lord Eversley (George John Shaw-Lefevre), who founded Britain's first countryside pressure group, the Commons Preservation Society (CPS), in 1865; Lord Avebury (Sir John Lubbock), the engineer of the 1882 Ancient Monuments Act; the Liberal MP James Bryce, who tried to do for wild places what Lord Avebury had done for ancient monuments; Octavia Hill, Robert Hunter and Hardwicke Rawnsley, who founded the National Trust for Places of Historic Interest or Natural Beauty in 1894; the artist-philosophers William Morris and John Ruskin; and the Egyptologist Flinders Petrie.

The interests of the preservationists overlapped with one another to a significant extent. Most were members of the CPS, the Selborne League (for wildlife protection, established in 1885), and the National Trust. Some were active in the Kyrle Society (established in 1876 and also concerned with issues of public access), the Society for the Protection of Ancient Buildings (1877), and the Society for Checking the Abuses of Public Advertising (1893). (Burchardt 2002: 93–100)

They were, moreover, all genuinely radical. When the CPS was founded, its establishment members took on its own people, re-establishing the grievances against enclosure that had been most recently expressed by the Chartists and the political journalist William Cobbett, the author of *Rural Rides*, whose 'portrayal of enclosure as a process by which the rural poor were cheated out of their rights resonated powerfully with agrarian radicalism.' The preservation groups believed that 'where private property rights threatened natural or man-made beauty, they should yield to the good of the community as a whole.' (Burchardt 2002: 44, 100)

Over enclosure, the CPS took the struggle back to the thirteenth century and campaigned successfully 'to repeal those clauses of the 1235 Statute of Merton which gave legal comfort to would-be enclosers of commons.' Their victories, including Hampstead Heath and Epping Forest, were significant, and they were also unafraid of direct action, hiring 200 navvies to dismantle the iron fencing erected around Berkhamsted Common in the dead of night in March 1866. Similar direct action was undertaken in the Lake District by Hardwicke Rawnsley and the Lakes preservation groups, and in the south by members of another group campaigning for access, the National Footpaths Preservation Society, founded in 1884. (Burchardt 2002: 124, 100; Marsh 1982: 40–52)

In Parliament, the reformers faced a similar struggle. Lord Avebury's Ancient Monuments Act was only finally passed after years of wrangling with less enlightened landowners. A typical example was the Tory MP Francis Hervey, who asked with incredulity, 'Are the absurd relics of our barbarian predecessors, who found time hanging heavily on their hands, and set about piling up great barrows and rings of stones, to be preserved at the cost of the infringement of property rights?' Such was the extent of the opposition that, when the Act was finally passed, its major concession was that the co-operation of the landowner was discretionary. An owner could sell a monument to the state or ask the state for protection, but could not be coerced by law. (Bommes and Wright 1982)

James Bryce's 'access to mountains' bill was even more fiercely resisted. Aimed at legislating for unfettered rights of access to uncultivated land, it was repeatedly defeated from 1884 onwards. Nearly fifty years later, when militant ramblers occupied Kinder Scout, Bryce's concerns had still not been addressed, and not until 1949, and the passing of the National Parks and Access to the Countryside Act, was any measure of success achieved. Even today, with additional legislation underway (the Countryside and Rights of Way Act 2000), the Victorian reformers' universal 'right to roam' is still an unfulfilled dream.

1901: the first enclosure

Ironically, Stonehenge's owner, Sir Edmund Antrobus, was immune to the proposals of the reformers. Lord Eversley tried on two occasions to persuade him to let the government place Stonehenge under the protection of the Ancient Monuments Act. In 1882, just after the Act had been passed, Antrobus 'resented any suggestion that he was neglectful of his duty to protect the monument from injury, or that it was necessary for the government to intervene for that purpose.' In 1894, a letter from Antrobus explained that he considered himself as 'holding the monument in trust for the public, and that he recognised their right of access to it.' He was apparently under the impression that if he fenced off the stones 'an indignant public might act as the London public did in regards to the railings of Hyde Park, when the claim to hold meetings was interfered with.' (Eversley 1910: 162)

While Sir Edmund lived, he fulfilled his obligations, allowing both unfettered access to the monument and the impromptu solstice festivals of the late nineteenth century. The problem for the reformers was that his successor might think differently, and that the monument would be unprotected by the new legislation. His nephew, who took over the estate when his uncle died in 1898, confirmed their worst fears. He 'felt Stonehenge was a dubious asset to the estate, yielding no income yet a source of trouble.' After trying, unsuccessfully, to sell it to the nation for £125,000 (while still retaining his hunting and grazing rights), he finally fenced it off and began charging admission in 1901, prompted by the collapse of a sarsen on New Year's Eve 1900 and 'on the specious grounds that the new military camp on Salisbury Plain might result in damage.' (Chippindale 1990: 15; Bender 1998: 113)

Residents of Amebury protesting en masse against the raising of the fence and the entrance charge, from a 1901 postcard.

The majority of preservationists were appalled, even though Antrobus' plans had been approved by an advisory committee of local and national archaeologists from the Society of Antiquaries, the Wiltshire Archaeological Society, and the Society for the Protection of Ancient Buildings. Lord Avebury resigned from the committee beforehand, saying that it was 'not sufficiently insistent on the rights of access of the public.' Hardwicke Rawnsley, raging against all kinds of enclosure, reminded readers of *The Manchester Guardian* that 'Stonehenge has stood for ages on a wild barrow-haunted down' where 'men's feet all up the ages have been as free as air to come and go.' Now, however, 'this barbed wire fencing, with all its association of suburban privacy and petty ownership, insults the eye and offends the heart.' Lord Eversley, meanwhile, recognised a link between commerce and the desire to turn a living monument into a museum piece: 'The erection of the fence has entirely altered the character of the monument. The effect has been to rob it of its peculiar character – a strange relic of the twilight of the world, standing untouched through countless centuries – and to convert it into an antiquarian's specimen.' (Hutchinson 1914: vol. 2, 136–7; *The Manchester Guardian*, 27 December 1902; Eversley 1910: 164)

In the wake of the enclosure, Amesbury parish council 'asserted the local tradition of free access to the downland', and the National Trust 'led a group of amenity societies insistent on public rights to a national monument.' Even *The Times* chipped in, describing the fence as 'not only unnecessary but also highly mischievous.' (Chippindale 1994: 164; Michell 1986: 9)

Eversley set about mounting a legal challenge to the fence. Flinders Petrie was recruited and members of the Commons Preservation Society consulted over the legality of obstructing tracks 'used from time immemorial.' The CPS made offers to Antrobus: 'if he would remove the fences and place the monument under the protection of the Ancient Monuments Act, it would repay all the expenses he had incurred' or, if he preferred to sell it, the CPS 'would appeal to the public for £10,000 for the purpose.' Antrobus was unmoved, and when the case came to court his indifference was rewarded. It seemed that the judge had already decided that 'the owner of the monument had been compelled, as a matter of duty, to erect the fence for its protection. He assumed that damage had already been done to it, though there was no evidence to this effect', and the case was dismissed. It was the first major defeat for the CPS and, somewhat ironically, the first enclosure of the twentieth century was at Stonehenge. Eversley's sorrowful conclusion was that the judge 'appeared to regard with equanimity the exclusion from the monument of the great bulk of the public. He was evidently under the impression that the vulgar populace had, by their destructive propensities, disqualified themselves as visitors to a place of antiquarian interest.' (Eversley 1910: 165–6)

Gowland's excavations

Arguably the only good thing to come out of this fraught situation was Antrobus' acceptance that something had to be done about the more unstable parts of the monument. Several sarsens of the stone circle were leaning precariously, and the response of his uncle – to prop them up with wooden supports – had done little to assuage fears that large parts of the monument were on the verge of collapse. In 1893, General Pitt-Rivers, the first Inspector of Ancient Monuments, had concluded that 'Some stones were sure to fall, more probably soon than later', and had proposed that 'the only remedy was to raise the leaning stones to the perpendicular, and to set them in new foundations of concrete or masonry.' The collapse of a sarsen in 1900 only confirmed the gloom of the more pessimistic commentators. *The Times* commented, 'Little we fear can be done to keep the remaining uprights standing. They will fall when their time comes.' (Chippindale 1994: 161; *The Times*, 4 January 1901)

The widespread indignation that greeted the newspaper's fatalistic pronouncement ensured that something would indeed be done, although initially there was little agreement about how to proceed. Full restoration of the monument, which had been a popular proposal in the eighteenth century, was no longer fashionable, partly due to the efforts of the preservationists, who followed John Ruskin's maxim that 'Restoration is a lie'. From Egypt, Flinders Petrie sent a letter to *The Times* urging the same caution regarding 'over-eager restoration', and in the end the reticence proved infectious. After Antrobus had consulted the same worthies who had approved the fence, he decided that a further round of timber supports was largely sufficient and that just one stone would be restored to the vertical – the surviving pillar of the central trilithon, which was leaning at an alarming angle of sixty degrees, pushing over a neighbouring bluestone, which was beginning to crack under the pressure. (Chippindale 1994: 205, 166)

In September and October 1901, the sarsen was duly raised to the vertical and set in concrete, although it was what happened before and after that was ultimately to prove more significant. In the course of limited excavations around the base of the stone and its fallen partner, the supervising archaeologist, Sir William Gowland, a Fellow of the Society of Antiquaries, concluded from a careful study of the implements used to shape the stones and secure them in their holes that Stonehenge was built 'during the latter part of the Neolithic age, or the period of transition from stone to bronze, and before that metal had passed into general practical use.' (Gowland 1902: 37–118)

William Gowland supervising the raising of the
surviving pillar of the central trilithon, 1901.
Reproduced by permission of Wiltshire Archaeological and Natural History Society.

It was not a novel idea. It had first been proposed in 1793 by James Douglas, who had suggested, in his book *Nenia Britannica*, that Stonehenge was 'a pre-Celtic sun-temple, which may have remained in subsequent use as a place of assembly down to Anglo-Saxon times.' Lord Avebury, a pioneering prehistorian as well as a preservationist, had expanded on the theory in *Prehistoric Times* (1865), in which he confirmed earlier attempts by Thomas Leman and the Danish antiquary Christian Jurgen Thomsen to divide prehistory into three distinct phases – the Stone Age, the Bronze Age and the Iron Age – and located Stonehenge in the former, 'a more ancient period than even our most imaginative antiquaries have yet ventured to suggest.' Gowland, however, provided judicious proof, and ironically the first carefully thought out modern archaeological interpretation of the monument's origins, which finally proved that the ancient Druids had nothing whatsoever to do with its construction, coincided with the first published reports of the arrival at the monument of their modern-day counterparts. (Michell 1982: 24; Lubbock 1865: 52–3; 1866)

Hawley's excavations

Gowland's limited excavation and restoration was not the end of the monument's necessary restoration. In 1918, when the Ministry of Works took over the management of Stonehenge after nearly two decades of inactivity by either Antrobus or Cecil Chubb, a structural engineer was immediately sent to assess the risk of the temple's imminent collapse, and during 1919–20 six lintel-crowned sarsens of the circle, including the four that frame the midsummer sunrise, were duly restored and set in concrete. After the caution of the 1901 restoration, it was a belated vindication of Pitt-Rivers' appraisal, voiced nearly thirty years before, that all the leaning stones needed to be secured.

The restoration is widely regarded as the high point of Colonel William Hawley's eight seasons of excavation, which took place between 1919 and 1926, and which have been regarded as a failure since the 1950s, when Richard Atkinson described Hawley's work as melancholy, mechanical, inadequate, destructive and lamentable. Chris Chippindale, for example, summed up the Hawley years as 'a disaster', noting that by the end of the project, despite having excavated every square inch of half of the monument's total surface area, Hawley 'was finally convinced he knew nothing about Stonehenge at all. Like a Zen master he had achieved complete detachment from his subject.' (Atkinson 1979: 196–7; Chippindale 1994: 183)

As Mike Pitts has recently pointed out, however, the denigration of Hawley's work is more than a little unfair. Under-funded and increasingly belittled by the Society of Antiquaries, who wanted hoards of gold rather than flint and bone, Hawley – and his assistant Robert Newall – nevertheless produced important information about many of the monument's outlying features. Excavation indicated that the north-eastern entrance to the bank and ditch had been widened in prehistory, as well as confirming the theory, first proposed by Flinders Petrie, that the bank and ditch were older than the stones they enclose. Hawley and Newall also uncovered countless stone-holes and timber post-holes that constituted a hidden history of the monument. These include the stone-hole of the Slaughter Stone's partner; the ring of pits discovered by John Aubrey (which were named in his honour); two other rings of pits between the Aubrey Holes and the central stones (which were the last to be dug before the site was abandoned in the Bronze Age); and complex and confusing arrangements of post-holes at the entrance to the bank and ditch and inside the stones, which defied easy analysis. (Pitts 2001: 93–8; Petrie 1880)

Above all, Mike Pitts observed, the detailed field notes left by Hawley and Newall have proved invaluable to all the archaeologists who have succeeded them, and who have struggled to get a measure of the enigmas they uncovered. In this they contrast favourably with the other great excavation of the time in the Stonehenge area. Between 1926 and 1928, Maud Cunnington excavated a lost timber monument whose post-holes were first observed from an aeroplane in 1925 in a field just under two miles to the east of Stonehenge. Dubbed 'Woodhenge' because of similarities to its more celebrated stone neighbour, this geometrically precise, six-ringed structure, aligned on the summer solstice sunrise as accurately as Stonehenge and containing a dark secret at its heart – the skeleton of a young child with its skull split in two – added a whole new dimension to the history of Stonehenge and its landscape. But, although Cunnington emptied every single one of the 156 post-holes that made up the structure, she left no field notes whatsoever, and subsequent archaeologists have been dependant on the details provided in her publications at the time. (Cunnington 1927, 1929)

*Woodhenge today: an unsatisfactory arrangement of
colour-coordinated concrete posts.
Copyright Andy Worthington.*

The right-wing drift of the preservationists

With Hawley's departure leaving Stonehenge more or less secure physically, its
curators and admirers were free to turn their attention to the land around. There were
certainly reasons for concern. An aerodrome had been built nearby during the First
World War, which had been converted initially into a store for surplus government
bricks and then into a pig farm. There was also a café, cottages for the custodians,
and talk of a colony of bungalows. In 1927, the National Trust launched an appeal
'to restore and preserve the open surroundings' of Stonehenge, and by 1929 it was
able to buy 1,500 acres of the land around. Although all the unsightly buildings were
removed, the Trust's promise that the land was 'inalienable' and would be kept safe
in perpetuity was soon broken, and for decades the precious, archaeologically
sensitive land around Stonehenge was rented out to tenant farmers who turned it into
arable land. Rodney Legg, author and modern-day rural activist, lamented that 'The
Trust was to regard its Stonehenge estate as an agricultural asset, rather than a
moment from the national dream', although this was typical of the right-wing drift of
the preservation societies at the time. (Chippindale 1990: 16; Legg 1980: 176)

By the 1930s, the leading figure in the Commons Preservation Society was Sir
Lawrence Chubb, who considered that the Kinder Scout trespass was funded by
'Russian money', and Jeremy Burchardt noted that the National Trust 'became less
concerned about access than it had been and switched its attention away from
landscape towards country houses, which had previously been a very minor aspect
of the Trust's work, quite subordinate to preserving "places of natural beauty".' Also
at this time the Conservative party, under Stanley Baldwin (Prime Minister for most
of the 1920s and the early 1930s), began to associate itself explicitly with an
idealised myth of the countryside. Baldwin assiduously cultivated an image of
himself as a kind of rural Everyman, despite the fact that his money came from the

Stonehenge as it appeared in a postcard c.1930.

iron industry. The illusion he created was so successful that it remains more or less intact to this day – think of John Major and his evocation of 'village cricket and warm beer' as what was best about Britain. Furthermore, the Tories' myth-making began to undermine the efficacy of the claims on the countryside that were made by the radicals and the Romantics. (Hill 1980: 77; Burchardt 2002: 103–6)

Archaeologists and the Great Goddess

When 'normal' life resumed after the Second World War, the right-wing drift of the conservation bodies was not yet evident at Stonehenge. The Druids, for example, found that they were 'tolerated by the Establishment'. They were 'exotic', and 'quite good for the tourist trade' (Bender 1998: 126). In 1956, O.G.S. Crawford, the founder and editor of *Antiquity*, described them as 'quite harmless and… entitled to carry out their rites without molestation.' From the 1930s to the 1950s, the prevailing mood amongst the archaeologists was about as far from Baldwin's Little England Conservatism as was possible. Crawford in particular was a fervent pre-war supporter of socialism, with its promise that, for a forward-looking archaeologist at the forefront of a new science, socialism's triumph was 'the natural corollary of science in human affairs… Science applied to society, cooperation in place of competition', as he wrote in 1938. (Crawford 1956; Stout 2001)

By 1953, with the Cold War looming and the ascendancy of the anti-socialist USA as apparent in science as it was in most other fields, Crawford had retreated into the past, counselling 'those suffering from the prevalent epidemic of pessimism… to stop looking forwards, for after all "it may never happen", and to look backwards at what actually did happen when the civilisation we talk so much about was young and full of promise.' As a result, his tolerance of the Druids may have had less to do with a measured appreciation of their contribution than with a kind of intellectual exhaustion following the failure of his political dreams. (Crawford 1953)

Looking for a golden age in the past, Crawford found the Great Goddess, a cult of the Mother Goddess that he described as 'the Archaic Religion of the Old World with its roots in the Old Stone Age.' After travelling to Crete, Ireland and Brittany in search of her, in 1957 his book, *The Eye Goddess*, was published just before his death. Other converts to the Great Goddess cult were the eminent archaeologist V. Gordon Childe, and even Glyn Daniel, Crawford's outspoken successor at *Antiquity*, who wrote of settlers arriving in Iberia from the eastern Mediterranean 'bringing with them the custom of collective tomb burial and a strong religious belief in an Earth Mother Goddess.' Jacquetta Hawkes was a particularly eloquent enthusiast, writing that 'Early farming communities seem to have focused their worship upon fertility and the life creating forces, expressed through a maternal figure in human form' and stating with bold conviction that 'Nothing can shake the evidence of hundreds upon hundreds of little clay, bone and stone effigies of the mother goddess... present in almost every cultural province between Sialk and Britain, and from Persia to Badari.' (Crawford 1957: 15; Childe 1954: 64–5, 268; Daniel 1958: 74; Hawkes 1968: 25; Woolley and Hawkes 1963: Part II, Section II, 337–8)

The conversion had been a long time coming, and ironically both the archaeologists and Gerald Gardner found the goddess around the same time. Gardner's influences – Aleister Crowley, Dion Fortune and Robert Graves – overlapped with the archaeological converts of the 1950s in the figure of Jane Harrison, the Cambridge classicist who had conceived the notion of the threefold Great Goddess in 1903, thereby influencing not only Crowley, Fortune and Graves but also several generations of archaeologists. However, the first conversion to the idea of a 'single mighty goddess' had actually preceded Harrison. It occurred to Sir Arthur Evans at Knossos in 1901, but both Evans' and Harrison's theories were soon augmented by three others. These were Joseph Dechelette (who in 1908 identified the origins of the cult in Asia Minor); G.D. Hornblower (who added the Palaeolithic 'goddess' figurines to the theory in 1929); and E.B. Renaud (who, the same year, compared the female figurines of the Pueblo with those of prehistoric Europe and concluded that the goddess had been worshipped throughout the world before the coming of civilisation). (Evans 1902; Dechelette 1908; Hornblower 1929; Renaud 1929)

Atkinson and Piggott's excavations

Behind the apparently unstoppable rise of the Goddess, the archaeologists at Stonehenge maintained their traditional status. Richard Atkinson and Stuart Piggott, aided by J.F.S. Stone, were in charge of the last major excavations at the monument, which took place in seasons from 1956 to 1964. As part of the establishment, they still held enormous privilege at Stonehenge. Chris Chippindale reported one particular instance when 'Lord David Cecil, allowed as a personal friend of Stuart Piggott to slip through the fence into the holy excavation precinct, turned and said in a stage whisper: 'I do enjoy privilege, especially when publicly displayed'.' (Chippindale 1994: 204)

The viewpoint of the privileged was also apparent in Atkinson's *Stonehenge* (1956), the first modern, full-length archaeological book devoted to the subject. Although some aspects of this widely-read primer have weathered well – the chronology for the raising of the monument's different phases that he established, for example – his proposal that Stonehenge was a creation of immigrants from Mycenae has not. This was an idea that had come from Piggott in 1938, as part of the popular diffusionist

A sarsen being raised during the excavations of the 1950s. Copyright Austin Underwood.

model of prehistory, in which a slow drift of influences from the cradle of civilisation in the Near East established the roots of culture in western Europe. (Piggott 1938)

The importing of the sophisticated goddess of the Aegean clearly underpinned much of the conversion to Crawford's cult of the Mother Goddess that took place in the 1950s, but it was also the most complacent viewpoint for social evolutionists like Atkinson and his colleagues, who believed that 'societies evolve inexorably from simple to complex, from good to better.' Adam Stout commented wryly that social evolution 'has, funnily enough, always been popular with people who see themselves as being at the top of the heap.' Unable to conceal his motives at the time, Atkinson aimed to quell dissenters with the question, 'Is it then any more incredible that the architect of Stonehenge should himself have been a Mycenaean, than that the monuments should have been designed and erected, with all its unique and sophisticated detail, by mere barbarians?' The put-down of the native population was clear: Atkinson identified with the élite, and the élite had to have come from abroad. (Stout 2001; Atkinson quoted in Renfrew 1973: 539)

Despite this typically self-regarding notion of prehistory, the physical consolidation of the monument under Piggott and Atkinson was a success. After Ruskin had once more been invoked, and proposals to restore the monument as fully as possible dismissed, the archaeologists and bureaucrats decided to re-erect only those stones that had fallen since reliable historical records began: the north-west trilithon of the central horseshoe (which fell down in a violent storm on 3 January 1797), and the sarsen that fell in 1900. Not only were the fallen stones resurrected, but a number of other sarsens were also straightened and set in concrete: three in 1959 and three in 1964, including one that fell down in March 1963 as the result of a blow received during the restoration of its neighbour. The monument was restored to such an extent that only seven of the twenty-five uprights that stand today are still in their original state. (Chippindale 1994: 205)

1962: the second enclosure and the goddess denied

With the archaeologists under the influence of the Mother Goddess and the monument more physically secure than ever, the start of the 1960s was an unlikely occasion for their tolerance of both the Druids and the crowds attending the solstice at Stonehenge to come to an end. Yet by 1961, the popular line in the media, as interpreted by Glyn Daniel in *Antiquity*, was that 'Stonehenge should be prevented from becoming a centre of neo-Druidism and hooliganism at Midsummer.' As he was to remain for the rest of his life, Daniel was implacably opposed to the occupation of Stonehenge during the summer solstice. In 1961, he fulminated, 'This is a monstrous, wicked and most undesirable state of affairs, and one which the Minister must bring to an end; and certainly by next Midsummer.' He complained that the Druids had 'no claim to an association with Stonehenge', that 'the existence of these strange ceremonies attracts crowds some of whom behave deplorably' and concluded that, 'on grounds of archaeology and the conservation of ancient monuments', admission to the monument at Midsummer should be prohibited. (Daniel 1992: 21, 25)

Daniel's was a prominent soapbox, and he was instrumental in the second enclosure of Stonehenge, the additional fencing and the exclusion zone that was established from 1962 onwards. It was, however, a short-lived triumph for the archaeological establishment. That same year, Peter Ucko, a young archaeologist, challenged the theory of the universal Mother Goddess in a paper for the Royal Anthropological Institute that looked in detail at the figurines of the Near East. As with all theories and counter-theories about prehistoric, pre-literate cultures, it was impossible to prove conclusively that the goddess theory was mistaken, but the mere proposal that 'the evidence concerned admitted of alternative explanations' was sufficient to send the majority of archaeologists scuttling back quietly to the safety of their former agnosticism. (Ucko 1962; Hutton 1999: 282)

As the decade progressed, the backlash continued. Stuart Piggott, who had only reluctantly subscribed to the theory in the 1950s, now delighted in savaging it, and at the end of the decade Peter Ucko expanded his criticisms to include the figurines of Egypt, Crete and Greece, and was joined by another young archaeologist, Andrew Fleming, who dissected the weaknesses in the association of the goddess with the megaliths of western Europe. Noticeably, however, the criticisms of the goddess theory were largely confined to the learned journals of academia, and in the wider sphere of popular culture the damage had already been done. The Great Goddess, like Margaret Murray's witch religion, had already taken on a vibrant and

WAITING FOR THE SUN TO RISE AT STONEHENGE, 3.30 A.M., JUNE

THE ATTEMPT TO SOLVE THE AGE OF STONEHENGE.

THE SUN'S PRESENT POSITION COMPARED WITH THE AXIS OF THE BUILDING ON THE LONGEST DAY, JUNE 21, WILL, IT IS EXPECTED, GIVE THE DATE OF STONEHENGE.

MEASURING THE SUN'S POSITION
At Stonehenge with the theodolite, which records the angles with marvellous delicacy

THE FRIAR'S HEEL STONE
Looking northward. The picture also shows the new railings to the right

A 1906 newspaper report on Sir Norman Lockyer's Stonehenge and Other British Stone Monuments Astronomically Considered.

irrepressible life of her own, a life that was aided by the continuing commercial success of Jacquetta Hawkes, the only prominent archaeologist to stand by the theory. Taking advantage of the fact that a conclusive denial of the Goddess' existence was impossible, Hawkes continued to believe in her as a personal opinion. (Piggott 1954: 46, 1965: 114-5; Ucko 1968; Fleming 1969; Hawkes 1978: ix)

'The dark forces of unreason'

The goddess' embarrassing exclusion from the cloisters of academia was just the beginning of the archaeologists' woes. In most ways, in fact, the archaeological establishment spent the majority of the 1960s and beyond fighting a rearguard action against emerging issues that they had either failed to address or that they had dismissed out of hand. Prehistoric astronomy, ley-lines and earth energies topped the list of what Glyn Daniel referred to as 'the dark forces of unreason', a counter-cultural uprising that, despite his bullish rhetoric, was to overwhelm the archaeological establishment as surely as the hippies and pagans were to undermine the authority of the state and the church. (Daniel 1982)

The onslaught began in 1966, when Gerald Hawkins, an American astronomer, published *Stonehenge Decoded*, in which he proposed that the monument was raised as a giant computer for the prediction of eclipses. The book immediately became a best-seller, although the idea that Stonehenge was an astronomical observatory had never been popular with the archaeological establishment, which only reluctantly acknowledged even the most basic in-built astronomical considerations in the monuments of prehistory. In 1906, when the eminent astronomer Sir Norman Lockyer published *Stonehenge and Other British Stone Monuments Astronomically Considered*, in which he identified stone circles and dolmens as the observatories and dwelling places of a ruling class of 'astronomer-priests', the archaeologists duly closed ranks against him, and his research, as John Michell put it, was 'denigrated and then ignored.' (Michell 1982: 29)

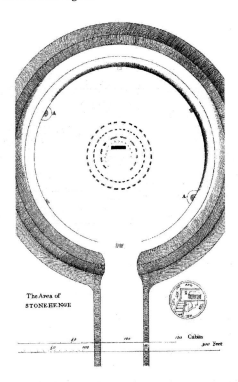

The Station Stones, clearly visible in a plan of Stonehenge by William Stukeley, from Stonehenge (1740).

The Area of
STONEHENGE

In light of Lockyer's achievements, it was a particularly harsh judgment. At Stonehenge, for example, Lockyer was the first to point out, in 1901, that the Heel Stone did not actually stand on the axis of the monument, but that 'the Sun must have completely risen before it was vertically over the summit of the stone', and he also provided a valid astronomical explanation for the rectangular shape marked out by four small, unshaped sarsens – only two of which still remain – which stood just inside the ditch. These two stones – and their lost partners – had been the object of speculation since 1846, when the Reverend Edward Duke, who named them the Station Stones, realised that the short sides of the rectangle were directed towards the summer solstice sunrise. Over a century later, Hawkins, with the aid of a rudimentary computer, established that the long sides of the rectangle were aligned on the most northerly setting of the moon, but Lockyer had made the even more astonishing discovery that, by laying out the stones in the form of a rectangle rather than a more obvious square, the builders had aligned its diagonal on the Beltane sunset. (Lockyer 1901; Duke 1846: 144; Hawkins 1966: 110; Lockyer 1906: 93)

In the aftermath of Hawkins' book, Glyn Daniel's attempts to undermine its findings backfired spectacularly when he invited Professor Fred Hoyle, a leading British astronomer, to comment on the calculations in the pages of *Antiquity*. Hoyle failed to fault Hawkins' findings, even though they demanded 'a level of intellectual attainment... higher than the standard to be expected from a community of primitive farmers', and concluded, 'A veritable Newton or Einstein must have been at work – but then why not?' (Hoyle 1966)

More subversive than Hawkins was Alexander Thom, a retired professor of engineering at Edinburgh University, who spent his retirement surveying a dizzyingly large number of stone circles. Less easy to dismiss were his conclusions that they revealed detailed astronomical knowledge, conformed to complex geometric patterns, and were laid out according to a fixed unit of measurement that he called the 'megalithic yard'. Thom's *Megalithic Sites in Britain* (1967) brought Lockyer's astronomer-priests back to the fore, and it was followed almost immediately by John Michell's *The View over Atlantis*, whose revolutionary impact was discussed in Chapter Three.

'The wreckage of academic history'

In addition to these attacks, the archaeological establishment was also stymied by its own failures to engage with and inspire its potential audience. The most prominent example of this failure was Richard Atkinson's excavation of Silbury Hill, Europe's largest man-made prehistoric mound and an integral part of the Avebury complex, which was broadcast live on BBC2 over sixteen months in 1968–9. To be fair, Atkinson's excavations uncovered invaluable knowledge about how the mound was constructed, but it was an unglamorous process. The most immediate result of this experiment was a widespread sense of anti-climax when nothing more than an old bottle from a previous excavation was discovered, instead of the 'treasure' that Atkinson had confidently predicted in 1967, when he had written that 'Some archaeologists believe that Silbury Hill is the largest of all Bronze Age barrows, and is likely to contain a royal burial of exceptional richness.' (Atkinson 1967: 13)

At the same time the radiocarbon dating methods used to determine the age of prehistoric objects were substantially overhauled, a recalibration precipitated by the discovery that the key component in the process, the radioactive isotope Carbon 14, displayed significant fluctuations in its rate of decay, which had previously been thought of as constant. The majority of the great stone monuments of western Europe were suddenly pushed back from the Bronze Age, where the archaeologists had confidently placed them for decades, to the Neolithic, and the notion that the culture had been imported from the east went with it. As Adam Stout put it, 'Atkinson's Mycenaean architect and all his diffused colleagues disappeared overnight', and the archaeologist Colin Renfrew admitted on Radio 3 that 'The rejection of the diffusionist model leaves something of a void in European prehistoric studies. In consequence our profession is in a state of flux… we have to adjust our thinking to the realisation that our barbarian ancestors were just as creative as ourselves.' (Stout 2001; Renfrew 1971)

By 1975, Richard Atkinson had converted to the theories proposed by Alexander Thom, undermining the establishment further by confessing that archaeologists found Thom's ideas disturbing 'because they do not fit the conceptual model of the prehistory of Europe which has been current during the whole of the present century.' In triumph, John Michell crowed that Atkinson was 'the first of the leading archaeologists to leave a sinking ship', adding that 'archaeology is in a state of embarrassed shock as its professors contemplate the wreckage of academic history.' (Ruggles 1999: 8; Michell 1977: 83–6)

Durrington Walls today: unmarked and uncelebrated.
Copyright Andy Worthington.

Such was the despondency of the archaeologists at the time that their successes were overshadowed. Foremost amongst these was the work undertaken by Geoff Wainwright, an ambitious young archaeologist who mobilised giant machinery to undertake telling excavations of vast but little-known henge monuments in Dorset and Wiltshire between 1966 and 1971: Durrington Walls, just across the road from Woodhenge; Mount Pleasant in Dorchester, forty miles south-west of Stonehenge; and Marden, in the Vale of Pewsey between Stonehenge and Avebury.

Wainwright's excavations uncovered the remains of timber monuments within the enclosures, indicating that the giant henges, along with the unexcavated Knowlton Circles, mid-way between Dorchester and Stonehenge, represented the social and ritual *foci* of five distinct but inter-related tribal areas, each of which was clearly of significant influence around the time of the great works at Stonehenge and Avebury. Significantly, however, his reports and conclusions – which remain fascinating to this day – were only finally published outside the immediate confines of the archaeological establishment in 1989. (Wainwright 1989)

It was into this void, where John Michell had been happily frolicking since the 1960s, that an academic called Michael Dames arrived at Avebury with an exciting and influential mythological template that will be discussed at length in Chapter Eleven, and Phil Russell, Bev Richardson, John Pendragon, Sid Rawle and others arrived at Stonehenge.

Chapter Seven

Revolution

1979: a glorious sunrise

In 1979, one event took place which ensured that the Stonehenge Free Festival would not only grow and become more political, but also that it would become an even greater source of outrage to the establishment: Margaret Thatcher was elected as Prime Minister. The transformation did not happen overnight. Although one attendee recalled that 'the festival had grown noticeably in size of attendance' and there were 'fewer of the old hands around', it was still a predominantly old-fashioned hippie affair, and its low-key, homespun charms remained intact. One regular festival-goer, recalling a wealth of spontaneous, open-ended jam sessions and hand-painted cardboard signs declaring 'feel free to use these instruments', observed that 'Little things like these were what made Stonehenge so totally unlike going to a commercial festival like Reading, which I also went to in 1979.' (Shark 2003d)

For the celebration of the solstice, David Loxley made a point of noting that the barriers came down and that members of the public, including a substantial proportion of the festival-goers, entered the circle to join the Druids, although there was clearly some confusion over the precise timing of the event. According to a contemporary press report, 'Thousands of disappointed tourists' turned up on the night of 20 June, 'but they had forgotten the Druid calendar which makes this a leap year and thus a day later.' Accordingly, the main event took place on the night of 21 June and the following morning. The Druids, led once more by *Coronation Street*'s William Roache, 'heralded the dawn after a midnight vigil', and 'the golden sun rose magnificently in a cloudless blue sky' that 'brought cheers from the watching crowds and a welcome warmth.' It was the first clear dawn since 1976, a 'perfect sunrise' particularly significant to both the Druids and the festival-goers in light of the events of the year before: the blanket ban on public access to the stones, the unprecedented hostility towards the festival-goers that was voiced by the police and the National Trust, and Glyn Daniel's mounting criticism of both the festival and the Druids. (Loxley 2003; Weird Wiltshire 2003)

Also 1979 was the year that the migratory May to September free festival season became firmly established. Stonehenge was preceded by the first of several free festivals at Horseshoe Pass near Ruthin, north Wales, and was followed by Priddy Pool in Somerset and Severn Vale in Gloucestershire in July, Deeply Vale in August, and several festivals in Wales in September, including Meigan Fayre and the Psilocybin festival at Pontrhydygroes in mid-Wales. (Lodge 2001)

The Druids arrive at the Stonehenge Free Festival in the 1980s.
Copyright Ian Oakley.

Rainbow punks and the Crass Collective

Elsewhere, the latest impetus for revolutionary change – one that was to collide spectacularly with the older festival culture – was happening in the towns and cities, where the Sex Pistols' cynical mottos 'Never trust a hippie' and 'The only good hippie is a dead hippie' persisted. It was only when the Crass Collective allied the youthful energy of punk to the hippies' purest legacy – anarchy – that a new synthesis occurred, the 'rainbow punks' who brought a new urgency to the festival scene.

There was a certain irony in all this. Crass was formed in response to Phil Russell's death. Jeremy Ratter said that 'Phil's death marked, for us, the end of an era. Along with him died the last grain of trust that we, naively, had had in the "system", the last seeds of hope that, if we lived a decent life based on respect rather than abuse, our example might be followed by those in authority.' He added, 'In a very real sense... Crass was Phil's band.' Jeremy produced a pamphlet about Phil's life, *The Last of the Hippies: An Hysterical Romance*, which was given away with a Crass LP, *Christ the Album*, and which contributed significantly to the Wally/Stonehenge cult. He admitted to C.J. Stone that 'while he was writing it, he knew that he was engaged in iconography'. The subsequent success of Crass' uncompromising vilification of the sickness at the heart of contemporary society shows clearly that, in the falling out with Sid Rawle over the box that contained Phil Russell's ashes, it was Jeremy and his fellow band members who took on the role of Phil's prophets with the most aplomb, 'consciously fulfilling Phil's famous axiom: "Guitars the tommy-guns, drums the missiles, sun the bomb".' (Stone 1996: 97, 80)

The Tibetan Ukranian
Mountain Troupe.
Copyright Andy Hope.

1980: the expansion of the free festival scene

Inspired by the new influx of politicised youth, the free festival scene began to grow significantly in 1980. Festival Welfare Services identified forty-seven alternative fairs and festivals throughout the summer, from the fields of East Anglia to the hills of Cornwall, in cities from Norwich to Bristol and Bath, and from the plethora of pagan-tinted psychedelic events in Wales to the peace-oriented Moon Fair in the Lake District. Significant free festivals which began that year, and which carried on until the late 1980s or the early 1990s, included Cantlin Stone in Clun, near the border of England and Wales, which took place in early July, and the Avon Free Festival (known in its first year as a New Age Gypsy Fair), which occupied Inglestone Common in Wickwar, ten miles north east of Bristol, later in the month. Penny Mellor of Festival Welfare Services attended the Cantlin Stone festival, which, like all its predecessors, began small, attracting up to 300 people for an acoustic event with a free food kitchen and stalls selling food, crafts and other produce that 'went very smoothly with few problems' apart from a disproportionate and heavy-handed police presence. (McKay 2000: 102; Mellor 1980a)

At the heart of this movement, the Stonehenge Free Festival more than doubled in size, with Penny Mellor estimating that there were 17,500 people present for the solstice. Despite atrocious weather and the widespread application of stop and search tactics by the police, Penny concluded that 'On the whole the atmosphere of the festival was very pleasant.' The festival also provided the first major outing for the most prominent of the new nomadic collectives, the Tibetan Ukranian Mountain Troupe, 'the creative, surreal, prankster Circus of the travelling scene', in the words of Convoy Steve, whose marquee became a focal point for much of the festival's best music (and whose misspelling of the word 'Ukranian' was, apparently, deliberate). (Mellor 1980b; Tibetan Ukranian Mountain Troupe 2003)

The Psilocybin Festival

Particularly significant in the sequence of festivals that followed Stonehenge was the Psilocybin Festival, which had begun the year before with around a hundred people attending, but which now grew to accommodate over a thousand, raising tipis, tents

A horse and cart at the Psilocybin Festival, 1980.
Copyright Alan Lodge.

and benders on a gentle curve in the River Ystwyth surrounded by mountains. The festival's organisers – a 'hard core of "New Gypsies" who travel with horse and cart' – came together to celebrate what for many of the festival-goers was their holiest sacrament: the compact, mind-opening, indigenous psychedelic fungi known as magic mushrooms. Once more the police presence was unnecessarily large and intimidating, but the festival had 'a gentle carnival atmosphere', according to a sympathetic press report, and Penny Mellor observed that it was 'a festival of doing. Almost everyone on site was trading in some way, mainly in food and crafts. People were very ingenious at thinking up new ways of exchanging money. The trading wasn't worked out on a high profit basis, but more on people working with whatever money and resources they had to generate enough money or basic supplies to live on themselves whilst providing a service for other people at the same time.' (Shark 2003k; Mellor 1980c)

The festival also confirmed the overlapping interests of the Stonehenge festival and the free festival scene in general. Bev and Del Richardson were there, as were the Tibetan Ukranian Mountain Troupe, who organised the digging of latrine trenches, and who 'for a modest sum' delivered 'breakfast with a smile' to the festival-goers' tents. Bev, 'sipping coffee in his bender', chatted happily to the press, effortlessly incorporating the use of magic mushrooms into his unique blend of paganism. He pointed out that the mushroom pickers constituted 'a hippy cottage industry', and added, 'The strange thing is that these things have never really caught on. The Beatniks used them, but it's never really been a popular thing.' (Shark 2003k)

113

The revival of political protest

The Psilocybin Festival was the last festival of the season, and alongside the 'high spirits', Penny Mellor noted 'a subterranean feeling of sadness as people discussed with each other where they were going over the winter and what they would be doing at the festivals next year.' Those who made it back to London found that in the wider sphere of national politics, opposition to the government of Margaret Thatcher was growing, represented in particular by a major revival in the fortunes of CND. The organisation had been mostly dormant throughout the 1970s, apart from a few large-scale events over the Easter period in the early years of the decade: an anti-war Festival of Life in London's Victoria Park in 1970, a Peace Festival in Alexandra Park in 1971, and a revival of the Aldermaston marches in 1972, when Hawkwind had rocked the gates of the Weapons Research Establishment with a sustained sonic barrage. (Mellor 1980c; McKay 2000: 94-6)

In October 1980, 70,000 people attended a national CND demonstration in London, and the drift towards a new radicalism in politics was also evident that summer, when the first Ecology Party Summer Gathering was held at Worthy Farm in Pilton. This small but significant step for the nascent ecological movement was convened by Michael Eavis in the absence of the Glastonbury festival, which he had been forced to cancel for a year while he juggled the financial loss sustained in 1979 with his ambitious plans for a larger festival in 1981. Significantly, the Summer Gathering brought the existing green pioneers, including Jonathan Porritt, into contact with the ecological leanings of the free festival scene for the first time. Music was provided by Roy Harper and Nik Turner's Inner City Unit, and Sid Rawle became so involved that he was duly elected to the Party Council at the Autumn Conference in Cardiff, when 'a controversial motion for the legalisation of cannabis was passed.' (McKay 2000: 102; Barnett 1998)

1981: the growth of a social, spiritual and political alternative

In 1981, the Stonehenge Free Festival became a truly massive event, with up to 35,000 people attending over the two-week period. There were a number of reasons for the increase in the popularity of both the gathering at Stonehenge and the free festival scene in general. Dissatisfaction with the Thatcher regime reached the first of several breaking points in 1981. The Specials caught the mood, topping the charts with *Ghost Town*'s sinister dub lament, and that summer riots broke out in Brixton, Toxteth, and dozens of other inner city areas across the UK. Across the country, people from all walks of life who were opposed to the new mood of intolerance in the Tory government discovered that at Stonehenge a social, spiritual and political alternative was already well-established, and from 1981 onwards an increasingly large number of young people in particular – an all-embracing cross-section of the left-leaning and the excluded that effortlessly took in students, workers and the unemployed – converged on the great festival on Salisbury Plain. Hilary Jones, for example, was one of the many people who adopted festival life – and the significance of Stonehenge – at this time: 'For years I'd watch Bournemouth empty of young people for that couple of weeks. And then I became old enough to join the exodus. 1980, 1981. It literally was an exodus. I remember the first time I got on the

The Stonehenge Free Festival, 1981.
Copyright Adrian Arbib.

bus and said, 'Salisbury, please', and the conductor said, 'Are you going to Stonehenge, because you can buy a through ticket?' They knew that anybody around seventeen, eighteen, nineteen, getting on the bus and asking for Salisbury was going to Stonehenge.' (Jones 1998: 198–9)

The eviction of squatters from the London boroughs was also on the increase from the late 1970s onwards, and was one of the main reasons for the growth of the travellers' movement, with thousands of people buying up old vehicles and taking to the road each year. A dynamic, expanding, alternative economy was developing, and for all these new nomads Stonehenge and its free festival assumed a central position. Big Steve, stage manager of the Polytantric stage from 1981 to 1984, recalled 'how together and hopeful the people were' at the beginning of the 1980s, when travellers were 'relatively free of hassle', and every year saw a 'nomadic drift from Stonehenge to Bristol to East Anglia and Wales from fayre to festival.' (Big Steve 1988)

In addition, with a commercial festival at Glastonbury up and running once more, the Stonehenge Free Festival became, semi-officially, Glastonbury's madder neighbour, with many of Michael Eavis' bands, who could not be named in advance for contractual reasons, sloping off to play the wilder party down the road, bringing fans in their wake.

The crossover continues: free festival regulars maintain the spirit of the Stonehenge festival at Glastonbury, 1982. Copyright Alan Lodge.

The Greenham Common Peace Camp

All these new influences combined to increase the potency of the free festival circuit throughout 1981, with small, impromptu travellers' camps springing up everywhere, and new, overtly political events joining the already impressive roster of established free festivals. Smokey Bear's Smoke-In, a one-day festival set up to publicise the campaign for the decriminalisation of cannabis, took place in Hyde Park in May (nearly twenty-three years after the Summer of Love's 'Legalise Pot' rally), and a larger Ecology Party Summer Gathering took place at Worthy Farm in July – after the reconvened festival, which raised £20,000 for CND. That same month, a Rock Against Racism Carnival took place in Leeds, with the Specials and Misty in Roots spreading the multi-cultural message, and this was followed by a peace festival in Aberystwyth in August. (Big Steve 1988; McKay 2000: 102; Lodge 2001)

The most significant political events of the year, however, focused in particular on the government's plans to base Cruise missiles on British soil. On 24 October, a demonstration in London in support of CND turned into one of the largest political protests in British history, and at the same time a new form of protest was beginning to take place outside the gates of Greenham Common, near Newbury in Berkshire, the first proposed airbase for the weapons. The Greenham story began on 6 September 1981, when a group of protestors – thirty-six women, six men and four babies in pushchairs, collectively campaigning under the name Women for Life on Earth – arrived on foot from west Wales to hold a demonstration. They subsequently set up a Peace Camp outside the base, and in the months that followed eight other camps were set up around the perimeter in a colour-coded rainbow coalition. The original camp was known as Yellow Gate, and it was followed by, amongst others, a

116

'Women for Life on Earth': one of the many banners created by the women of the peace movement.
Copyright Thalia Campbell.

women-only camp at Green Gate, nearest the missile silos, a New Age camp at Blue Gate, a religious camp at Violet Gate, and a collective of artists at Red Gate. (The Women's Library 2001)

In February 1982, the Peace Camps declared themselves women-only, a stance that was based on a radical sharpening of feminist rhetoric. As Penny Welch, Lecturer in Politics and Women's Studies at the University of Wolverhampton, put it, 'Many Greenham women argued that aggression, the nuclear arms race and militarism were associated with men/masculinity whereas women were associated with life-affirming characteristics', and it was this association that 'gave women the responsibility to campaign for peace.' In practice, only one of the camps – Blue Gate – was exclusively for women, and the other camps all admitted men in the daytime, but the women's focus on their own power to effect immense change became a beacon of such intense inspiration that the majority of those who were, to some extent, excluded by the process were ultimately won over. (Welch 2003)

Representatives of CND, for example, described how 'There was some opposition within CND and the larger peace movement to the fact that men were barred from the camp, but this largely melted away as the determination, imagination and the energy of the Greenham Women became clear.' As the conflict intensified, and the women were subject to 'press hostility and physical abuse including repeated, often quite brutal evictions', it became clear that, in addition to the protestors' self-professed aim of empowering women, they had also succeeded in establishing an innovative form of direct action that was smaller in scale than CND's national demonstrations but that was to prove, ultimately, both more persistent and more enduring. (Allum 2000)

1982: the Peace Convoy

As the events of 1982 unfolded, the movement's political aspirations increased even more sharply It was the year that Margaret Thatcher went to war in the Falklands. 250,000 people promptly turned up for another CND demonstration in Hyde Park on 6 June. And at Stonehenge the political mood threatened to overwhelm the festival's social and spiritual components. It was, nevertheless, a successful solstice. Jeremy Sandford (who back in 1974 had written the first in-depth analysis of the festival scene, *Tomorrow's People*) reported that 'This year officialdom actually cut the wire around Stonehenge on solstice day so that a procession of hundreds of people could cross the road and enter the shrine, where three weddings and several namings of babies took place.' He concluded that 'People related to the divinity which many still feel resides in that place in various ways that they felt appropriate.' (Sandford 1982)

The most lasting impression of the 1982 festival was, however, the travellers' collective adoption of the peace movement. Hundreds of the free festival regulars formed themselves into a Peace Convoy, and on 30 June, as the festival came to an end, 135 vehicles set off to join the Women's Peace Camp at Greenham Common and to hold a 'Cosmic Counter-Cruise Carnival.' The carnival's inspiration was a CND rally and mini-festival – featuring assorted Stonehenge regulars – that had taken place at Greenham in March, shortly after the protestors' first blockade of the base, when thirty-four women had been arrested. (The Women's Library 2001)

After a sustained campaign of misinformation that was deliberately leaked from the festival site, and that resulted in 2,000 police officers being sent off to guard seventeen possible festival sites, including Inglestone Common, Old Sarum and even Windsor, the convoy scored an early victory at Greenham itself, avoiding a police roadblock that had been set up at short notice by ducking down a previously reconnoitred alternative route to the camp, a track at the back of the base that was overgrown but just passable. Once on site, the convoy established a number of stages, participated in direct action – pulling down sections of the fence – and endured random acts of police brutality. Big Steve recalled one morning when 'the police arrived in large numbers in riot gear and everyone sat in a circle... as the police seemed to pick out indiscriminately various members of the convoy.' (Shark 2003l)

In time-honoured fashion, a free news-sheet was produced, which combined typical bravado with an awareness of the importance of the peace movement: 'The unstoppable convoy has taken another site. But not just another site; the most

The Peace Convoy on the road to Greenham Common, 1982.
Copyright Alan Lodge.

important site we have ever taken… It's what we've been practising for all these long years. Every Deeply Vale, every Inglestone, every Windsor free festival, every Stonehenge has in a way been a preparation for this – this is the one that really matters.' Thalia Campbell, one of the original protestors from Women for Life on Earth, recalled how the convoy's commitment to direct action shocked not only the police, but also a large number of the women protestors. She commented that 'It was some time before the women decided that cutting the fence was OK', adding that 'if they had known their Suffragette history, they would have acted faster. The Suffragettes decided that violence to property – especially men's property – was OK, but violence to people was not.' Even so, the most poignant event at Greenham in 1982 was the 'Embrace the Base' gathering on 12 December, when 30,000 women linked hands to encircle the airbase, decorating the fence with pictures of loved ones, messages and flowers. (Shark 2003l; Campbell 2003)

A summer of protest and celebration

Although the established free festival circuit was still in existence, by 1982 radical politics had permeated almost every event. The Vines Cross free festivals in East Sussex, which began around this time, attracting up to 3,000 people for an old-fashioned diet of music and drugs, were overshadowed by those which successfully mixed protest and celebration. On 23 May, 5,000 people gathered for a Cannabis Law Reform Rally in Brockwell Park, Brixton, which brought together London's rastas – through the Jah Shaka, King Sounds and Coxsone sound systems – and the travelling festival scene, including Nik Turner and his Pyramid stage, and various members of the festival's crew. (Shark 2003m, 2003n)

*A tipi overshadowed by the Sizewell 'B' nuclear reactor
at the Pure Energy Fair, September 1982.
Copyright Alan Lodge.*

In July, the first Green Gathering took place at Worthy Farm, a development of the Ecology Party meetings that attracted over 5,000 people. As well as widening the scope of the green movement, the gathering also established a template for sustainable gatherings that were able to maintain the ethos of the free festivals in the face of a growing influx of less focused 'consumers.' The music was restricted to acoustic music only, everyone was encouraged to participate – financially, physically and spiritually – and it is significant that the Green Gatherings, as well as other small-scale gatherings along the same lines, are still running today. (McKay 2000: 103)

The final explicitly political travellers' event of the summer took place in September. The Pure Energy Fair, in Westleton, Suffolk, was a three-day protest against the building of the nearby Sizewell 'B' nuclear reactor that saw the Peace Convoy organising a stage and bands for local anti-nuclear campaigners, setting up camp on the beach, and balancing their political input with a dose of old-fashioned hedonism. As Big Steve put it, 'we had the luxury of hot showers on site and communal nude hippie showers were much appreciated by the dusty travellers.' To complete what seems to have been an idyllic protest party, free food was provided by the ubiquitous Hare Krishnas. (Shark 2003o)

1983: the cracks begin to show

By 1983, the increasingly intertwined expressions of celebration and dissent – the free festival scene and the political protest movement – expanded beyond anyone's

The main drag, Stonehenge 1984.
Copyright Ian Oakley.

wildest dreams. At Stonehenge, Penny Mellor estimated that 'There were at least 30,000 people attending the festival over the solstice weekend, with as many as 70,000 people visiting the festival over the duration.' It began amiably enough, with a search for the location of the main stage that encapsulated the organisers' ongoing commitment to the increasingly pagan-tinted earth mysteries movement as espoused by John Michell. Big Steve described how 'Sid Rawle and I wandered across the fields... clutching a dowsing rod; it twitched downwards and I opened my eyes to find myself in a circle of daisies – this had to be the place for the stage.' (Mellor 1983; Big Steve 1988)

As the numbers of attendees grew, however, the festival began to show signs of cracking under the pressure. In many ways it was an inevitable downturn for an event that had only a minimal infrastructure and, more crucially, little or no support from outside, apart from the welfare and medical volunteers. Penny Mellor noted ruefully that 'There seemed to be less caring amongst the festival people.' Hundreds of trees were cut down in the nearest plantation – until the National Trust provided alternative supplies – and the stage crews threatened to walk out unless something was done about the heroin dealers who had begun to make their way onto the site. To their credit, the representatives of the festival's leaderless tribes – who were as appalled as anyone else by these developments – took the problem seriously, and those that could be found were subsequently evicted. (Mellor 1983; Shark 2003d)

In other ways, however, the festival was a resounding success, an integrated, cosmopolitan stew of alternative sub-cultures, in which old hippies shared spliffs with young punks, and travellers traded socialist banter with bunking undergraduates. For students like myself, visiting for the first time, this seasonal settlement of impossibly weathered and wildly decorated tents, tipis, vans, buses and old army vehicles was little short of a revelation, an alternative state within Thatcher's Britain that seemed to have rooted itself to the ancient sacred landscape

121

Afternoon crowds of festival-goers and the general public, summer solstice 1984.
Copyright Ian Oakley.

with nonchalant ease. In between the chattering and the laughter, the streets throbbed with the chugging and wailing of electric guitars and the pounding of drums from innumerable small stages, a cacophony of skin and metal punctuated only by the regular cries of 'Hot Knives! Speed! Acid!' that rang through the sultry afternoon air like a mantra. Less conspicuously, groups of elfin wanderers brewed up pots of magic mushroom tea or stood, beaming beatifically, beside barrels full of the previous year's harvest.

As dusk descended, thousands of tiny lights lit up the streets, and the festival assumed the guise of an ancient city. As Jeremy Sandford described it, 'For those like myself who have always felt a tinge of envy for the Duke in *As You Like It* setting up his court in the Forest of Arden, there is an unending fascination in these tent cities, rising up overnight in the midst of the countryside. I like to fancy that we can see the everyday world recreated here in a better light, dedicated to good health, peace, cooperation, conviviality and music.' (Sandford 1982)

Maximum dissent

At the end of the festival, the Peace Convoy continued its summer itinerary, which had begun in May with free festivals at Rhayader in Wales and Oswestry in Shropshire, travelling first to Inglestone Common for the Avon Free Festival, then to mid-Wales for a festival in Montgomery and then to Somerset, to join the Green Gathering, which had moved from Worthy Farm to Lambert's Hill Farm, near Shepton Mallet. The season continued at Cantlin Stone in August and concluded with a magic mushroom festival in Hay-on-Wye in September, but it was the combination of events at the Green Gathering that was to retain a particular resonance. (Lodge 2001)

The three-day event, which featured the largest tipi circle so far seen outside North America, was successfully convened as a Children's Gathering, 'with entertainments and workshops based around their needs and desires', but was blighted by persistent harassment from the police, something that was becoming commonplace to the travellers but that came as a shock to everyone else. Although the convoy had made a contribution to the gathering's coffers and had been given a 'broadly sympathetic welcoming space' by its organisers, members of the Green Collective felt that they were 'virtually besieged by the largest police operation ever seen at a Green event in this country. Large numbers of people – many of whom had never had much dealings with the police beyond asking a bobby for the time – found themselves being stopped, searched and treated in an intimidating fashion.' (McKay 2000: 104, 175)

In the wider political arena, the year began sedately enough with a CND carnival in Brockwell Park in May, but a national CND demonstration on 22 October became the second largest political rally in British history – after the noble and colossal women's suffrage rally of 1909 – assuming greater significance when taken as part of a new development that transcended national boundaries for the first time. Similar demonstrations, taking place throughout the whole of western Europe, brought the total number of anti-nuclear protestors to over five million people, and the prevailing reaction against the dawn of a terrifying new world order was reinforced in Britain by the extraordinary mushrooming of the Greenham women's cause, with twenty-four hour vigils taking place outside all of the 102 airbases in the UK that were used by American forces.

1984: the biggest free festival in British history

Against this backdrop of concerted political activity, widespread social agitation and a deeper, darker undercurrent of anger and frustration that was to see riots breaking out across the inner cities once more, the Stonehenge Free Festival grew even larger in 1984. Despite the continuing problems of managing the unmanageable without any official leadership, conspicuous problems were tackled head-on. Heroin dealers were dealt with even more sharply than the year before, and a burnt-out car, dumped at the entrance, carried an explicit warning: 'This was a smack dealer's car.'

Overall, there were reasons for those involved in the organisation of the festival to feel, as the Festival Zone website put it, that 'the fun far outweighed the fear.' The unprecedented mingling of the tribes continued unabated, breaking down social barriers that were all too noticeable in the 'real' world, and John Pendragon tried to counter the drift towards chaos by establishing a mini-festival within the larger festival, a dealer-free zone with its own stage that sought to recreate the spirit of the early gatherings. He was also one of the founder members – along with the pagan George Firsoff – of 'Robin's Greenwood Gang', another internal organisation that was set up to counter the damage caused to the nearby woods through a process of guidance and education. Musically, there was a more diverse line-up than ever before, and even the traditional headliners, Hawkwind, tried to top their performance of the year before (when they had played a two-hour set at sunrise on

An aerial view of Stonehenge and its festival, summer solstice 1984.

solstice morning) with a conceptual performance – Earth Ritual – that was spread over two days. (Shark 2003d; Lodge 1998; McKay 2000: 104)

Most spectacularly of all, on solstice morning the fences came down, the sun shone out in all its summer glory, and the Druids and the festival-goers were once more at the stones together. There were pagan weddings, children were blessed, there was nakedness, and all manner of other rituals were performed, from the profound to the impenetrable. For myself, the occupation of Stonehenge was an opportunity to appreciate for the first time the sheer scale of the monument and the skill of its construction, giving me a visceral rush of astonishment and admiration that has not left me to this day, despite the fact that, behind the scenes, the authorities responsible for the temple and its immediate environment – the government, English Heritage (a quango that took over management of the monument on 1 April 1984), the National Trust, local landowners and the police – were already working on plans that would deny access to the stones at the summer solstice for the overwhelming majority of people for another sixteen years.

The heart of the Stonehenge Free Festival, summer solstice 1984.
Sid Rawle, arms outstretched, welcomes the sun.
Copyright Alan Lodge.

Chapter Eight

Suppression

Porton Down, Boscombe Down and Nostell Priory

Oblivious to these developments, the majority of the Peace Convoy headed to the west of England and Wales after the Stonehenge festival had run its course, to continue the established run of festivals that had begun in May at Rhayader and Hay-on-Wye with festivals in Montgomery, Clun (the ongoing Cantlin Stone festival), Castle Caereinion (near Welshpool) and Hay-on-Wye (again) from July to September. (Lodge 2001)

In the meantime, the first signs of a new and disturbingly violent intolerance on the part of the authorities occurred near Boscombe Down airfield in southern England and at Nostell Priory in West Yorkshire. The first of these incidents came about after a group of militant travellers hijacked a peaceful animal rights protest at Porton Down in early July, pulling down fences before moving on to the US air force base at Boscombe Down, where a peace camp was already in existence and a free festival had been held just a few weeks before. At Boscombe Down, the fences came down once more, 'undoing weeks of careful confidence-building between peace activists and the USAF base security', as one erstwhile supporter put it. The authorities took their revenge shortly after, when the protestors were 'cut up by riot vans, boarded, attacked and trashed by a squad of "Special Branch" police.' (Kibblewhite 2003)

In some ways, this retaliation by the police could be regarded both as the end result of a deliberately confrontational game of cat-and-mouse and as a premonition of the violence that was to come at the end of the summer, when riots erupted throughout the inner cities and a Stop the City demonstration took place in London on 27 September – following an inaugural event that Easter at which Class War activists had hurled bricks at the Bank of England – when minor damage was caused to branches of Barclays Bank, sex shops in Soho and the offices of Saatchi and Saatchi, the Trafalgar Square fountains were dyed red, and 470 people were arrested. (Green Anarchist 1984)

At Nostell Priory, however, the police violence was unprovoked and far more severe. At the end of a licensed weekend festival, riot police, fresh from suppressing striking miners at the Orgreave coking plant, raided the site at dawn, ransacking vehicles and arresting the majority of the travellers – 360 people in total – with a savagery that had not been seen since the end of the third People's Free Festival at Windsor in 1974. The travellers were held without charge for up to a fortnight in police and army

Porton Down, July 1984: the fence comes down.
Copyright Celia Kibblewhite.

prisons, finally appearing before a magistrate who 'systematically went through us all, finding us guilty and nicking us for whatever it was.' As one of the accused, Phil the Beer, put it, 'I got two lots of suspended sentences for six months each for just being there at a festival and complaining that these people were smashing my home up. I felt quite bitter about that, really.' (Rosenberger 1989; Goodwin 1995, 2003)

Molesworth

Some of the battered survivors made it to Molesworth in Cambridgeshire, a disused World War II airbase that had been designated as the second Cruise missile base after Greenham Common, where they joined peace protestors from Greenham and members of various Green organisations to become the Rainbow Village Peace Camp. Molesworth swiftly became a rooted settlement and, in many ways, was the epitome of the free festival-protest fusion. One resident, Phil Hudson, noting that there was 'every kind of "alternative" freak, dissident and outcast inhabiting the converted buses, trucks, ambulances, horse boxes, tipis, geodesic domes, and the most splendid benders I've ever seen', recalled the extent of the experiment: 'There was a village shop (a double-decker bus), a postman, a freaky chapel ("Eirene", Greek for peace), a peace garden (largely built by a former RAF man who was badly irradiated at Christmas Island in the '50s), a small plantation of wheat for Ethiopia (planted weeks before Michael Buerk "broke" the famine story in the mainstream media), and the legendary Free Food Kitchen.' (Hudson 2002)

Molesworth: preparations for a dragon parade of children at the peace chapel, 1984.
Copyright Celia Kibblewhite.

Lasting throughout the winter, the Rainbow Village – now numbering about 150 people – was finally evicted at the start of February 1985 by 'the largest peacetime mobilisation of troops in this country': 1,500 Royal Engineers, 600 MoD police and a thousand police. The eviction took five months to plan, and the armed forces were led by Defence Secretary Michael Heseltine, who wore a flak jacket for the occasion. (Schnews 2000; Rosenberger 1989)

Although overlooked by the authorities, the date chosen for the eviction was highly symbolic to the convoy: Imbolc, the festival of rebirth in the Celtic calendar that many of the travellers had been drawn to over the previous decade. As their relationship to the land intensified the festival season, centred on the summer solstice at Stonehenge, began to be constructed around a cycle of ancient pagan festivals that were far more resonant than the Bank Holidays with which they had pragmatically begun.

After various attempts to reoccupy the site (which was eventually refortified with an extra security fence at a cost of £3 million), the convoy shifted uneasily around the country for the next few months, gathering in Sharnbrook in Bedfordshire in April, and attending the first major free festival of the year, the Tree Fair at Long Marston airfield near Stratford-upon-Avon, over the Bank Holiday weekend at the end of May. On 1 June, after stopping overnight in Savernake Forest near Avebury, 140 vehicles set off down the A338, heading for the A303 and Stonehenge, unaware that they were entering a trap.

Police violence at the Battle of the Beanfield. Photographer Tim Malyon, spotted by the policeman on the left, started running as soon as he had taken this incriminating image.
Copyright Tim Malyon.

The Battle of the Beanfield

That day, after eleven years of begrudging tolerance on the part of the authorities, the Stonehenge Free Festival came to an abrupt and bloody end at the notorious Battle of the Beanfield, an otherwise unremarkable field in Cholderton, on the Wiltshire border. Under the pretext of an injunction taken out by English Heritage, the National Trust and seventeen local landowners against eighty-three named individuals who supposedly made up the organisation of the festival, the road was blocked off and police in full riot gear attacked the defenceless convoy with unprecedented brutality, smashing windows, beating people up and dragging women and children out of their vehicles through shattered windscreens. After part of the convoy broke through a fence and drove into a nearby bean field, there was a chilling and surreal stand-off for nearly four hours, with all attempts at negotiation refused, until the terrifying violence began again, with helicopters wheeling overhead, and an officer on board shouting through a loudhailer, 'You're doing a great job. This is how they like it.' (Stone 1996: 159)

Few outsiders witnessed the events of the Beanfield. Most of the media had obeyed police instructions to stay away from the main action 'for their own safety.' The few who did make it through saw a one-sided rout of heart-breaking brutality. Nick Davies of *The Observer* wrote that 'There was glass breaking, people screaming,

129

One of the victims of the police violence at the Battle of the Beanfield.

black smoke towering out of burning caravans and everywhere there seemed to be people being bashed and flattened... men, women and children were led away, shivering, swearing, crying, bleeding, leaving their homes in pieces... Over the years I had seen all kinds of horrible and frightening things and always managed to grin and write it. But as I left the Beanfield, for the first time, I felt sick enough to cry.' (Carey 1997)

Kim Sabido of ITN was so shaken by what he saw that he declared live to camera, 'What we, the ITN camera crew, and myself as a reporter, have seen in the last thirty minutes here on this field has been some of the most brutal police treatment of people that I've witnessed in my entire career as a journalist. The number of people who have been hit by policemen, who have been clubbed whilst holding their babies in their arms, in coaches around this field, is yet to be counted... There must surely be an inquiry after what has happened here today.' (Stone 1996: 159; Goodwin 1995)

A complete travesty of justice

By the end of the evening, 420 people had been arrested, taken to holding cells throughout southern England, in Aldershot, Bristol, Plymouth, Portsmouth, Southampton and Yeovil. Immediately after arrest, several dozen women were strip-searched in a police garage. All those detained were charged with obstruction of the police and obstruction of the highway, and in addition 241 of them were charged with unlawful assembly, a grave and antique transgression, which in theory carries a maximum sentence of life imprisonment. Representatives of social services were on hand to take children into care, and in the meantime, back at the Beanfield, the remaining vehicles 'were systematically looted and smashed', some were burnt out, and seven travellers' dogs were destroyed by the RSPCA. (Goodwin 1995; Stone 1996: 160)

Ironically, the main obstacle to this complete travesty of justice was provided by the most unlikely of spectators. The Earl of Cardigan, secretary of the Marlborough Conservative Association and part of the family that owned Savernake Forest, had travelled with the convoy on a motorbike, accompanied by a friend, thinking 'it would be interesting to follow events personally.' In court, the Earl described 'a heavily pregnant woman with "a silhouette like a zeppelin" being "clubbed with a truncheon" and riot police showering a woman and child with glass.' When his honesty provoked outrage in the conservative media, he commented, 'if I see a policeman truncheoning a woman I feel I'm entitled to say it is not a good thing you should be doing', and it was chiefly his testimony that saw off police charges against the convoy in the local magistrates' courts. (Carey 1997)

Significantly, no inquiry into the bloody events of 1 June 1985 has ever been held, and noticeably, with the exception of Nick Davies, every media witness to the events of the Beanfield discovered that their evidence was either tampered with or that it mysteriously disappeared. When Kim Sabido's report was broadcast later that day, his agonised commentary had been replaced by a bland voice-over, and he later confirmed that 'some of the nastier, more controversial shots that were taken at the Battle of the Beanfield, like the woman being dragged out by her hair' through the shattered windscreen of her vehicle, had 'disappeared' from the ITN library. Similar disappearances were noted by the freelance journalist and photographer Tim Malyon, and the photographer Ben Gibson, who was working for *The Observer* with Nick Davies, and whose negatives vanished from the newspaper's archives during an office move. (Goodwin 1995; Carey 1997)

Justifying the unjustifiable

Despite the heavy-handed manner in which the travellers were suppressed, some argued that the end justified the means by which it was achieved. The tabloid press in particular delighted in attacking the travellers at every opportunity. Headlines screamed, 'Invasion of the "Giro" Gypsies', 'Sponging Scum', and 'Sex-mad junkie outlaws make the Hell's Angels look like little Noddy.' The tabloids' crusade to create modern day 'folk devils' was echoed in *Antiquity*, where Glyn Daniel concluded merrily, 'The Wiltshire police dealt firmly with the invaders, and the so-called Battle of Stonehenge, in all its violence, was seen on British television. The pop festival desecrators were routed and the Midsummer Solstice passed off without any due incident.' (Daniel 1992: 178)

The authorities' justification for the events of 1 June 1985 was farcical. In an press advertisement issued earlier in the year by the National Trust and English Heritage to

STONEHENGE

THE NATIONAL TRUST AND ENGLISH HERITAGE
REGRET TO ANNOUNCE THAT THE FREE FESTIVAL
WILL NOT BE ALLOWED ON THE LAND AT
STONEHENGE CARED FOR BY THEM THIS YEAR
OR IN FUTURE

The monument and the area around it form one of the most important archaeological sites in Europe, and for this reason must be given careful protection. The festival which has taken place in June in recent years has caused serious damage, particularly in 1984, to the National Trust land near the monument which contains many achaeological features associated with the stone circle itself. The Trust has consequently decided, that it should no longer make its land available for the festival. This decision is fully supported by English Heritage. Please do not make plans for a festival at Stonehenge in 1985 and help safeguard our heritage by supporting our efforts to protect Stonehenge and its setting.

 Warren Davis
Information Office
National Trust,
36, Queen Anne's Gate
London SW1H 9AS
Tel. (01) 222 9251

Gillian Raikes,
Information Office,
National Trust,
Wessex.
Tel. (0747) 840560

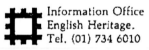 Information Office
English Heritage.
Tel. (01) 734 6010

Help us to preserve the past for the future

*Zero tolerance: the 1985 advertisement announcing
that 'the free festival will not be allowed.'*

announce that 'the free festival will not be allowed on the land at Stonehenge cared for by them this year or in the future', it was claimed that the festival had 'caused serious damage, particularly in 1984, to the National Trust land near the monument which contains many archaeological features associated with the stone circle itself.' It was certainly true that in 1984 someone had dug a hole for a bread-oven in a barrow (albeit one that had already been excavated), that in some years damage had been done to trees and that every year it cost £20,000 to clear up the field after the festival was over, but these transgressions paled into insignificance compared with the long-term effects of agriculture, the depredations of the army, the trench – fifteen feet long and six feet deep – that was dug across the entrance to the festival field in 1985 to prevent access, and the estimated £5 million that the Beanfield operation and the subsequent court cases cost the establishment – and by extension the nation's tax-payers. (Fowler 1990: 139, 147; Stone 1996: 160)

In a less brutal world, the money spent on the Beanfield would have been sufficient to clean up after the free festival for the next 250 years. In addition, the threat to the stones, which was implicit in the authorities' complaints, was effectively countered by Bill Kendall, a custodian, who told Tim Malyon in June 1985 that 'The "hippies" have never done any damage to the stones over the six year period I've been on duty at Stonehenge. They are respected by the custodians. They come with black bags and collect up all the rubbish when they leave, even the cigarette ends.' (TAT 1988: 21)

With hindsight, it is clear that the suppression of the Stonehenge Free Festival, which took place between similar attacks on the Miners at Orgreave in 1984 and the printers at Wapping in 1986, was actually part of a wider political agenda that was authorised from the highest possible level. For years, the establishment had been unable to stop the festival. In more innocent times (as recently as 1982), the sociologist Michael Clarke had asked, 'How is it that a somewhat motley collection of young and not so young people managed to impose their taste for festivals on the English countryside in summer, in spite of the rooted opposition of many of the residents?' and had concluded that a significant part of the answer was 'the assumption in the British legal system of a right of assembly without prior state permission.' (Clarke 1982)

If this was one explanation of the legal loopholes by which the festival thrived, at ground level the inadequacies of the existing laws occupied the police. In a 1981 report, Frank Lockyer, Chief Superintendent of the Wiltshire Police, conceded that the authorities' only legal weapon against the festival-goers – injunctions – were as inadequate as they had been against the Wallies in 1974: 'For an injunction you have to have certain things [like] a set venue. We never know which field they will use, and which persons to serve it on.' In the face of this powerlessness, Lockyer resigned himself to a policy of containment, although his number two, Chief Inspector Alex Morrison, went for a more hands-on approach. Throughout the history of the festival, Morrison, often alone and nearly always smiling, maintained a persistent presence in what would otherwise have been a complete no-go area, filling the small but significant role of community liaison officer. (Wiltshire Police 1981)

At the Beanfield, when Frank Lockyer and Alex Morrison were nowhere to be seen, the police's Operational Commander was Lionel Grundy, the Assistant Chief Constable of Wiltshire, whose previous record included interrogating the Guildford Four, the four innocent Irishmen whose conviction and imprisonment for an IRA bomb attack was one of the major miscarriages of British justice in recent history. In the lull after the violence of the afternoon, it was Grundy, now accompanied by 1,363 police officers, who addressed the travellers, insisting that there would be no negotiations, and that everybody in the field was to be, in his words, 'arrested and processed', and at 7 p.m. Grundy stood by while his men interpreted the concept of 'arrest' with licensed bloodlust. Something had changed significantly in the intervening years. (Malyon 2003; Stone 1996: 156)

Thatcher's vengeance

Nick Davies was undoubtedly correct in commenting that 'The whole of the Wiltshire Establishment had sat down to decide what to do about the Convoy', and that, because 'there wasn't really a law that would enable them to keep the Convoy out... they came up with the civil injunctions to justify all that then happened.' The clues were there in advance: the press advertisement cited above; the injunction, which was delivered to the convoy at Sharnbrook in April, but which was dismissed out of hand (as one of the travellers put it, 'it was difficult to take it seriously, it seemed meaningless, almost comical, just a bit of paper'); and in particular the last minute attempt by John Pendragon 'to persuade the National Trust that the problems they quoted as leading to the ban had already been addressed by the festival community.' As Alan Lodge described it, 'After some progress, "London" said "no talking", and the die was cast.' (Goodwin 1995; Craig 1986: 5; Lodge 1998)

Clearly, everything that took place after the injunction was raised was illegal. The Beanfield took place eight miles from Stonehenge, outside the jurisdiction of the injunction, and in any case the basis on which the names of the 'ringleaders' were compiled was dubious to say the least. A leaked police report commented on a 'known hierarchy' within the convoy, a 'small nucleus of leaders' whose decisions were fulfilled by 'lieutenants' or 'warriors' who intimidated other groups on site. The presumption of innocence before guilt was not only turned on its head; it was done away with completely. The travellers were presumed guilty, and punished without a trial. (Carey 1997)

What Nick Davies omitted from his analysis of the establishment closing ranks to authorise and justify the events of the Beanfield was the presiding figure of Margaret Thatcher. At Orgreave, Stonehenge and Wapping, it was Thatcher's new army, a faceless, paramilitary police force, bussed in from outside the area, that broke dissent with extreme violence. At Stonehenge, as at Orgreave and Wapping, people were left physically and emotionally scarred, livelihoods were destroyed and communities torn apart.

'Anarchy in action'

Maureen Lodge, one of those arrested on the day of the Beanfield, summed up the real reason for the brutality of that day: the travellers' movement was a 'threat to the State.' It was 'anarchy in action, and it was seen to be working by so many people that they wanted to be a part of it too.' So attractive was this lifestyle that 'for four years, from 1981 to 1985, the numbers of people taking to the road had been doubling, year on year.' At the heart of the travellers' year was the Stonehenge festival, the centrepiece of a seasonal procession of free festivals that roamed around the country on a continuous basis throughout the summer months, generating its own rolling economy and relying on a high degree of co-operation and common sense. (Goodwin 1995; Stone 1996: 153)

There were problems along the way – a few thugs and casualties on the fringes, the collateral damage of the modern world – and there were hard drugs too, above and beyond the heroin dealers who were dealt with so firmly. Cocaine, which arrived in 1983 in a blizzard of narcissism and greed, undermined the supremacy of psychedelics and hash, an established and largely successful arrangement, which had only previously been punctured by a deranged spate of barbiturate abuse in the late 1970s – and which led to the 1977 festival season being described as a 'harrowing' experience by Robert Nightingale of Release. The most notorious incidents in the festival's history, however, focused on one particular group that was beyond the control of the festivals' organisers. This was the Windsor chapter of the Hell's Angels, the only large surviving outlaw chapter, who were involved in altercations with the punks in 1980 – ironically, when Crass, the band inspired by Phil Russell, tried to play the festival for the first time – and the Peace Convoy in 1982. (Nightingale 1978; Rimbaud 1981; Shark 2003d)

In general, however, it was the travellers' success in creating a kind of loose, self-regulating social alternative that led to the suppression of the Stonehenge Free Festival. One of the festival's great mottos, along with 'It's never too late to have a happy childhood' and the amusing 'Fuck all for sale', was 'what can you bring or are willing to contribute for free?' 1977's flyer urged, 'Bring wot you expect to find. If you want to contribute in any way, don't wait to be asked: do it.' Nik Turner, who lent his pyramid stage to the festival each year, provided an eloquent summary of its principles: 'Nothing is free, but a free festival is what everybody brings to it. I'd take the stage but I didn't want any money for it. I saw it as my contribution. This is what free festivals were about: what people could contribute to them.' For eleven years, the Stonehenge Free Festival ran itself on donations. That last year, Convoy Steve and a mate 'spent an hour a day extracting (with love) a tax from lots of the traders and the money was shared out amongst the rubbish collecting teams, the kids area, Festival Aid… and St Johns Ambulance.' Steve's conclusion was that this was 'pretty together for hippies eh?' and it is an opinion that I share. (Hutchinson 1977; Stone 1996: 221; Shark 2003d)

'For the people': a poster by Nick Mann from the back page of 'Stonehenge '85', a pamphlet produced by travellers and festival-goers to commemorate the Battle of the Beanfield.

The aftermath

After the Beanfield, the travellers and hard-core festival-goers tried to regroup themselves. Some of the battered survivors fled to Glastonbury, where they received a welcome in the orchard of Greenlands Farm in the nearby village of Wick. Bruce Garrard, part of the Rainbow Village Peace Camp at Molesworth, commented that 'Glastonbury was the only place that seemed to offer any kind of sanctuary at all.' Others limped back to Savernake Forest, where more travellers, oblivious to the carnage occurring down the road, had continued to gather. The police approached the Earl of Cardigan for permission to evict the site. 'They said they wanted to go into the campsite "suitably equipped" and "finish unfinished business",' the Earl told *Squall* magazine. 'Make of that phrase what you will. I said to them that if it was my permission they were after, they did not have it. I did not want a repeat of the grotesque events that I'd seen the day before.' With the police rebuffed, the travellers had a few days to recuperate before a legal eviction order was raised, but it was clear that the area around Stonehenge was to remain off-limits to them throughout the solstice period. (McKay 2000: 52; Carey 1997)

On the morning of the solstice, the great sarsens of Stonehenge were guarded, imprisoned and alone. Even the Druids were banned. The Ancient Druid Order performed a midnight ceremony at the familiar 'double circle' on Normanton Down, before heading down to Maiden Castle in Dorset for the solstice dawn. Pagans for Peace, a group of fifty people who had walked to Stonehenge from London, were the only observers of the solstice dawn at the monument, strung out along the perimeter fence like refugees catching a glimpse of forbidden freedom. *The Times* ran a report: 'Shivering beneath their protective blankets they held hands and chanted 'I am at one with the infinite sun', although 'The object of their worship remained hidden behind the cloud which dispensed unremitting rain.' (Loxley 2003; *The Times*, 22 June 1985)

In the end, 2,000 people held a reconvened Stonehenge Solstice Celebration at Bratton Castle, an Iron Age hill-fort and, appropriately enough, a former Neolithic ritual site, complete with a long barrow, above the Westbury White Horse just twelve miles north-west of Stonehenge. Hawkwind turned up to play, and the police stayed off-site. To this extent it was a triumph, although the fall-out from recent events was still readily apparent. Margaret Greenfields, a festival regular and welfare volunteer, recalled, 'It was like a refugee camp – mud, rain, wind, people shocked and dazed, a man with a broken leg in plaster hauling water in the mud, people with dysentery.' (Greenfields 2003)

Throughout the summer, the travellers attempted to hold their lives together. In late July, some of the Peace Convoy made it to Cleeve Common in Gloucestershire, where an impromptu free festival took place, comprising a few hundred people at most. Others held a festival at Cannock Chase in Staffordshire, and in August the survivors moved onto the Cantlin Stone festival, which must have seemed like a rare and dependable oasis. In September, a brave collective of agitators on the south coast organised the first Torpedo Town free festival, at which Hawkwind made another appearance, and as the season came to an end, many of the travellers returned to rest in the welcoming orchard of Greenlands Farm. The worst year of their lives was over, but the violence and intimidation was not yet complete. (Shark 2003p; Lodge 2001; McKay 2000: 105)

An unhappy ending

In fact, the story of the Beanfield does not have a happy ending. Six years after the bloody events of 1 June 1985, twenty-four of the travellers set upon that day won a long, drawn-out court case against the Wiltshire Police for wrongful arrest, assault and criminal damage. Even then, the judge arranged for all their compensation to be swallowed up in legal costs. The travellers' legal representative, Lord Gifford QC, commented that the decision 'left a very sour taste in the mouth.' (Carey 1997)

I leave the final word to Alan Lodge, who was one of the twenty-four, and who captured the human tragedy of the day when the English state donned jackboots to destroy its new gypsies: 'There was one guy who I trusted my children with in the early '80s – he was a potter. After the Beanfield I wouldn't let him anywhere near them. I saw him, a man of substance at the end of all that nonsense wobbled to the point of illness and evil. It turned all of us and I'm sure that applies to the whole of the travelling community. There were plenty of people who had got something very positive together who came out of the Beanfield with a world view of "fuck everyone".' (Carey 1997)

Chapter Nine

Exclusion

'Medieval brigands'

In 1986, the larger war on travellers and the whole free festival scene began. In the House of Commons, Margaret Thatcher gleefully declared that she was 'only too delighted to do anything we can to make life difficult for such things as hippy convoys', adding that 'if the present law is inadequate, we will have to introduce fresh law' to deal with them. Douglas Hurd, the Home Secretary, called the travellers 'nothing more than a band of medieval brigands who have no respect for the law or the rights of others', and at the heart of this onslaught the defending of Stonehenge became, yet again, a quasi-military operation. (House of Commons 5 June 1986, 3 June 1986)

The build-up began in December 1985, when the National Trust and English Heritage announced that no festival would be tolerated the following year. In February 1986, Wiltshire County Council recorded its own formal opposition to a festival at Stonehenge, and in April, Wiltshire police, the National Trust and English Heritage applied to the Chief Clerk of Wiltshire Council for permission to close part of the A344 between 9 May and 30 June. In early May, razor wire fencing was erected around Stonehenge, and the Forestry Commission blocked all but one entrance to Savernake Forest with felled trees. On 13 May, English Heritage, the Ministry of Defence and twenty-three other landowners sought a High Court injunction banning forty-nine named people from approaching within a four-mile radius of Stonehenge, and the following day, when festival organisers met up with senior officers in the Wiltshire police to discuss the solstice, they were told in no uncertain terms that drivers would be stopped within five miles of the stones, and that even pedestrians would be stopped a mile away. (NCCL 1986: 6-7)

The injunction was granted on 20 May, although in the meantime a convoy of 200 travellers in seventy vehicles scored an early victory, spontaneously – and symbolically – occupying the old festival site opposite the stones on 17 May. Their eviction was swift but surprisingly peaceful. In the afternoon, a judge was interrupted during a round of golf to sign a writ, in the early evening the Sheriff read out the order under a darkening sky, and as the heavens opened the convoy duly left unmolested under the watchful gaze of hundreds of bedraggled police officers. (Krystof in Garrard and Hieronymous 1986: 6)

Writing shortly after the event in *Festival Eye*, a new magazine set up to report on the free festival scene in general and the negotiations for the Stonehenge festival in

A poster from 'Stonehenge '86', one of the many campaigning pamphlets that were produced during the years of exclusion.

particular, editor Alex Rosenberger was optimistic, suggesting that 'The way that the police dealt with what was a tricky situation showed that a new sense of realism is emerging over what is likely to happen this year at – or near – Stonehenge: there was no violence, no one was arrested, and the travellers moved, when the police insisted they should, without causing any trouble.' (Rosenberger 86)

Sadly, Alex's judgement was premature, and from then on the travellers were subjected to a barrage of harassment, intimidation, evictions and arrests that continued throughout the build-up to the solstice. What follows is taken mainly from contemporary accounts by members of the convoy and other travellers, and reports by observers from the National Council for Civil Liberties (NCCL).

Established in 1934 by the journalist Ronald Kidd, 'after he observed the use of police agent provocateurs who were inciting violence during the hunger marches in London in November 1932', the NCCL brought together 'eminent journalists, writers, lawyers and MPs to observe the behaviour of police at mass public gatherings', and it had been monitoring human rights and civil liberties in Britain ever since. In the 1960s and 1970s it became 'involved in the problems of policing and the administration of justice', warning in 1971 that 'the virus of political intolerance has arrived in Britain' and that the country was showing signs of a 'drift to tyranny', and during the post-Beanfield conflict at Stonehenge the evidence of its observers constituted a damning indictment of the legally dubious methods employed by the government, the courts and the police in dealing with the travellers. (Phillips 1999; Neville 1995: 258, 285)

Harrying the convoy

After the injunction of 20 May, the convoy, supervised by police officers, made its way westwards from Stonehenge along the A303, leaving Wiltshire and entering Somerset, where the vehicles came to a temporary halt forty miles from Stonehenge at Camel Hill near Sparkford. Evicted after five days, the expanding collective – now numbering 300 people and a hundred vehicles – proceeded to nearby Lytes Cary, occupying private land belonging to a farmer named Attwell, who promptly collapsed with a heart attack. Atwell recovered, but his collapse was an unexpected boon for the reactionaries of the establishment. Agriculture Minister John Selwyn Gummer visited the convoy and called them 'common criminals', the newspaper *Today* launched a vitriolic campaign against the travellers and offered to pay the £5,000 that it cost Atwell in legal fees to take out a High Court eviction order, and the National Farmers Union, whilst conceding that the government should find a permanent site for the festival on MoD land, pressed for a change in the law that would make trespassing on private land a criminal rather than a civil offence. (NCCL 1986: 7–8)

From Somerset, the convoy was shunted into Dorset, enduring further humiliation on the border, when 300 police 'in riot gear, protective headgear and capes without identifying numbers', checked vehicles, checked individuals for criminal records and warned them that moving on would cause a breach of the peace. Paddy Ashdown, then the Liberal MP for Yeovil, attempted to negotiate a compromise between the travellers and the police, and eventually the three-mile long convoy was allowed to proceed in five smaller groups. Ashdown later told the press that he could not understand the actions of the police and that he doubted that they had the legal power to stop the convoy on the main highway. (NCCL 1986: 8–9)

After resting the next night on a by-road outside Corfe Castle, the convoy ended up in Hampshire, at Stoney Cross, a disused Second World War airfield in the New Forest, on 1 June. During the next week, as the travellers recuperated, Margaret Thatcher and Douglas Hurd launched their rabble-rousing attacks on the convoy in the House of Commons. In response, Labour's Clive Soley – like Paddy Ashdown, outside the establishment coterie that was condoning the persecution – compared the government's actions to those of Adolf Hitler: 'when they talk of making people conform, that is precisely the language that was used in Nazi Germany, and that when people failed to conform they were put in concentration camps and gas chambers.' (NCCL 1986: 10)

'Operation Daybreak'

The government was impervious to criticism. On 9 June, Operation Daybreak, a dawn raid on the Stoney Cross encampment by 440 officers from five counties, revived the spectre of the Beanfield. Although there was none of the brutal violence of the year before, in other ways the tactics were just as worrying. Sixty-four people were arrested, even though no resistance was put up by the convoy, and surveillance had been stepped up to such an extent that the police now had files on all the vehicles that they were determined to destroy. All but two of the 131 vehicles on site were duly impounded, often for the most trivial infringements of the law. (Oubridge 1986)

The only vehicles to escape destruction were a bus and a small van that were used to carry small children and pregnant women to safety, although their departure took place under the most alarming circumstances of all. A social worker from Hampshire Social Services turned up in the middle of the night to warn the convoy of the impending eviction, telling them 'my conscience won't live with this', and advising them 'to get your kids away because they're coming on at four o'clock. The police have got care orders for forty-seven kids.' Veteran traveller Spider recalled that the bus drove straight to Glastonbury, where Michael Eavis provided the children with a refuge. Spider called it 'a very emotional night' and added, 'the thought of what lengths the authorities would go to to drive us down was frightening.' (McKay 2000: 53)

At Stoney Cross, deprived of their vehicles, a number of the travellers allowed themselves to be transported in a coach provided by Hampshire Social Services to an emergency reception centre at an old aircraft hangar in nearby Calshot, but seventy convoy members confounded the authorities by setting off on foot for Glastonbury. They walked for fourteen hours that first day, a forced march of twenty-three miles, with 'constant harassment from the police' and at least fifty people arrested for doing 'absolutely nothing', but as they passed through the villages along the way, people came out to talk to them and they elicited widespread sympathy. In Horton, a farmer

*The Stonehenge Campaign
logo, from a 1989 pamphlet.*

let them stay overnight on his land, and the villagers provided them with 'supplies of food and bedding and wood for the fire.' (NCCL 1986: 11–12; Dawn in Garrard and Hieronymous 1986: 20)

The walkers arrived at the festival site in Pilton three days later, where Rainbow Village members 'set up their domes as spare shelter, and got a free food kitchen going.' Along the way, they had scored a massive PR coup, allowing the villagers of three counties the opportunity to see the 'folk-devils' conjured up by the government and the media at close-hand, and for some the bonds between convoy members that were formed as they made their way on foot across the contested countryside of southern England were stronger than anything that had come before. However, by allowing the travellers to make their way to Glastonbury, the authorities succeeded in their primary objective: keeping them away from Stonehenge for the solstice. (Garrard and Hieronymous 1986: 22)

The Stonehenge Campaign

While the convoy endured these ordeals, several hundred other people were walking towards Stonehenge from London, Southampton, Bristol and East Anglia on a number of peace pilgrimages that were known as the Stonehenge Freedom Marches or the Stonehenge Walks. The pilgrimages evolved from meetings of the Stonehenge Campaign, an alliance of festival-goers dedicated to 'the reinstatement of the Stonehenge People's Free Festival and religious access to Stonehenge itself.' Hilary Jones attended the early meetings and commented that 'theatre groups, community groups, housing groups, all the alternative things that went on at Stonehenge were represented.' (Jones 1998: 203)

The campaign was launched at the end of April and included, along with the planned marches and the publication of *Festival Eye*, an impressive raft of additional measures: lobbying the House of Commons, picketing the London headquarters of English Heritage and the National Trust, picketing the Beaulieu Motor Museum, owned by English Heritage chairman Lord Montagu (ironically, the landowner responsible for the first 'proper pop festival' in the 1950s), and approaching the National Trust for permission to hold a free festival, limited to ten to fifteen days' duration, on an old airfield site near Stonehenge. The campaign's motivation was

The Salisbury protestors, June 1986.
Copyright Alan Lodge.

deliberately non-confrontational – 'how can we get to Stonehenge without it seeming like a call to arms?' – although in light of the authorities' entrenched opposition, it was clearly a rhetorical question. (NCCL 1986: 6; Jones 1998: 203)

On 1 May, when the London group had set off, they had declared their intention to hold a nude protest in Salisbury on Saturday 14 June. It was a suitably provocative gesture, and the council promptly banned them from the centre of town. When the day came, however, and the walkers from London arrived on the outskirts of Salisbury, their numbers rising from 30 to 150 as others joined in along the way, they were met by another hundred people who had gathered outside the Guildhall to support the protest. As the police herded them out of town, their numbers were swelled by hundreds of locals, and by early evening a cavalcade of fifty vehicles, 'all with people sitting on the roofs and leaning out of windows and playing musical instruments and having a wonderful time', set off for Grovely Wood, five miles to the west, between the valleys of the River Nadder and the River Wylye. (NCCL 1986: 6–7; Garrard and Hieronymous 1986: 25–6)

Hanging Longford

By the next day, the new convoy had moved a few miles to the north, and was winding up and down the Wylye valley, looking for a place to stay that was within

144

striking distance of Stonehenge. They settled near Hanging Longford, 'where the villagers were found to be communicative and helpful', and enjoyed 'a happy hazy few days' with 'the festival spirit running high.' (Firsoff 1992; Garrard and Hieronymous 1986: 29–33)

When it came to the solstice, however, the police were still in charge. On Wednesday 18 June, in the first of many attempts to establish a ticketed event, English Heritage, through the police, offered 300 tickets for the solstice, provided that the travellers obeyed six conditions, which included the restriction of ceremonies to three groups of a hundred for an hour each, and complicated travel arrangements involving the use of privately hired coaches, 'the firm or firms used to be previously identified by the police.' (Smith 1986)

Committed to free access for all, and understandably wary of leaving their vehicles and trusting the police, the travellers refused the offer. Their refusal coincided with the swift passing of an eviction order, and when the convoy moved off as requested, on the morning of Friday 20 June, heading away from Stonehenge, they were almost immediately stopped by the police, and over 300 people were arrested for obstructing the highway and obstructing officers in the course of the duty. The charges were groundless, of course, and both sides knew it. The travellers offered no resistance to the police, and when the processing was over – during which they were 'denied access to telephones and lawyers due to the "exceptional circumstances"' – and they had all been dispersed to prisons as far away as Gloucester and Portsmouth, Steve Hieronymous noted that 'even the constables guarding us slowly admitted they found the whole thing farcical (except for the overtime they were all getting paid).' (Garrard and Hieronymous 1986: 29–33)

The next day, the prisoners were taken by coach to Salisbury, where they spent the afternoon behind the courts, 'sexes segregated, one coachload handcuffed all day.' When they finally left the coaches, hundreds of supporters were there to greet them, 'the whole festival drinking, smoking, dancing in front of the courts.' Steve Hieronymous noted that 'the good burghers of Salisbury [got] a carnival two weeks running', but in the end the authorities triumphed once more. As the NCCL observed, 'the effect of the arrests was to ensure that 230 travellers were off the roads and in custody over the period of the solstice.' (Garrard and Hieronymous 1986: 29–33; NCCL 1986: 28)

Solstice 1986: why don't we do it in the road?

In the end, only a few hundred spectators made it through to Stonehenge on the morning of the solstice, where they were begrudgingly allowed to watch the sunrise from behind the perimeter fence. There were 'shirt-sleeved, dazed looking locals… wandering down the road, having exercised their ancient rights of access', Druids of the Secular Order, a new Order born out of the festival years, who 'went into a mantric chorus of "The sun machine is coming down and we're gonna have a party, uh-huh"' (from David Bowie's *Memory of a Free Festival*), and the Reverend David Penney, who said a prayer for life and peace, which included the poignant line, 'Lead us from fear to trust, from hatred to love.' Even the Ancient Druid Order,

Punks, police and Druids: the summer solstice 1986.
Copyright Chris Chippindale.

prohibited from approaching the stones as they had been the year before, joined the rest of the excluded outside the perimeter fence and defiantly performed their ceremonies on the road beside the Heel Stone. (Richie in Garrard and Hieronymous 1986: 34–6; Loxley 2003)

The convoy was represented by a single group of travellers, including festival veteran Brig Oubridge and members of the Tibetan Ukranian Mountain Troupe, who arrived by car from Glastonbury with enough 'blag-power' to secure access. Brig irreverently blew a conch horn before the Druids' ceremonies were over, at which point a cloud uncovered the sun and 'there was awesome silence as the glow of the sun's amber brilliance lit upon the assembled company.' One of his companions, Ritchie, felt that 'an almost paternal tolerance of our clumsy intrusion flowed from the Druids', and suggested that 'there was a real magick' at work that morning. On the way back to Glastonbury, another of the travellers, Penny, a 'High Priestess of the Daughters of Albion', spotted 'a lone naked figure dancing her celebration of the year's round' on a distant rise. (Garrard and Hieronymous 1986: 34–7)

For most travellers, however, the solstice involved exile from Stonehenge. The convoy at Hanging Longford may have risen above it all, but many of those stranded at Glastonbury were not in the mood to forgive and forget. Bruce Garrard spent solstice night 'on a hill overlooking the festival site at Pilton, watching day appearing in the east and the huge full moon setting into the last of the night on the other.' He met a man who had been at Stoney Cross, who had walked to Glastonbury as 'more-or-less a refugee', and who was 'overcome with the fact that such a rare and

Circle around the stones, 1987.
This photo was taken at the winter solstice that year.
Copyright Alan Lodge.

impressive cosmic event should (and it really should) have been witnessed at Stonehenge.' (Garrard and Hieronymous 1986: 2)

Solstice 1987: 'The earth is our mother'

The events of the solstice in 1986 marked the Druid Order's penultimate gesture of solidarity with the travellers and festival-goers (the last took place in 1988 when David Loxley attended a Stonehenge Campaign meeting at which he said that the Order was 'in favour of the festival-goers' presence at the stones, and that attempts would be made to sort out a ritual for both groups to take part in together'). For the 1987 solstice, English Heritage offered 500 free tickets for dawn at the stones in advance, and the Druid Order accepted. The Stonehenge Campaign and others who were pressing for free and open access refused, but what could have been a night of confrontation was resolved with a display of unexpected tolerance on the part of the authorities. At 6.30 in the morning, after the Druids had performed their rituals, about 300 people were allowed into the temple, where they joined hands in a circle around the henge and spiralled into the stones, chanting 'The earth is our mother, we shall take good care of her.' (Hicks 1988a; Firsoff 1992)

For some who were there, the limited access provided in 1987 was regarded as a success. George Firsoff called it 'a great victory for conciliation and good sense', although most travellers were unconvinced. Some again observed the solstice at the Glastonbury festival, where the highlight was undoubtedly the Mutoid Waste Company's Carhenge, a witty and poignant tribute to Stonehenge, with gigantic trilithons made out of old cars. For the most part, however, it was difficult to regard the tolerance of 300 people for a few hours as a success when measured against the events of the Beanfield, the many thousands who had gathered at the stones for the solstice during the festival years, and the ongoing persecution of the travellers' very existence. (Firsoff 1987)

The Public Order Act

In 1987 the Beanfield's legal successor, the 1986 Public Order Act, came into effect, with its notorious 'anti-hippy' clause 39, which edged closer to the criminalisation of trespass. Under the new clause – which applied to scheduled monuments (including Stonehenge), 'land forming part of a highway' and agricultural buildings – the police were enabled to arrest two or more people for trespass, provided that 'reasonable steps have been taken by or on behalf of the occupier to ask them to leave.' In addition, the previous requirement for arrest under these circumstances – damage to property – was amended to include the use of 'threatening, abusive or insulting words or behaviour' and/or the presence of twelve or more vehicles.

In its report on Stonehenge, published before the Act was passed, the NCCL had been particularly wary of giving the police increased public order powers, when the ones that they already had, 'ranging from powers to prevent breach of the peace, to enforcement of road closure orders, to the use of Road Traffic Act, were stretched to their limits to exclude, contain and, in the words of the Chief Constable of Hampshire, to 'neutralise' the travellers.' In almost every case monitored by the NCCL in 1986, grave misgivings had been expressed – about the legality of confiscating vehicles, the charges of obstruction and the extent of information gathering, as well as the road blocks and closures. (NCCL 1986: 23)

Doubts were also expressed about the legality of various procedures undertaken by the institutions that sustained the police: Salisbury District Council's order banning the planned demonstration on 14 June; the bail conditions imposed by magistrates, which required travellers to leave Wiltshire immediately; and the insistence of the police and courts in Salisbury that the defendants on 21 June were handcuffed in court. Subtly underlining the disproportionate hysteria that surrounded the travellers, the NCCL noted that the handcuffs were only removed when the defence lawyers pointed out that 'even those accused of terrorist bombing offences in the Old Bailey the previous week... had not been handcuffed in court.' (NCCL 1986: 29)

The NCCL's closing comments accused the government, as well as all the institutions above, of a general failure to implement the terms of the Caravan Sites Act of 1968, which required local authorities to provide sites for Gypsies – defined as 'persons of nomadic habit of life, whatever their race or origin' – and which empowered the Secretary of State for the Environment to force them to do so. Noting that in January 1986 less than 40 percent of 'official' Gypsies had been housed, that the Secretary of State had failed to enforce a single omission and that the 'new' travellers were not catered for, despite fulfilling the criteria outlined in the 1968 Act, the NCCL proposed immediate action to quell the traditional conflict between travelling people and settled people and to bring to an end the current situation whereby 'both central and local government sat back and waited for the police to use their public order powers to deal with the inevitable conflict.' (NCCL 1986: 33–5)

Predictably, the government ignored the advice of the NCCL. When the Public Order Act became law, some of the worst fears of both the travellers and the NCCL were confirmed (and it was noticeable too that despite assurances that traditional Gypsies,

Confrontation at the summer solstice 1988.
Copyright Alan Lodge.

the long-suffering victims of the state's aversion to a nomadic way of life, would not be targeted, a group of Gypsies in Somerset were evicted as soon as the Act became law). By the time the solstice came around, many travellers were too preoccupied with the problems caused by Clause 39 to worry about Clause 13 of the Public Order Act, in which 'two people proceeding in a given direction can constitute a procession and can be arrested as a threat to civil order.' Clause 13 was aimed at Stonehenge. It was the prop that held up the exclusion zone and kept the majority away from their temple at the solstice.

Solstice 1988: the return of the riot police

Seemingly satisfied with this arrangement, English Heritage expanded the free ticket scheme for the 1988 solstice, this time offering a thousand tickets in advance. Once more, the Druids accepted, along with locals, archaeologists and other interested parties, and once more those who were pressing for free access for all refused. By the week before the solstice, 4,000 people had gathered in Cholderton Woods, outside the exclusion zone to the east of Stonehenge, a great, defiant coming together of the tribes, with groups of travellers arriving from all over the country, their numbers swelled by hopeful festival-goers from the towns and cities, as well as those who had arrived on foot – the Stonehenge Walkers, whose numbers continued to grow, with representatives from an increasing number of towns around the country.

On 20 June, a representative of English Heritage came to Cholderton to offer 500 tickets for the solstice to the travellers, but they were rejected outright. Brig Oubridge told a reporter, 'Everyone here said no. We don't believe in tickets and anyway we

*A peace movement banner
commemorating the
violence in 1988.
Copyright Jo Bradley.*

can't select 500 to go'. Sid Rawle declared, 'The tickets are illegal and immoral. They have no right to be handing out tickets and we have no right to take them'. And no one was mollified by English Heritage's concession that 'If people do turn up without tickets, and there are spare places, we may consider allocating them.' (*The Guardian*, 21 June 1988; *The Western Daily Press*, 21 June 1988; Suburban Guerillas 1989)

As night fell, the festival-in-exile set off on foot from Cholderton Woods to Stonehenge, where the vast entourage, its numbers swelled by others who were still arriving on foot or by car, attempted to gather by the perimeter fence once more. It was an ugly night. Helicopters roamed the skies, casting searchlights over the stones, and an uneasy stand-off ended after five people from Bristol 'flying the ragged flag of anarchy' climbed on the Heel Stone, and others – perhaps Class War activists whose motto, in Wiltshire at least, was 'Avenge the Henge' – hurled bottles and crowd barriers at the police. The actions of this minority were clearly provocative, but the majority of people were 'relaxed if a bit confused', in the words of George Firsoff, and almost everybody was shocked by what happened next. Hundreds of riot police with truncheons and heavy shields made repeated charges, forcing the crowd back towards the A303, while the Druids and the others with tickets, safe in the stones again, for the most part turned a blind eye. (Firsoff 1988a, 1988b)

The reaction of the police was widely regarded as disproportionate and heavy-handed. Women with babies were part of the crowd, numerous people were nearly trampled underfoot, and observers reported the indiscriminate truncheoning and arrest of others who had done nothing. Throughout this whole period, the only retaliation noted by George Firsoff came from a group of youths in a field to the north, who were throwing stones at the advancing police lines. Although there was no repeat of the gruesome events of the Beanfield, there were casualties, amongst them Andy Smith, the successor to Alex Rosenberger as editor of *Festival Eye*, who finally received a £10,000 out of court settlement from Wiltshire police in 1995 for a truncheon wound to the head that resulted in post-traumatic stress syndrome. (Firsoff 1988b; Carey 1997)

Solstice 1989: the final clampdown

In 1989, with helicopters patrolling once more, the authorities hit on a new plan, so successful that it rolled on down the years. The four-mile exclusion zone was enforced so tightly that almost everyone who tried to make it to the stones was either stopped or arrested. Even the Druids were excluded once more, forced to reprise the 1985 combination of Normanton Down at midnight and Maiden Castle for the solstice dawn. (Loxley 2003)

On the night, about 500 people tried to break through the exclusion zone, although another 2,000, with Michael Eavis' permission, were holding a free festival at the site of the Glastonbury festival in Pilton, which had finished on 18 June. At Stonehenge, a reporter for *The Southern Evening Echo* celebrated the success of the first year of the new, improved exclusion zone: 'Police arrested about 200 people as they tried to reach Stonehenge to celebrate today's Summer Solstice. A huge operation involving 800 officers from 12 forces successfully enforced a four-mile "no-go area" around the ancient monument.' For those who were there, the bland statistics failed to capture the surreal terror of the situation. Andy Hemingway, who works in community arts in Norwich, and who had hitched down with a friend, found himself cowering in a bush a mile or so from the monument, with a helicopter hovering no more than twenty feet above his head. Wind-whipped and half-deaf from the down draft and noise of the rotor blades, he compared the experience to 'films such as *Escape from Colditz*, where escapees are hunted down by uniformed authoritarians', adding, 'but this was real. And they were looking for us!' (Hemingway 2003)

By the end of the solstice period, most of those connected with the free festival and the travelling community had given up trying to negotiate a settlement with the authorities. The National Trust had never been willing to negotiate, but sporadic meetings between English Heritage and representatives of the Stonehenge Campaign had taken place throughout the previous few years. Paul Aitken recalled that at the first meeting 'there was a room full of people, and what they essentially did was

Defiance at the spring equinox 1989.
Copyright Alan Lodge.

express their passion. And English Heritage sat white-faced and started to realise what sort of an impact they had on people. [They] said they'd try and find a site, talk to accommodating land-owners', but in subsequent meetings 'they just repeated themselves. In the end we got disillusioned and stopped talking to them.' (Aitken 1998: 204)

The equinoxes and the winter solstice

For most travellers and festival-goers, access to Stonehenge in the years following the Beanfield was restricted to the other festivals of the solar year: the winter solstice and the equinoxes. These had been observed for many years, though not necessarily at Stonehenge, by Druids and other pagans, including those involved in the festivals. After 1985 many other festival-goers, in response to their exclusion from the summer solstice, began to focus on these other turning points in the ritual year instead. Bearing in mind what was taking place at the summer solstice, these gatherings seem to have taken place in a parallel universe.

In 1988, there were 300 people at the spring equinox when a long line of travellers' vehicles parked up along the by-way and access to the stones was allowed, 300 at the autumn equinox, when the security guards let people stay inside the stones the night before, and a thousand at the winter solstice, when bands played outside the perimeter fence, the police presence was negligible and the crowd was once more allowed into the stones. (Harrison 1989)

Access continued in 1989, with 300 vehicles and 800 people at the spring equinox, when the celebrants were once more allowed in to see the dawn. Similar numbers

The exclusion zone in force, summer solstice 1990.
Copyright Adrian Arbib.

attended the autumn equinox and the winter solstice, and the momentum continued at the spring equinox in 1990 with over a thousand people partying in the stones from before dawn until 9 a.m.. Many of the most prominent campaigners for access at the summer solstice were in attendance: Alex Rosenberger, the 'festival' Druids (whose role will be discussed at length in the next chapter), and Willy X – free festival veteran, Polytantric member and originally one of the youngsters who had fallen under Phil Russell's spell at the first Stonehenge festival. (Hughes 1990)

By the time of the autumn equinox, even these privileges came to an end. Despite apparently successful negotiations between various Druid orders and the monuments' curators, the stones were closed to all. Some visitors jumped the fence, prompting the security guards to withdraw so that they could hold a ceremony, but 'the Druids and their stewards were still refused official access and remained outside.' (Firsoff 1992)

At the winter solstice, the clampdown was complete. Although the travellers enjoyed a roadside party with fires, drums and jugglers, the stones remained off-limits, guarded by several hundred security guards. A similar stand-off took place at the spring equinox in 1991, and in September a spokesman for English Heritage stated that they were 'no longer interested in conditions for access being met', and that 'there was to be no access at the quarters again.' (Pete in Suburban Guerillas 1991; Firsoff 1992)

The breakdown of the travelling community

Outside of Stonehenge, the wider harassment of travellers continued unabated. In some quarters, defiance only made people stronger. In *Festival Eye*, Alex Rosenberger wrote, 'By the time the authorities got around to banning the festival in 1985, our spirit was too strong for anyone to kill it. All the attempts to stop the festival and to make life harder for the "so-called Peace Convoy" have served only to make the culture, and the spirit that holds it together, stronger.' (Rosenberger 1989)

Despite Alex's optimism, the events of the Beanfield – and the persecution that was still prevalent – contributed significantly to breakdowns in the travelling community and brought widespread misery. With the free festival circuit under constant attack, the autonomous economy that went with it collapsed. Alan Lodge described the process as follows: 'As soon as they scared away the punters, it destroyed the means of exchange. Norman Tebbit went on about getting on your bike and finding employment whilst at the same time being part of the political force that kicked the bike from under us.' By 1987, the festival circuit was a skeleton. Cantlin Stone and the Avon Free survived, and a new festival – Ribblehead, in West Yorkshire – began that year, but it was not enough to support a living. (Carey 1997; McKay 2000: 106–7)

Demoralised and angry, some travellers turned to hard drugs and alcohol. Decker Lynn, veteran traveller and mother of six, recalled, 'At one time smack wasn't tolerated on the road at all. Certainly on festival sites, if anybody was selling or even using it they were just put off site full stop.' Lynn observed acutely that 'Heroin is something that breaks up a community because people become so self-centred they don't give a damn about their neighbours', and in the years that followed the Beanfield the battered community was put under more pressure as families like Lynn's were 'forced to vacate sites that became "dirty"', dividing the travellers still further. (Carey 1997)

The final threat came from the Brew Crew, the hard-drinking, mutant offspring of the travellers' scene. Mostly young males – some from within the movement, others arriving in droves from the inner cities – the Brew Crew developed 'a penchant for nihilism, blagging and neighbourly disrespect' that spiralled into violence at some of the surviving free festivals of the time. At a festival held ten days before the solstice in June 1988 at Calleva Roman Town (beside the Aldermaston Weapons Research Establishment), Willy X was set upon by thugs and 'beaten so badly that he ended up in hospital with a broken nose, a torn ear and other injuries.' The attack was apparently motivated by revenge. At a festival the year before, Willy had exposed 'a group of alcohol-sodden thugs [who] had been ripping people off and putting the stolen property into a large bender.' (Carey 1997; Hicks 1988a; 1988b)

Given the sheer scale of the problems they were facing, unsurprisingly some travellers abandoned their way of life at the end of the 1980s. Some emigrated to mainland Europe, and others, broken by the struggle, sank into twilight existences on the fringes of urban society. For those who remained, salvation came from an unlikely source. The hybrid manifesto of punk and hippie values that had fuelled the

154

*Nant Gawr, the Avon Free
Festival, 1987.
Copyright Alan Lodge.*

free festival circuit found its way into the Acid House movement that exploded into riotous life at the end of the 80s, when warehouse parties and outdoor raves brought the free party scene back with a vengeance.

Revival: the birth of Acid House

The new movement, in which powerful, sequenced dance music came of age, was fuelled by a man-made stimulant – ecstasy – that had been invented in 1914, but that only reached Britain via the hedonistic outpost of Ibiza in the summer of 1987. Widely credited with thawing British reserve as no previous narcotic had done, turning football hooligans into love puppies and creating a euphoric and boundlessly optimistic counter-cultural community whose energy and positivity rivalled – or even exceeded – the headiest days of the 1960s, ecstasy and its attendant music scene began to spread like a benevolent virus throughout the country. In 1988, the Second Summer of Love was declared, and even *The Sun* was caught up in the furore. 'It's groovy and cool – it's our Acid House T-shirt! Only £5.50 man', cooed the 'Bizarre' column, relegating its health concerns – '10 reasons to say no to evil LSD' (and ecstasy) – to the bottom of the page. DJ Paul Oakenfold told the *NME*,

From a poster for the Treworgey Tree Fayre, 1989.

'The key, the secret to the whole thing, is fun. People have never had so much fun.' (*The Sun*, 12 October 1988; Bussman 1998: contents page)

In its early days, the use of ecstasy was a largely urban phenomenon, about as far from the travails of the travellers and the traditional free festivals as it was possible to get. One of the first outdoor parties took place outside Guildford in spring 1988. It was organised by Boy's Own, a posse of clubbers who went from producing a cheeky, topical fanzine to running an influential record label in the space of a few short, hectic years. Steve Hall recalled the ignorance of the authorities at the time, with a description of the event that would certainly have seemed like an alternative universe to the travellers of the same period: 'The police didn't have a clue what was going on. They hadn't even heard of ecstasy. There were all these people smiling, going up to the police and chatting, offering them Lucozade. One of the policemen looked around and said, "I think we can leave this lot: they're a silly old bunch of cunts, aren't they?" and left.' (Bussman 1998: 40)

By the end of the year, the media had turned. 'Evil of Ecstasy: Danger drug that is sweeping discos and ruining lives', screamed the same rag that just a few weeks before had been flogging Smiley T-shirts. More worrying to those inside the scene was the haste with which unscrupulous entrepreneurs jumped on the bandwagon, expanding into the countryside but only so far as to throw expensive parties in prototype superclubs. By 1989, as a representative of the Nottingham sound system DiY put it, 'The revelatory had been assimilated and corrupted. And so the creative, the idealists, the believers, moved again.' The wheel miraculously turned full circle, and the revolutionary sound systems – including DiY, Sweat, CircusWarp and Circus Normal – relocated themselves 'in the fields, in the free festivals of the hippies and travellers, in the ancient fields of England, so long denied to the landless.' (Bussman 1998: 30; DiY 1997a)

When the radicals took to the countryside, they not only established an underground network of hundreds of parties and festivals across the UK, but by returning to the land of the travellers and the pagans, they ensured that the gap between the traditional free festival scene (with its emphasis on live music) and the new free party scene would begin to blur. In May 1989, a thousand people – a dawning rainbow coalition of travellers and ravers – tried to hold a Beltane free festival at Barbury Castle, an Iron Age hill-fort on the Ridgeway to Avebury. Chased out of Wiltshire, they eventually settled near the Uffington White Horse, further east along the Ridgeway in Berkshire. Their success prompted over 5,000 people to turn up for the Avon Free Festival on Inglestone Common at the end of the month. At Glastonbury, house sound systems and travellers came together in the same place and in significant numbers for the first time, and in 'the dust-battered chaos' of the Treworgey Tree Fayre, a pay festival in Cornwall that August, the disparate tribes came together as one during a set by veteran reggae militants Misty in Roots. (Suburban Guerillas 1990; DiY 1997a)

Jane Bussman, in her gloriously irreverent survey of dance culture, *Once in a Lifetime*, commented, 'Until 1989, sunrise was something for milkmen, teething babies and druids. No one could have predicted that by summer hundreds of thousands of us would be not only awake at dawn, but dancing in a field.' She added that sunrise was 'the best time to study man's tenancy agreement with nature.' One of the most highly regarded parties of the summer took place in East Grinstead in August, set up yet again by Boy's Own. Steve Hall recalled 'people lying about on haystacks, dancing around as the sun came up. A hippie vibe still prevailed, rather than techno till you drop. It was a bit more "love and peace".' (Bussman 1998: 48, 41)

'Raves as big as towns'

By 1990, the transition was complete, but first there was some unfinished business to take care of. April's 'Poll Tax Riot', a demonstration against Thatcher's loathed Community Charge – a replacement for the rates that charged every individual over 18 years of age the same amount regardless of income – brought together agitators and idealists of all persuasions, sounding the death knell for the Iron Lady and providing many of her opponents with their first taste of victory in a struggle that had lasted over a decade. Sadly, however, the destabilisation of the Tory leadership was not enough to unsettle other fanatics within the Conservative party.

In the first legal move to suppress the festival spirit since the Public Order Act of 1986, Luton MP Graham Bright sponsored the Pay Parties (Increased Penalties) Bill, which advocated fines of up to £20,000 and/or six months' imprisonment for the organisers of parties on unlicensed premises and outside legal licensing hours. 15,000 people took to the streets of London to protest against the Bill in February, and William Deedes, former editor of *The Daily Telegraph*, made the memorable comment, 'What troubles me about this Bill is the smell of moral outrage attached to it. A politician is safer when he is slightly tipsy and accompanied by a prostitute than when he is under the influence of moral outrage.' Ignoring all criticism, Parliament passed the Bill in July, and the new Act was immediately used to justify one of the largest mass arrests in British history. At a party in Leeds, 836 people were arrested, although almost all were released within a few hours, and an official complaint was made against the police, who were subsequently sued for assault and unlawful arrest. (Bussman 1998: 54)

Elsewhere, however, the parties continued to proliferate as though nothing had happened. At Glastonbury, in the Travellers' Field, sound system pioneers Tonka, DiY and guests including the KLF and the Happy Mondays presided over a non-stop dance party whose energy and euphoria blew the rest of the festival away. In DiY's words, 'For the first time at a major festival, travellers united with their urban counterparts, utilising their generators, buses, marquees and knowledge with the systems, decks, DJs and music of the dance posses.' (DiY 1997a)

Sadly, conflict between on-site security teams and a group of recidivist travellers on the Monday morning (resulting in £50,000 of damage to equipment and facilities) brought an end to Michael Eavis' accommodation of the free festival scene that had lasted since 1985. Implicated by default, the whole of the travellers' movement was now effectively banned from both Stonehenge and Glastonbury over the solstice period.

Undeterred by the actions of a sociopathic minority, the new traveller-sound system alliance moved on to Pepperbox Hill near Salisbury in July, throwing a free party that lasted for weeks and drew thousands of people. In August, the travellers got together with Liverpool's urban clubbers at the Moreton Lighthouse festival, and a similar crossover, this time involving ravers from across the south of England, occurred later the same month at Torpedo Town. (DiY 1997b)

Despite the government's attempts to put the new movement down, its momentum was relentless. For the most part, the anonymity of the organisers and the sheer numbers of people attending the events kept the legislation at bay. In this respect, the situation was similar to the last few free festivals at Stonehenge, although the party-goers often took the 'Go for it!' mentality of the convoy to new extremes. In September 1989, ravers at Risley in Cheshire drove a forklift truck at riot police, and in January 1990, at a party in Rugby, revellers stopped dancing and attacked the police instead. (Bussman 1998: 32, 54)

The free parties continued throughout the autumn and winter of 1990, and by 1991 the enthusiasm for them had grown to such an extent that 'there were raves bigger than towns... self-ruling mini-cities that appeared on Saturday afternoon and were gone by Sunday, leaving no trace apart from a mountain of Evian bottles and a man no one knows in a poncho asleep in a hedge.' Over 15,000 people came together for the Avon Free Festival, which took place near Chipping Sodbury at the end of May. DiY DJs played non-stop for 130 hours, and a London-based crew called Spiral

Spiral Tribe poster.
Image provided by Chris Riley.

Tribe, who had been hosting a series of wildly successful parties in a variety of squatted buildings in the capital, were immediately inspired to put the free party focus back on Stonehenge and the summer solstice. (Bussman 1998: 81; DiY 1997b)

Spiral Tribe

The activists of Spiral Tribe presented a sharp, unified image – shaven-headed, all dressed in black, with distinctive graphics that aped the corporate world in order to subvert it – and their beliefs combined an appreciation of new technology with the ecological mysticism of the free festivals and overt political aims: to 'turn the purely hedonistic rave scene into a political medium.' Their creed, as described by the journalist Simon Reynolds, was 'crystallized in the buzzword 'terra-technic': using technology to unlock the primal energy of Mother Earth.' One of their records quoted the lament of a nineteenth century American Indian chieftain – 'I am a savage and I can't understand, How the beauty of the Earth can be sold back to man' – and their spokesman and *de facto* leader, Mark Harrison, spelled out explicit parallels with contemporary pagan practice: 'At our parties, you step into the circle and enter ritual space.' After spending time with the group, Simon Reynolds agreed that a Spiral party was 'like a pagan gathering', and observed that 'Dancing with the stars overhead, it's hard not to succumb to the back-to-nature Romanticism.' (Stone 1996: 176; Reynolds 1998: 142)

For Reynolds, the philosophy of Spiral Tribe (and of the free party scene in general) constituted an 'uncanny fulfilment' of the prophesies of Hakim Bey, a radical

159

American author who called for the establishment of a 'festal culture' based around 'spiritual hedonism' and the 'jubilee concept', the latter harking back yet again to the radical agrarian Thomas Spence who, 200 years before, had been inspired by the jubilee proposed in the Book of Leviticus, 'an institution occurring every fifty years whereby land was redistributed to ensure that all members of the community remained equally well provided for.' (Reynolds 1998: 143; Burchardt 2002: 36)

In particular, the free party scene fulfilled Bey's concept of the Temporary Autonomous Zone (TAZ), 'a microcosm of "that anarchist dream" of a free culture', 'a guerrilla operation which liberates an area (of land, of time, of imagination) and then dissolves itself to re-form elsewhere/elsewhen, *before* the State can crush it.' This was similar to what the free festival circuit had done in the late 1970s and early 1980s, and Bey himself noted that 'The sixties-style "tribal gathering", the forest enclave of eco-saboteurs [and] the idyllic Beltane of the neo-pagans' were all '"liberated zones" of a sort, or at least potential TAZs.' However, Bey saw the situation in the 1990s as demanding more than had been attempted previously, and John Michell's notion of 'the Lord of Misrule' as a regular punctuation in the established order was effectively replaced by a manifesto for permanent revolution. At its most extreme, the TAZ blurred traditional distinctions between people and place. Bey's 'spiritual project' was 'the creation or discovery of pilgrimages in which the concept "shrine" has been replaced... by the concept "peak experience"', an experience that must be 'on the social as well as [the] individual scale.' (Bey 1991: 101, 106, 134)

Solstice 1991: Longstock and Stonehenge

At the summer solstice in 1991, Spiral Tribe took their party-protest fusion back to the Stonehenge area. With Wiltshire effectively off-limits, the Longstock festival took place in a pretty Hampshire valley sixteen miles from the temple. Over a thousand people turned up, strung out along a narrow by-way known as Rats Lodge and 'hell-bent on serious fun.' One reveller asked, 'What's fascinating about a pile of rubble on Salisbury Plain? We can celebrate the solstice anywhere', but for many of the travellers Longstock was 'The Stonehenge People's Free Festival 1991' in exile, as many of the banners around the site declared, and for the die-hards the focus of the celebration shifted back to Stonehenge on the day of the solstice. (*The Guardian*, 22 June 1991)

Alex Renton of *The Independent* joined a van of ten, including festival veterans Willy X and Hilary Jones, on a mission to break through the exclusion zone. Willy X's commitment to the campaign for free access to Stonehenge was one of the most enduring in the whole period of exclusion, and Renton noted that he took 'a philosophical view of the troubles, telling him, 'All this is a fleeting moment in 4,000 years of the stones'.' Hilary Jones was angrier. She told Renton that Stonehenge was 'a central part of our cultural and religious life' and that visiting it at the solstice was 'an aid to making sense of things, trying to find out where we went wrong.' (Renton 1991)

Illustration by Mike Heath, from the cover of Stonehenge 1991, *another campaigning pamphlet.*

*Willy X in combative mood.
Photo supplied by Chris Riley.*

After parking up three miles south of Stonehenge, the Longstock pilgrims approached the monument on foot, diving into woodland on one occasion to avoid the searchlights of a low-flying police helicopter. When they arrived at the entrance, a 'grumpy sergeant' warned them 'to process away' to prevent a breach of the peace and handed them copies of clause 13 of the Public Order Act, but Willy X provocatively took 'a slow, hilarious five minutes to read it out loud, while the police [grew] restive', and as they left, figures rose from the misty fields to shout 'Happy Solstice!' It wasn't much of a triumph, but Hilary was satisfied: 'I think we made our point. And that's all we can do, these days.' (Renton 1991)

'Complete ecstasy-fuelled illegal madness'

Throughout the rest of the summer, the parties and festivals continued to proliferate – throughout the whole of southern England and the Midlands, on airfields and in quarries, on building sites and in fields. In early August, for the Celtic festival of Lughnasa, Spiral Tribe held a party at Cissbury Ring, at which the violence threatened by two rival gangs of gate-crashing football supporters was defused when an MC called Adrenalin Reggie took the mike, calming them 'like a shaman performing a magical act', according to Debby Staunton, whose Advance Party of activists and party organisers was inspired by the Spirals' example. At the end of the month, the Spirals joined several other sound systems at the White Goddess festival in Cornwall, which began with a full moon on the Bank Holiday weekend and ran for 'two glorious, sun-soaked, pumping, full-on, heavenly weeks' of sleepy days and dancing nights, with Reggie calling out at dusk, 'Come on, all you dance warriors!' Battle stations! Battle stations!' and the crowd dancing till dawn. (Stone 1996: 177–9)

At the same time, in the north of England, an intrepid vanguard of the travelling free party convoy smashed through a police cordon in Liverpool to take the Moreton Lighthouse site again. The ensuing five-day festival was constantly monitored by helicopters and ringed by riot police, and and the presence of numerous TV cameras may have been the only obstacle to a violent, Beanfield-style clampdown. DiY called it 'Complete ecstasy-fuelled illegal madness' and wondered 'will we ever see such lawlessness again?' The short answer was 'Yes', as the parties continued to thrive, but in the longer term, as the authorities finally realised the scale of the social insurrection they were facing, the opposition was mounting. (DiY 1997b)

The first big festival of 1992 took place in the middle of May near Lechlade, north of Swindon. 10,000 people turned up, and the media's dormant sense of outrage was reawakened. Behind the scenes, a massive police operation was at work to prevent the Avon Free Festival from taking place over the Bank Holiday weekend at the end of the month but, despite a number of police forces shunting convoys of travellers and sound systems from county to county in the vain hope that they would somehow disappear, they found themselves incapable of preventing the festival from establishing itself on common land at the head of a valley at Castlemorton in Gloucestershire. (DiY 1997b)

Castlemorton

By the Saturday night, with hotlines and mobile phones literally spreading the word like wildfire, up to 50,000 people had come together to create the largest free gathering since the last Stonehenge Free Festival in 1984. In this eight-day collision of twenty-four hour sound systems (including Spiral Tribe, DiY, Bedlam and Circus Irritant), survivors of the free festivals met nascent road protestors and anti-capitalists, ashen-faced Essex boy racers on ecstasy, mixed with New World Travellers, fresh from the beaches of Goa and Thailand and tripping on Californian acid, and hardly anyone at all met the Brew Crew, pumping white urban dub music out of mobile pigsties. It was the most exhilarating clash of bewildering alternatives to be seen for nearly a decade, an epic event of myth-making proportions, in which Castlemorton and the Bank Holiday weekend – neither sacred place nor holy time of year – to some people became both, the forbidden solstice at Stonehenge mutating into a vibrant contemporary alternative.

The comparison with Stonehenge and the older free festival scene was sustained in other ways too. Debby Staunton remarked of the free party scene that 'People give what they've got', and called it 'an *ad hoc* economy without too much importance being placed on profit. A circulatory process. People are making money, then spending it again, and the whole thing goes round and round.' At Castlemorton, the alternative society envisioned by the free festival pioneers was revived. There was excellent food, there were stalls selling clothes, jewellery and artwork, and – to counter the illusion that everything could run smoothly in a crowd this size – there was even a return to the self-policing that had seen heroin dealers banished from Stonehenge. One of Castlemorton's more celebrated anecdotes concerns the capture of a member of a group of thieves who was 'persuaded' (the myth claims that acid was administered) to recant his crimes on stage, which he duly did, emphasising the depth of his conversion by encouraging his companions to return the rest of the stolen goods. (Stone 1996: 179–83)

Castlemorton.
Copyright Alan Lodge.

Like Stonehenge, however, Castlemorton was followed by a clampdown. Thirty-nine people were arrested for conspiracy to cause a public nuisance, although the ensuing trial – in which Willy X caused widespread mirth in the courtroom by claiming that he alone had organised the entire event, and one of the Spiral's barristers took pride in wearing a 'Make Some Fuckin' Noise' T-shirt beneath his robes – resulted in acquittals for all. Once more, however, the tax-payers were required to pick up the most extraordinary bill: over £4 million for the court case alone, a figure that did not even include the cost of the police. West Mercia alone deployed over 600 officers, including, rather alarmingly, twenty 'tactical firearms personnel', at a cost of over £600,000. (Stone 1996: 187–8)

The Castlemorton trial may well have been a public humiliation for the government, but most of the planned clampdown on the nation's subversives was taking place quietly behind the scenes. Police forces across the country began collaborating in Operation Snapshot, the creation of a massive database of names and licence numbers that was intended to ensure that nothing like Castlemorton would ever happen again. The process was just as legally dubious as the information gathering that had been taking place around Stonehenge for nearly a decade, but even this was just the beginning of the government's response. Just as the Public Order Act had followed the Stonehenge Free Festival, so a new and even more disturbing piece of legislation – the Criminal Justice Act – began sailing through a quiescent parliament almost as soon as the last vehicle had left Castlemorton Common. (Reynolds 1998: 140)

Chris Riley of Spiral Tribe relaxes after the Castlemorton trial collapses.
Photo provided by Chris Riley.

Nothing like Castlemorton would ever happen again, but in the two-and-a-half years before the Criminal Justice Act became law, the protests against it not only mushroomed, as will be discussed in Chapter Eleven, but they also reintegrated fully with a kind of pagan righteousness that had been in danger of being lost in ecstasy's hedonistic rush.

Chapter Ten

New Druids and archaeologists

While some representatives of the free party scene began slowly to perceive the sanctity of the landscape they were occupying, and some of the older travellers sought to preserve the pagan spirit of the golden era of the free festivals in a political climate that often seemed bent on nudging them towards nihilism, other groups of motivated individuals continued to focus on Stonehenge. Significantly, the Ancient Druid Order was not the only Druidic group campaigning for access to the temple in the years after the bloody events of the Beanfield. Five groups in particular were established at this time, one derived from the historical Druid tradition, one from Wicca and the other three from the years of the free festival.

Philip Carr-Gomm and the Order of Bards, Ovates and Druids

The resurrected Druid Order was the Order of Bards, Ovates and Druids (OBOD), which had effectively ground to a halt on the sudden death of its founder, Ross Nichols, in 1975. The Order was revived in 1988 by Philip Carr-Gomm, a psychotherapist and play therapist, who had been a teenage disciple of the elderly Nichols in the 1960s, and who had been initiated into the Order by his mentor on Glastonbury Tor on May Day in 1970. In 1984, after a kind of visitation from Nichols, in which he suggested, 'Have a look at my teachings again, and you will find that they are immensely relevant to the problems of our time', Carr-Gomm began a search for Nichols' lost papers, in particular the manuscript of *The Book of Druidry*, which he had completed shortly before his death, and which combined a history of the Druids, a guide to ancient sites (including Stonehenge) and an anthology of Druid wisdom. (Carr-Gomm 1992: 11)

The quest led not only to the refounding of the Order, but also to the publication of *The Book of Druidry* in 1990, which revealed the extent to which Nichols had paved the way for his particular branch of Druidry to play a major role in the growth of modern paganism. In its pages were references to 'the Great Mother' and 'the Horned God', Nichols' take on the divine polarity at the heart of Wicca, a wide-ranging review of Druidry's Celtic antecedents (the adoption of the eight-fold year, with its ostensibly Celtic festivals, was justified on the basis that 'England had quite as good a title to be called a Celtic country as, say, the majority of France'), and several concepts from the counter-cultural rebirth of the 1960s: ley-lines and numerology from John Michell, and the complex geometry and megalithic yard proposed by Alexander Thom. (Nichols 1992: 112)

Philip Carr-Gomm is initiated into the Order of Bards, Ovates and Druids by Ross Nichols, Glastonbury Tor, Beltane 1970.
Copyright Brian Peacock.

Carr-Gomm duly added a contemporary ecological angle, noting in the first lines of his Foreword to Nichols' book that 'Many people these days are turning to the native traditions of various cultures in an attempt not only to reconnect with their roots and their heritage, but also in an attempt to find a living spirituality that can lead them out of the psychological wasteland that has been created by industrial society.' Following Spence and Nichols, he stressed that 'the Celtic tradition, whose spirituality is epitomized in the path of the Druid', could fulfil these needs, and he carefully pointed out the similarities and differences between Druidry and Wicca: both worked in a circle, both worked with the four quarters and the four elements, and both worked with the seasonal festivals. Druidry, however, tended towards a reverence for the sun, whereas Wicca emphasised the moon, and Wicca was more concerned with sexual polarity than Druidry, although on the latter point he banished the spectre of patriarchy by immediately committing OBOD to gender equality. (Carr-Gomm 1992: 9, 14)

He also maintained contacts with Christianity in a way that Wicca did not, and although he acknowledged that this would disappoint some who hoped that Druidry was 'exclusively "pagan"', he insisted that many of the priests of the early Celtic Church had been Druids and had helped to retain its connection with Nature. He professed an ambition to revive the Celtic Church, and in 1989 the Order participated in the first-ever conference of Druids and Christians, at which all parties aspired to 'return to the practice of a simple and pure spirituality which is in tune with Nature, rather than holding a position of superiority towards it.' (Carr-Gomm 1992: 14)

Despite these innovations, Carr-Gomm soon began to move away from the idea of reviving the Celtic Church, preferring to focus instead on the common ground shared by Druidry and Wicca. He became particularly interested in the celebrations of the eight-fold year, commenting in 1991 that performing ceremonies 'every six weeks or so' is 'a deeply satisfying experience.' (Carr-Gomm 1991: 77)

Overall the image of a vibrant contemporary Order that he projected, combined with the innovative ways in which he facilitated its expansion – first of all through a postal course and then through the possibilities provided by the Internet – ensured that by the start of the twenty-first century OBOD was the largest Druid Order in the world, with 4,500 initiates and 2,000 people taking its mail order courses. (Shallcrass 2001)

Philip Shallcrass and the British Druid Order

From Wicca came the British Druid Order (BDO), founded in 1979 by Philip Shallcrass, a musician, artist, poet and writer, whose route to Druidry was rather more tempestuous than that of Philip Carr-Gomm. As a teenager in the 1960s, he pursued many of that decade's enthusiasms: Zen Buddhism, Taoism, Hinduism, yoga and meditation, as well as psychedelic drugs, which, in his own words, 'led to both extremes of what Aldous Huxley described as *Heaven and Hell.*' Recovering in the early 1970s, he was drawn to the study and practice of ritual magic, the tarot, astrology, shamanism, astral projection and the cabbala, and it was at this time that he joined the Hermetic Order of the Golden Dawn. (Shallcrass 2002)

Shallcrass became interested in Druidry in 1974 after reading Robert Graves' *The White Goddess*, but when he could not find an existing Order he became a Wiccan instead, training to the degree of High Priest in a coven of Alexandrian witches, a potent off-shoot of Gardner's original, founded by a charismatic individual called Alex Sanders, that flourished from the late 1960s onwards. Having elected to compose rites for seasonal festivals, he began 'lacing them with as much Druidic lore as he could uncover in his researches in libraries and second-hand book shops', to such an extent that by the end of the decade the coven had dropped so much of the existing Wiccan rites that they decided to rename themselves the Grove of the Badger (a Grove being 'the standard designation for a Druid gathering'), which in turn became the Mother Grove of the BDO. (Shallcrass 2002)

From the beginning, Shallcrass was concerned to 'establish a native British spirituality', although as the Order grew its scope widened, and it now 'teaches and practices Druidry as the ancient native spirituality of Europe, re-kindling its sacred fire for the 21st century.' Eschewing any attempts to ally itself with false and immemorial histories, the Order does not seek 'to recreate a Druidry that may have existed 5000, 2000, 200 or 50 years ago', but sees Druidry instead as 'a process of constant change and renewal, whereby the tradition is continually recreated to address the needs of each generation.' From this relentlessly modern perspective, the Order has sought, nevertheless, to capture the spirit of the ancient native traditions, the roots of Druidry that it sees 'in direct communication with the spirits of nature, the ancestors and the gods.' (Shallcrass and Orr 2002a, 2002b; Shallcrass 2002)

In many respects, the BDO is similar to OBOD, so much so that the two Chiefs became firm friends and Shallcrass, acknowledging the success of OBOD's postal course, felt no need to establish his own. Where they differ most prominently is in Shallcrass' focus on elements drawn from traditions outside the Celtic world favoured by OBOD, and in particular the shamanic traditions of North America. After a sweat lodge rite in the mid-1990s – adopted from the 'living tradition' of the Lakota Sioux – Shallcrass took the name Greywolf, 'following a powerful vision of a wolf that came to him during the rite.' Inspired to pursue the shamanic elements that he saw as central to Druidry, he 'began to work more and more with his animal helpers, spirits and guides', and he has described the role of shaman as 'restoring the role of Druid to something close to its original form, that of a walker between worlds, mediating between them for the benefit of their communities', working directly with the 'spirits of place, of the land, of trees, plants, animals and ancestors.' Such is his pursuit of shamanism that Ronald Hutton recently described him as 'a shaman quite convincingly disguised as a Druid.' (Shallcrass 2002, 2001)

Neither OBOD nor BDO concentrated initially on the contentious issue of Stonehenge. Philip Shallcrass described Stonehenge as 'a powerful place in which to make ritual', but added 'It is not the most powerful place, nor is it central to my spirituality to work there. There are other places that resonate with my heart and soul more strongly.' Philip Carr-Gomm, perhaps in deference to the schism that had led to the establishment of OBOD in the first place, seems initially to have shied away from it, focusing instead on the alternative sites adopted by Nichols – Glastonbury in particular, where the official re-founding of the Order took place. In 1991, however, in an analysis of the rituals of the eight-fold year in which he commented that this was the time that the Druids held their 'most complex ceremony', he began to focus on the 'public outcry' that attended recent events at Stonehenge, and as the decade progressed both Orders became more involved in the struggle for access. (Shallcrass 1999: 12; Carr-Gomm 1991: 72)

This process will be discussed in detail later in the chapter, but for now it is sufficient to note that the focus on Stonehenge was driven by the three other new Druid Orders – the Secular Order of Druids (SOD), the Glastonbury Order of Druids (GOD) and the Loyal Arthurian Warband (LAW) – whose origins lay in the festival years and who came to prominence in the immediate wake of the Beanfield.

Tim Sebastian and the Secular Order

The first of these to be founded was the Secular Order. Arch-Druid Tim Sebastian, a free festival veteran and a member of a band called Gryphon in the early 1970s, described how the Order was 'initiated in the presbytery of the parish church in Amesbury' in 1975, with four aims: 'to spread the Druidic message to the youth of the nation and to act as voluntary guards to the Druidic ritual in a caring low-key way, to act as a catalyst in bringing together all the Celtic/pagan magical systems of England in a great debate on the future, and to promote the writings of John Michell.' (Sebastian 1990: 110)

'Memory of a Free Festival':
Tim Sebastian at Stonehenge,
summer solstice 1986.
Copyright Chris Chippindale.

The first two aims – guarding the Druidic rituals and catering for young people – were recognised by Philip Carr-Gomm in his survey of contemporary Druidry in 1991. According to Carr-Gomm, in 1975 Tim 'formed a support group for the Druids which he felt were being squeezed out of Stonehenge by the rock festival', a move which contributed to the solstices of 1976, 1979 and 1984, when the Druids and the festival-goers were at the stones together at sunrise, and it was only ten years later, when the festival was shut down with unprecedented violence, that the Order was founded and Tim specifically 'wrote new, progressive ceremonies aimed at the young.' (Carr-Gomm 1991: 39)

The Order's third aim – to be a catalyst for a great debate on the future – began in 1986 at the Stonehenge Forum in Salisbury, which Tim described as 'an amazing event' at which 'all the major spiritual bodies came together... to debate the Stonehenge issue', and at a Beltane gathering, 'deep in the woods of Wilton', which brought together 'Christians, pagans, Egyptologists, astrologers, Druids, hippies, rainbow warriors, anarchologists, feminists, quakers, Crowleyites, witches, Wallies, Kabbalists, and some who were a bit of everything.' For Tim, the Beltane event as 'one of the great spiritual meetings of all time to be seen near the Temple.' (Sebastian 1990: 112)

STONEHENGE '86

NEW EDITION

STONEHENGE, ITS HISTORY, MEANING, FESTIVAL, UNLAWFUL MANAGEMENT, POLICE RIOT '85 & FUTURE PROSPECTS

The cover of John Michell's influential 1986 pamphlet.

He was also involved in establishing the Solstice Trust, whose members and sympathisers included John Michell, David Loxley, Sid Rawle, Tim Abbott and Janet Cross, a Quaker. The Trust proposed creating a 'World Garden' at Stonehenge, 'an arena for all, especially designed with the help of artists and environmentalists with an interest in folklore and ritual', established 'on the harmonious principles of the New Jerusalem' and with the 'utmost attention… paid to environmental enhancement and community participation.' Plans for the Garden included a museum, a reconstruction of Woodhenge, a herbal clock, and the welcoming of 'The world-famous Tipi Circle' at the summer solstice. In the end, however, Tim's most lasting contribution to the dialogue may well have been his involvement in the interfaith conferences held in the early 1990s, which will be discussed in the next chapter. (Sebastian 1990: 113–6)

The Order's fourth aim – to promote the writings of John Michell – was in some ways a long-overdue recognition that the godfather of the earth mysteries movement was intrinsically involved in the flowering of paganism in the 1970s. Certainly, Michell's spirit was once more abroad. He published an old-fashioned dissenters' pamphlet to coincide with the solstice exclusion just three weeks after the events of the Beanfield, which was reprinted in an expanded version in 1986 as *Stonehenge, Its History, Meaning, Festival, Unlawful Management, Police Riot '85 & Future Prospects.*

Michell's was a poetic and sensitive analysis of the situation, a stillness at the heart of a raging storm. In the aftermath of the Beanfield, he wrote that 'The violence and brutality which desecrated Stonehenge in the summer of 1985 made it the saddest year in the history of the monument. Those who knew not of Stonehenge, who had never experienced its weird and lasting attraction, were astounded. What is this old pile of rocks which inspires such intensity of popular religious feeling and such vicious expressions of official jealousy?' He maintained, moreover, that 'The matter of Stonehenge is not merely parochial. Whatever happens there is crucially important to the future of the country and may well determine the shape of things to come and the pattern of a new order on earth.' It was a bold claim, easy to ridicule perhaps, for a rational élite, but unparalleled as a tenet of belief for mystics and political radicals. (Michell 1986: 12, 25)

As well as being influenced by John Michell, Tim Sebastian also brought irreverence to the world of Druidry from the days of Fort Wally, when the prankster was the other face of the preacher. At Beltane, for example, the Order recreated May Day customs including maypole dancing, a hobby horse and racing round loaves down a steep hill. The bawdy side of the May tradition was evoked by their 'Cucumber Dancers', a folk ritual described as 'a boisterous, humorous and blatantly sexual Cucumber Dance in the Morris tradition' by Graham Harvey, a lecturer in Religious Studies, who concluded that their activities had 'a serious intention: to cause a much wider impact than a preciously spiritual event might attract.' The Order also slyly subverted the notion of the Triple Goddess, drawing on that old hippie staple, Aleister Crowley, and in particular his attitude to his female Muses, whom he referred to as his Scarlet Women. As Harvey described it, 'the celebration of sexuality without reference to fertility or reproduction is honoured as the fourth face of the Goddess: the scarlet woman.' (Harvey 1997: 10, 23, 71; Grant 1972: 135)

The Secular Order was prominent at the solstice in 1986. As well as inviting the crowd to chant along to the festival-loving lyrics of David Bowie, they 'lightly tripped into place with their minstrels and floral costumes, to announce "The battle for Stonehenge is over; let the battle for the soul of the Nation begin"' – somewhat prematurely, in light of later events. The following year, in keeping with their origins during the years of the free festival, they went in as part of the crowd of 300 who spiralled into the stones after the Druid Order had finished its rituals, and as the events of 1988 and 1989 unfolded, they duly ran up against truncheons and arrest. (Richie in Garrard and Hieronymous 1986: 34–6)

Rollo Maughfling and the Glastonbury Order

The Glastonbury Order was founded on Glastonbury Tor at Beltane in 1988 with similar aims to that of the Secular Order, namely 'to offer a new age alternative to the way druidism had been presented up till then.' Their Arch-Druid, Rollo Maughfling, was another free festival veteran with pagan credentials. As a child growing up in West Penwith, Cornwall, he recalled being carried on his father's shoulders to a Gorsedd of Cornish Bards in the Boscawen-Un stone circle. In his 'wild youth', he met John Michell, 'literary interpreter of the visionary kingdom', and he later became a pupil of Alex Sanders. (Maughfling 1990; Pendragon and Stone 2003: 80)

Rollo Maughfling leads a procession at Avebury, summer solstice 2003. Copyright Pete Glastonbury.

Almost as soon as they declared their presence, the Glastonbury Druids secured privileged access to Stonehenge for the coming summer solstice. They 'followed in behind the other druids and proclaimed an invocation from within the stones.' Overall, though, it was not a happy occasion. Remembering the violence that took place outside the perimeter fence that year, Rollo declared that 'The dreadful events of that day still ring in our minds, and we have vivid memories of seeing so many friends being brutalised as scapegoats for the authorities' mismanagement of the whole affair.' His conclusion about the Ancient Druid Order was even harsher: 'Though it is not our purpose to criticise any other druid order, it was brought to our attention that the then presiding order had not only lost touch with the people but with the whole situation at Stonehenge.' (Maughfling 1990)

By 1989, Rollo had conceived a plan to hold a Druid Eisteddfod at Stonehenge on the summer solstice, 'with prizes in poetry, music, theatre, dance, art, film, healing and geomantic archaeology.' With the agreement of several other Druid chiefs (an arrangement that will be discussed below), a petition for the Eisteddfod was delivered to the Queen on the summer solstice, after a meeting on Primrose Hill, where the Druids 're-performed the first Gorsedd ritual of Edward Williams... with a new circle constructed from stones sent by Druid groves from all over Britain.' (*The Guardian*, 21 June 1989; Sebastian 1990: 117)

Like Tim Sebastian, Rollo also subjected Druidry to the irreverence of the prankster. Although the festival Druids' rituals were largely based on established tradition – calling to the four quarters and reciting the Druid oath, for example – their 'sacred mantra', a long, drawn-out call of 'I-A-O', not only represents, through its individual sounds, the sun at the equinoxes ('I'), the sun at the solstices ('A') and the earth's passage around the sun ('O'); it also fulfils their particularly earthy take on the sexuality of the nature religion, with the 'I' as 'the phallus of the solar god', the 'A' as 'the lovely open legs of the Earth Goddess' and the 'O' as 'the sound of their cosmic lovemaking, from whence all creatures and all life are born.' (Pendragon and Stone 2003: 76)

Rollo and Tim also remained committed to their roots in the festival years. On the quarter days, they were both regulars at the travellers' festivals that survived at Stonehenge until autumn 1990. At the spring equinox that year, Rollo took centre stage at dawn, 'preaching/singing/speech-making to the bemused audience of hippies, druids, tourists and English Heritage.' He was joined by Tim Sebastian, and the robed Druids' free-form performance was only once interrupted by festival veteran Willy X cheekily encouraging the crowd to 'Beware the uniforms!' (Hughes 1990)

Arthur Pendragon

The final player in this festival-based triumvirate – John Rothwell – has been known since 1986 (when he changed his name by deed poll) as Arthur Uther Pendragon. The full story of how a restless, reckless army kid became first a soldier, then a renowned biker leader called John the Hat, and then King Arthur, the Once and Future King Reborn, is admirably told by Arthur and C.J. Stone in *The Trials of Arthur* (2003). Its subject – and his motives and beliefs – are central to the story of the summer solstice at Stonehenge in the 1990s.

Ronald Hutton has described Arthur as 'a sincere natural mystic, whose very strong libertarian political convictions are bound up with a sense of guidance by supernatural forces. His belief in reincarnation was stimulated by the experience of vivid dreams and memories, known since childhood, which seemed to him to be memories of previous lifetimes.' In Arthur's own story, a catalytic event was a near-death experience at the age of fourteen, when a dustcart he was in was hit by a munitions train on a railway line. After this event, he realised that 'death was not the end' and that 'There was nothing in life to be afraid of.' He began to investigate Zen Buddhism, witchcraft, the occult and mysticism, 'anything and everything that could give him some understanding', and by his early twenties he had joined a coven of witches in Lancashire, as well as briefly becoming a member of the Universal Free Church, where he was known as the Reverend J.T. Rothwell, psychic investigator. (Hutton 2003: 238; Pendragon and Stone 2003: 14–16, 26)

The most profound influence on his development, however, was his life as John the Hat, biker leader. The close-knit world of the bikers was held together by an unwritten code of honour – described by the bikers themselves as 'righteousness' – which centred on the prime importance of fidelity and integrity, of being true to

Arthur Pendragon and a devoted young follower. Copyright Pete Glastonbury.

yourself and your friends. In this spirit of 'righteousness' the principles of the Warband – 'Truth, Honour and Justice' – were first formed, and it was as a biker that Arthur first experienced the extraordinary allure of Stonehenge and its free festival: 'There was something about sitting around a camp fire at night, weaving tales, with the silhouette of the stones nearby... that called upon the spirits of the ancestors to join them at the party, to commune with them.' The bikers subsequently became involved in ridding the festival of its unwanted heroin dealers in its last few years, as well as convening wild full moon biker parties that sought to 'recreate the energy of Stonehenge' at Odiham Castle, a ruin in Hampshire. (Pendragon and Stone 2003: 32–3)

Although no brief account could explain fully the cumulative factors that led to the rebirth of John the Hat as King Arthur, Stonehenge retained a central significance. One night in June 1986, shortly after he had received his calling, when he was still wondering if he was possessed by a vision or a delusion, he drove down to Stonehenge to seek a sign. After vaulting the perimeter fence and somehow avoiding the attention of the security guards, he made it to the centre of the stones, where a

*Arthur Pendragon raising Excalibur, watched by
Rollo Maughfling. Avebury, summer solstice 2003.
Copyright Pete Glastonbury.*

raven, swooping low, brushed his face with its wing. He took it 'as an act of consecration. As if something from nature had, priest-like, laid a hand upon his forehead to offer blessings for his chosen course.' (Pendragon and Stone 2003: 44–5)

Over the next few years he consolidated his position, finding his Excalibur – aptly enough, the sword that was used in John Boorman's film – and attracting followers, initially through adverts in the bikers' magazine *Back Street Heroes* and Mensa's *International Magazine*, but increasingly by rumour and reputation. He also refined the concept of the Warband, a revived 'Round Table' that focused in particular on three categories of knights: Shield Knights, who, like Arthur, recalled their historic names and purpose; Quest Knights, who were convinced of their calling but unsure of their historic identity; and Brother Knights, 'people whose feet were firmly set in the 20th century but who were drawn to the Arthurian values of Truth, Honour and Justice.' Significantly, in a typical and rather touching attempt to play down his own role in favour of the larger mission, both the Shield Knights and the Quest Knights had returned 'not to press for the reinstitution of their own heroic values, but to be of service to the Brothers in their battle to make a better world.' (Pendragon and Stone 2003: 56–7, 65–9)

At Beltane 1990, Arthur met his Merlin on Glastonbury Tor. He turned out to be Rollo Maughfling, who claims his surname is derived from 'Merlin.' Rollo rang Arthur up the day before and invited him to the Glastonbury Order's ceremony. In the legend of Arthur's Druidic initiation, Rollo asked him to bring his sword. At the

Arthur Pendragon in his Druidic capacity, Avebury, vernal equinox 2003. The ceremonial arch of staffs is one of several innovations devised by Arthur himself. Copyright Andy Worthington.

very moment in the ceremony that Arthur was required to raise it skywards, the sun came out from behind a cloud, 'a shaft of sunlight hit the sword like a brand of fire' and 'everyone gasped at the sight of it, this shimmering, intense, brilliant, electric sword burning in the morning sunlight.' (Pendragon and Stone 2003: 77)

That day Arthur also met Tim Sebastian, who remembered him as John the Hat, roaring out of the Stonehenge-in-exile festival at Westbury in 1985 'at the head of a huge V-formation of bikes.' Tim recalled the bikers as 'barbarian hordes', although Arthur admitted that 'in fact, they had just been arrested, and [he] was leading them off site in a dignified retreat.' (Pendragon and Stone 2003: 83)

Arthur and Stonehenge

The Loyal Arthurian Warband duly became an enthusiastic new Druid Order, and Arthur's mission to free Stonehenge began at the autumn equinox that year. This was the occasion when, after several years' tolerance, access on the equinoxes and at the winter solstice was denied to all, but some of those excluded – including Arthur and others – scaled the fence and occupied the stones, later joining hands through the fence with those on the outside, to create a large, symbolic circle around the Heel Stone.

177

Arthur was so incensed at their treatment, and so inspired by the struggle for Stonehenge, that he left his job (as a freelance builder) and his home (a caravan in an apple orchard in Langport) and became Arthur full-time. He embarked on a one-man sit-in outside the temple – throughout winter – to protest at the charging of an entrance fee. With an eye for publicity, he campaigned under the slogan, 'Don't Pay, Walk Away', attracting media attention (he playfully told one reporter, 'I will stay here for ever and ever until they open the Stones for the Equinoxes and Solstices') and becoming a kind of tourist attraction, photographed by countless Japanese and American tourists. (Pendragon and Stone 2003: 85, 88)

For four months, he lived in a bunker between two trees, a modern-day mendicant reliant for food and drink on the generosity of strangers. He recalled that 'It was bloody cold and it was bloody damp but it had to be done. I survived a lot of the time on handouts from the Americans who seemed totally phased that they could walk along and almost fall over a bloke in robes who said he was King Arthur. By the time the winter was over I was in a bit of a state and I lost a lot of weight, but on the plus side I made my point and met a lot of interesting people.' (Russell 1996)

At the solstice, Arthur embarked on the first of a series of voluntary arrests for breaking through the exclusion zone that ran on down the years as persistently and pig-headedly as the authorities' intransigence endured. That first year, he was arrested – for possession of an offensive weapon (Excalibur) – with seven others at a party inside the exclusion zone. In 1992, he caused confusion in the police ranks by declaring that he and his four companions were not, in fact, forming a procession of two or more people (which was illegal) but were only attempting to have a picnic, and in 1993 he actually got through to the stones. (Pendragon 2000)

From the start, Arthur courted the media assiduously, holding press conferences outside the perimeter fence and sending other members of the Warband on high profile missions elsewhere. One year, for example, four of his knights – Lucan, Dagonet, Guy the Rant and Marcus the Black – were sent on a Dragon Quest. After sneaking into the Granada TV studios, they claimed squatters' rights on the floating model of Britain that was used for the weather forecast on *This Morning*, and they only withdrew – as transmission time neared – when they had been lent the model dragon that signified Wales, which was later used to raise money for the homeless. (Pendragon and Stone 2003: 100–4)

Conspicuously, other Druid groups sprang up during the fierce ballet of Arthur's solstice manoeuvres. Dylan Ap Thuin, a young, dreadlocked Wiccan who met Arthur for the first time at the summer solstice in 1993 (and who subsequently occupied the stones along with Arthur and a slightly bemused French Druid called Barnade) founded the Insular Order of Druids on the spot. (Ap Thuin 2001)

The Council of British Druid Orders

As the troubled 1980s yielded to a questionable new decade, all that these five new Orders – OBOD, BDO, SOD, GOD and LAW – had in common were: a certain attraction to Stonehenge, a certain attraction to the summer solstice, and a certain sort of ritual to acknowledge this conjunction of time and place. To add to the confusion of what, beyond these few concerns, was central to Druidry as a whole, these three criteria were also fulfilled by the surviving Orders, the Ancient Order of Druids – the friendly society that still had an antique antiquarian's fondness for Stonehenge – and the Ancient Druid Order, the original agitators for solstice access.

A truly surreal scenario ensued. All but the Ancient Druid Order joined together in a short-lived confederation, the Council of British Druid Orders (COBDO), which sought to agree on ways of dealing with their central concern: exclusion from their temple at the chosen time of year. It remains unclear why it was ever thought that such a coalition would ever reach consensus. As Philip Shallcrass put it, 'the visions of Druidry held by the various groups were so radically different, ranging from the social interests and mutual support of the Ancient Order through to the anarchic political activism of the Loyal Arthurian Warband, with every shade of opinion between.' Even so, the Council made a go of it at the beginning, with many representatives gathering for the Gorsedd on Primrose Hill at the solstice in 1989, at which the petition for the Glastonbury Order's proposed Stonehenge Eisteddfod was read out, which was later delivered to the Queen. When Arthur picketed Stonehenge in the winter of 1990–1, he declared that he was doing it 'on behalf of the Council of British Druid Orders, the Arthurian Warband and the Free Peoples of Britain.' (Shallcrass 1999: 10: Pendragon and Stone 2003: 85–6)

Within a few years, the coalition had broken up. Philip Shallcrass commented that 'The issue of Stonehenge proved particularly divisive, with the larger, older groups favouring peaceful negotiation while some of the smaller, recently formed groups supported a far more militant approach', and he also criticised 'the erratic, unpredictable and often aggressive behaviour of one of COBDO's officers.' Shallcrass himself maintained two views that ran contrary to the beliefs cherished by the more political Druids. Although he was appalled by the events of the Beanfield, his opinion of the Stonehenge festival, which he had attended in 1980, was that it was 'pretty dismal', and he cited vandalism to trees and burial mounds, shoplifting in Amesbury, residents' fears of burglaries and people 'pissing on other people's tents until large areas of the field and the nearby woods stank of stale urine' as examples of why it was reasonable for many people to want the festival closed down. (Shallcrass 1999: 9–10)

Shallcrass also resisted Arthur's notion of Stonehenge as a 'people's temple', commenting that this was 'ironic, given that the site was probably constructed as a symbol of the political power of a dominant social elite.' On this latter point (itself a revival of an ideological struggle that had raged for years between the festival-goers and the temple's curators), he was speaking for the majority of Druids. In the struggles over access, only a few of the leading 'pagan' personalities – Ross Nichols, John Michell and Arthur – have ever managed to put aside their identification with the supposed élite for long enough to embrace fully the concept of access for all. (Shallcrass 1999: 9)

In the wake of the Council's breakdown, the Ancient Order abandoned Stonehenge completely, and OBOD and the BDO began negotiations for their own special access on the days around the solstice, whilst maintaining a secondary commitment to open access for all. Noticeably, the Ancient Druid Order, the only group that had not been involved in the Council, regained their 'traditional' access for the solstice dawn in 1990, a privilege they held onto exclusively until 1995. (Loxley 2003)

The other Druids – the Secular Order, the Glastonbury Order and Arthur – were now well and truly excluded. Advocates of free access for all, they were back to their universalist festival roots, outmanoeuvred by the partisans, although they kept the Council going, and Arthur's commitment to access at Stonehenge was unwavering. In 1994, 'by the judicious method of having a Radio 4 documentary crew with him', he actually got through to the stones again, correctly predicting that the police would be reluctant to run through the whole embarrassing charade in the presence of a camera crew. At the same time that the journalists were being entertained at the stones, two of Arthur's knights – Guy the Rant and Dagonet – occupied Winchester Cathedral, claiming squatters' rights and sanctuary, declaring that they would not leave until the Archbishop of Canterbury issued a statement 'deploring the so-called 'Exclusion Zone'. In the end, the Canon obliged, and the knights left satisfied. (Pendragon and Stone 2003: 106)

Local support, official denial

The Druids were not the only ones striving for change in these years. Throughout the exclusion period, the Church of England frequently brought representatives of the various sides together to seek a solution. As early as 1985, in the aftermath of the Beanfield, a meeting was held to discuss a proposal put forward by English Heritage to hold 'a one-day Solstice festival at the stones, allowing the Druids and other groups to ritualise there.' Talks stalled over the provision of an official campsite, to divert 'the thousands who would otherwise have swamped the Solstice festival', and as John Michell described it, 'The National Trust and other local landowners closed ranks, refusing any festival camp on their properties.' (Michell 1986: 7)

On 21 March 1986 – the vernal equinox of the pagan solar year – a Church of England forum in Salisbury Town Hall, organised by the Reverend David Penney, was similarly inconclusive. Although the meeting was 'good-humoured and tolerant' and 'the majority of the Festival groups would doubtless have been appeased by even the slightest official concession', the main thrust of the meeting – that the National Trust should make land available for a free festival – was again thwarted when the Trust refused. (Michell 1986: 7-8)

In 1987, the Salisbury Civic Society took the initiative, convening a meeting addressed by the Assistant Chief Constable of Wiltshire, David Cooke, who proposed that 'consultation, not confrontation, was the answer' to the problems at Stonehenge. At the end of the meeting it was decided to ask the Ministry of Defence 'to make some of its gigantic holding of unused land available' for the festival instead, but this request was also turned down, and although *The Salisbury Journal* subsequently ran a report on the meeting under the headline 'Talks not truncheons', George Firsoff noted that Cooke 'soon found himself posted far away.' His last memorable transgression occurred in December 1987, when he dared to admit that 'In the past two years that I have dealt with the travellers, I have found them very reasonable people.' (TAT 1988: 21, 16; Firsoff 1992)

Throughout this period, the views of local residents – who were persistently presented in the media and by the authorities as the 'victims' of the festival – were also overlooked. Although there were many who were vehemently opposed to the festival, many others maintained an opposing point of view. Douglas Reid, a councillor in Amesbury, campaigned until his death in 1998 to reinstate the festival. In a letter to *The Salisbury Journal* in 1996, he reminded readers that three separate local petitions in 1985–6, showing significant majorities in support of a festival, had been presented to English Heritage and the National Trust, but had been ignored.

Reid focused on the loss of trade every June, both in the town and on the festival site, concluding that local businesses 'had all benefited considerably from the huge increase in spending money brought into the local economy.' He also noted that 'Most local people visited the festival at some time or other (even if only to gaze from the roadway) and a not inconsiderable number joined the campers on site for a free summer break, some taking their young families along', and added that the festival had initially 'filled a gap in Amesbury's entertainment caused by the temporary demise of its annual carnival' and that in its later years it had 'provided the only chance, without large expense, for many people to see famous national groups playing.' (Reid 1996)

Reid's was a prominent voice, but he was not alone. C.J. Stone encountered similar opinions about trade when he casually started a debate in an Amesbury hotel bar one night. The majority opinion was that the Co-op had lost money through shoplifting, but that everybody else had benefited. One man's father had run a phenomenally successful ice-cream van at the festival every year: 'He used to get all sorts. People coming up to him bollock-naked, buying an ice lolly. Didn't bother him in the slightest. They were all nice people.' (Stone 1996: 102)

All agreed that as the policy of exclusion was implemented, 'the police reaction was excessive', and life in the town was made almost intolerable. The landlady of the hotel remarked that '1988 was the worst. It was like a prison camp. The locals all had to carry ID cards' and there were 'Police and roadblocks everywhere. Cars were stopped coming into and going out of the town. It was a nightmare.' (Stone 1996: 103)

The archaeology/earth mysteries crossover

Increasingly, the archaeological establishment also became involved in the struggle for the solstice at Stonehenge. Not all archaeologists agreed with Glyn Daniel's opinions of the Druids and festival-goers. Richard Atkinson insisted that the free festival was 'an institution which I find amicable with the history of Stonehenge', and as early as June 1985 Michael Heaton defended the counter-culture and indicted establishment hypocrisy in a singularly passionate letter to *The Guardian*: 'The damage, if any, done to Stonehenge (by the festival) is piffling in comparison to the damage done by the Ministry of Defence, but because it is done by 'hippies'… it is singled out for analysis and hysterical reaction. It's on a par with outlawing children for picking wild flowers when everyone knows the real threat to our flora comes from farmers and industrialists producing things that nobody needs or wants. The 'hippies', anarchists and pagans have absolutely nothing to do with the destruction of our heritage. They revere the stones in a way that millions of tourists, farmers and police could never do. They are using Stonehenge for its original purpose and so actively partaking in a continuum that the rest of us can only stare vicariously at through pages and frames of historical romances.' (TAT 1988: 21; *The Guardian*, 24 June 1985)

Chris Chippindale, who had suggested before the Beanfield that 'A show of determined force is, regrettably, probably the only way to see the festival off', conceded afterwards that 'We need to find a site on land which is not archaeologically precious and within reasonable distance of Stonehenge for the festival-as-a-camp... and give access for the festival-at-the-stones on an agreed day, if at all possible the day of the solstice.' Chippindale's opinion of the Druids was that they were as bogus as Glyn Daniel insisted they were, but he accepted, as O.G.S. Crawford had, that they were a sort of 'antique curiosity – dotty, harmless and Englishly eccentric', and that they should 'sensibly be left to perform in peace.' (Chippindale 1985; TAT 1988: 17)

In addition, many of the younger generation of archaeologists were themselves part of the counter-cultural movements that had given rise to the earth mysteries movement, the revival of paganism and the free festival scene. In 1986, they showed their political colours at the World Archaeological Congress in Southampton, when a number of young archaeologists 'refused to cooperate with the official, Apartheid-backed, South African delegation', and as the 1980s wore on, the willingness of some archaeologists to see other viewpoints combined with a similar willingness in pagan practitioners and those involved in the field of earth mysteries, so that the distinctions between all three became increasingly blurred. (Stout 2001)

Leading the charge from the earth mysteries side were Paul Devereux and Nigel Pennick, two of the leading authors in the pursuit of geomantic truths. In 1989's *Lines on the Landscape*, they not only put forward the most coherent defence of the movement's objectives to date; they also dissociated themselves from '"New Age" cultists, would-be gurus, "soft" or popular theoreticians and journalistic hacks', and distanced themselves from the relentless subjectivity that was anathema to the objective scientists of the archaeological establishment. In doing so, they 'reject[ed] the notions of leys as energy lines, because the only way to demonstrate the reality of such energies is through the rods of dowsers who are themselves believers.' Within a few years, ley-lines were officially dead, and Paul Devereux began investigating landscape lines as 'spirit paths' for shamanic flight, a development that began to resonate with the prevailing trend towards shamanic investigations in both paganism and archaeology. (Pennick and Devereux 1989: 13; Hutton 1991: 123)

Ironically, it was the pursuit of ley-lines that had led many of those involved in earth mysteries to look at monuments in terms of their wider landscape contexts – something that traditional archaeology, focused on the minutiae of excavation, had

Volunteers undertake magnetic tests on the bluestones at Stonehenge in September 1987 as part of the Dragon Project, a research programme established to investigate unusual 'energies' at ancient sacred sites.
Copyright Paul Devereux.

often failed to do – and as earth mysteries began to move away from subjectivity, younger archaeologists began to embrace it. Chris Tilley of University College London, inspired by the missing dimensions in traditional archaeology, began putting himself back into the landscape, a process that he described as phenomenology, and that led to the publication of *A Phenomenology of Landscape* in 1994, which he described as 'an exercise in a 'blurred genre'.' (Tilley 1994: 1)

Throughout the archaeological establishment as a whole, there was a dawning awareness that archaeology's fabled objectivity was a deception and that subjective viewpoints were inevitable. As dogma duly gave way to doubt, the bold statements of the past were replaced by something altogether more slippery. One recent view of the Neolithic, for example, the 'Mobile Neolithic', whose landscape was 'held together by movement across its surface between a constellation of places, each of which was loaded with social and religious significances', finds nomads usurping the place of the permanently settled farmers conjured up in their own image by the older, landowning archaeological establishment. (Barrett 1994. 146-7)

'Who Owns Stonehenge?'

One of the first fruits of the breaking down of barriers between archaeology, earth mysteries and paganism was the publication in 1990 of *Who Owns Stonehenge?*, a collection of essays that brought together the differing viewpoints of Paul Devereux, Tim Sebastian, Rhys Jones – an academic and a member of the Gorsedd of the

National Eisteddfod of Wales – and the archaeologists Peter Fowler and Chris Chippindale. It was a valuable experiment. Paul Devereux rounded up the questions and answers offered by the earth mysteries movement, Tim Sebastian wove a mystical fable of Druids past and present, and Rhys Jones, a Welsh-born Senior Fellow of Pacific Studies at the Australian National University, put forward a Welsh land-claim on the monument that he then chose not to pursue, in the interests of preventing 'narrow sectarianism.' The most progressive contributions, however, came from the archaeologists. (Devereux 1990: 35–61; Sebastian 1990: 88–119; Jones 1990: 62–87)

Chippindale, who by now had become the late Glyn Daniel's successor at *Antiquity*, introduced his contributions with a succinct appraisal of the conflict at Stonehenge, a 'bubbling brew of issues concerning intellectual freedom, rational and intuitive knowledge, preservation, presentation and access, the place and role of religious beliefs, the state and its dissidents, the rights of dispossessed ethnic minorities, and even the concept of ownership.' He also changed his mind about the Druids, conceding that, however bogus their historical claims, their present-day response to the monument was perfectly valid: 'Stonehenge, in almost every opinion, was a place of religion and ritual in prehistory. The modern Druids treat it that way today; the State as custodians of the place, and archaeologists as scientists, do not.' (Chippindale 1990: 9, 23)

Peter Fowler also acknowledged pagan claims on the monument, reviving Daniel's musings, back in 1978, on the significance of the perceived sincerity of Stonehenge's contemporary worshippers: 'many people now see Stonehenge primarily as a living, religious place – indeed, more as a 'temple.' The majority in a secular society finds it difficult to sympathise with this view; far easier to ridicule it. But whatever the objections – the 'religion' is pagan, unauthentic, self-deluding, silly – the sincerity of the present-day religious beliefs centred on Stonehenge must, it seems to me, be accepted.' (Fowler 1990a: 142)

Fowler also extended sympathy to the travellers, accepting the significance of the festival as the central gathering of Britain's modern-day nomadic tribes. He admitted that because of 'incompatibility between settled and nomadic people', there had been 'no understanding that 'nomads' need a meeting place... related, by common understanding and convenience, to the cycle of their activities, the seasons and/or the movement of recognized heavenly bodies.' He wondered whether the existing arrangements questioned sufficiently the extent of police powers and personal freedom in a democracy, and he questioned the establishment's insistence that there was no room, 'literally as well as conceptually, for people of 'no fixed abode' in a bureaucratically-based, property-owning and, above all, settled society.' (Fowler 1990a: 150, 144)

Fowler was not, however, exclusively an apologist for pagans and festival-goers. In one chapter, he donned his heritage-guarding hat to rail against the interlopers from a preservationist viewpoint. Archaeology, he stated, 'contrasts in its altruism and public spirit with the motivation and efforts of nearly all other consumers of the Stonehenge phenomenon, whether they be latter-day druids, ley-liners, wallies,

A 'national disgrace': chaos masquerading as a worthwhile visitor experience.
Copyright Andy Worthington.

festivalists or tourists.' Their contribution was 'at best questionable', and was 'characteristically erosive, introverted and self-gratifying.' (Fowler 1990b: 128)

Nevertheless, the main libertarian thrust of the views put forward by Fowler and Chippindale was to resonate unnervingly in the staider corridors of academia. Fowler in particular had tackled a number of establishment taboos head-on, accepting that 'However correct management of the monument may be in secular terms, it will be defiling the "holy", and be seen as "unreasonable", from a "New Age" religious point of view', declaring that access to the monument was 'one of the major social issues of our time', and conceding that 'Whatever the illegalities, the inconvenience, even the damage of the Festival, something spontaneously creative has been destroyed... The Stonehenge festival, though anarchic, was eventually positive, the only pop festival that actually threw out heroin dealers. The dark side – the damage, the outrage caused to local people – in a sense was the product of official neglect.' (Fowler 1990a: 142-8)

His most controversial transgression, however, was reserved for the National Trust. As a Council member, Fowler was a party to the banning of the festival from 1985 onwards. It was a role that he undertook with reluctance, and he admitted to being shocked by the events of the Beanfield, but it wasn't until the AGM in autumn 1985 that he 'trembled with shame when fellow-members of the National Trust who had been subject to the 1985 police action were denied a fair hearing... by a hostile and, to my mind, perhaps deeply disturbed assembly.' (Fowler 1990b: 131)

'Stonehenge Belongs to You and Me'

In 1992, two young archaeologists at University College London and Cambridge – Barbara Bender and Mark Edmonds, supported by seven archaeologists from other universities – wrote to *The Guardian* to protest about the situation at Stonehenge. Their article echoed many of the sentiments put forward by Fowler and Chippindale.

'Stonehenge Belongs to You and Me': part of the travelling exhibition set up to raise debate about the ownership and management of Stonehenge. Copyright Polly Farquharson, with thanks to Barbara Bender.

They pointed out that for the establishment Stonehenge was 'a pre-eminent trace of our great past (the 'our' remaining unspecified)', that for the police it was 'presumably an unwelcome drain on resources and a public relations minefield', and that for at least some of the travellers, it was 'a spiritual mecca and an important seasonal meeting-point.' They proposed two solutions: 'In the short term, the potential exists for arrangements to be made for controlled access to the site at the Solstice and for the placement of a Free Festival at some distance from the stones. In the longer term, and at a rather broader level, what is at issue is intellectual as well as physical access.' (Bender and Edmonds 1992)

English Heritage declined to respond, but in truth the organisation had only just begun to think about the very broadest issues of access at Stonehenge, let alone the specific issues surrounding the summer solstice. A plan was being drawn up, in conjunction with the National Trust and the Tussaud Group, to create a 6,000 acre 'Millennium Park' around Stonehenge, which was finally launched in May 1997 through full-page advertisements in the national press. Under the heading, 'Before we can take down the fence, we have to dig up the road', the consortium presented a vision of 'a 6,000 acre prehistoric natural wilderness containing over 450 ancient monuments, as well as Stonehenge itself', and promised to submerge the A303 'through an underground tunnel where it passes the site', to 'close the A344 and return it to grassland', and to 'remove the existing (and woefully inadequate) visitor centre and car park and build a new Visitor Complex at least a kilometre away from the stones.' The consortium also suggested that 'By making Stonehenge harder to get to, we would make it more accessible. Visitors would be able to roam freely (and free of charge) among the monuments, unfettered by fences.' Throughout the whole of this period, however, no short-term solution was proposed, the exclusion zone returned every summer solstice, and the visitors' facilities at the monument were condemned as a 'national disgrace' by a House of Commons Select Committee in 1993. (CBA 2003)

Noticeably, Barbara Bender followed up her convictions by attending Stonehenge Campaign meetings and establishing, along with three prominent campaigners – Paul Aitken, Hilary Jones and Wesley Burrage – a travelling exhibition, entitled 'Stonehenge Belongs to You and Me', which featured the differing viewpoints of all the groups and organisations concerned with Stonehenge, each mounted on cardboard trilithons, and which toured around the country for three years from 1993, taking in venues as diverse as free festivals, village halls and the Museum of London. (Bender 1998: 145-171)

As an immediate follow-up to the article in *The Guardian*, however, Bender tried to get through the exclusion zone at the summer solstice in 1992 in a minibus full of archaeologists. Predictably, they were stopped by police, under the terms of clause 13 of the Public Order Act, the one that Druids, travellers, would be festival-goers and frustrated solstice-watchers of all hues had been running up against every year: 'two people proceeding in a given direction can constitute a procession and can be arrested as a threat to civil order.' Bender and her colleagues 'offered to go in with fifty yards between each person', but the police 'openly subverted the new law and order act' and 'said they would arrest us anyway.' The archaeologists went to Avebury instead, where 'in the misty dawn, people were chilling out, dancing, dowsing. Not a policeman in sight. It felt great.' They had discovered, as many others had at this time, that the charms of Stonehenge's neighbour were far more conducive to solstice revels than the caged and prohibited temple on Salisbury Plain. (Bender 1998: 148)

Chapter Eleven

Avebury and other sacred places

The festival diaspora

While Arthur and his Warband continued to challenge the exclusion zone at Stonehenge, aided and abetted by the Secular Order, the Glastonbury Order and all manner of other outraged individuals, the majority of those excluded from Stonehenge after 1985 found less contentious places to celebrate the summer solstice. P. Bennett and T. Wilson, the authors of a booklet entitled *The Old Stones of Rollright and District*, pointed out that, 'Whereas people annually visited the one site on Salisbury Plain, ignoring – or not even being aware of – megalithic sites in their own backyards, the closing of Stonehenge as a ritual centre took people back to their own local sites.' (Bennett and Wilson 1999: 7)

In the south of England, solstice pilgrims began to focus on Glastonbury, on Cissbury Ring and its near-neighbour Chanctonbury Ring on the South Downs, and on the many stone circles of Cornwall, in particular Boscawen-Un, which had been a regular focus for the ceremonies of the Cornish Druids – Gorseth Kernow – ever since the Order was founded in 1928. Although both John Michell and Rollo Maughfling had experienced the ceremonies at Boscawen-Un, it is noticeable that Gorsedd Kernow has never been involved with the struggle for access to Stonehenge. Like the Welsh Druids, the Cornish Druids function as a cultural organisation, rather than one with political or spiritual aims, and on their website they describe themselves as a 'non-political, non-religious' organisation that has 'no connection with Druidism or any pagan practices' and that 'exists solely to uphold the Celtic tradition.' (Gorseth Kernow 2002)

One of the most prominent of these alternative venues was the Rollright Stones in Oxfordshire, which had long been a favoured location for a number of covens. As early as 1959, a young Wiccan high priestess known as Dayonis held a ceremony at the Rollrights with her coven on Midsummer's Eve. All night long, the party of fifteen witches leapt over a bonfire and danced around the stones, and Dayonis later explained the intensity of her feelings about the ceremony in a letter to Gerald Gardner, in which she declared, 'I wanted to roll over and over like a young animal.' It was a statement that Ronald Hutton has described as a perfect expression of 'the feelings of release and blissful communion with nature and the past which the witch religion gave.' (Dayonis 1959; Hutton 1999: 250)

Nearly three decades later, at the summer solstice in 1987, the Rollrights was one of the first sacred sites to be taken up by the travelling festival community as an

Avebury: looking south from the remaining arc of the southern inner circle to the portal stones of the vast outer circle.
Copyright Andy Worthington.

alternative to Stonehenge. 'Hippies hold festival at Rollright Stones', trumpeted a local newspaper, and Douglas Hurd turned up to be harangued by his 'medieval brigands.' (Greenfields 2003)

Despite the awakening – or reawakening – of interest in these sites, there was one place in particular – Avebury – that began to attract the major share of the frustrated ritual attention that was being diverted away from Stonehenge.

Avebury

Even before the events of the Beanfield, the temple complex of Avebury was far from unknown. Just eighteen miles north of Stonehenge, the wonders of Avebury are almost beyond compare in the whole of the British Isles. The largest stone-chambered long barrows in the country – the East and West Kennet Long Barrows – are just two of around three dozen Neolithic barrows that radiate from a central area dominated by a natural hill known as Waden Hill, its colossal man-made companion Silbury Hill, and the largest henge monument in the country, hacked out of solid chalk and containing what was probably the largest stone circle in the world, the Great Ring or Outer Circle, measuring 1,100 feet in diameter.

Inside the remains of this vast circle stand the remains of two further stone circles, the North and South Circles, themselves the fifth and seventh largest examples in the UK. And running up to the henge are the remains of a stone avenue of paired

William Stukeley, 'A View of the South Temple. July 15 1723', from
Abury, A Temple of the British Druids, With Some Others, Described *(1743).*

standing stones, the West Kennet Avenue, the sole survivor of two original avenues, each nearly a mile and a half in length. Other significant sites include Windmill Hill, to the north west of the central area, which was home to the country's largest causewayed enclosure (a meeting place for seasonal gatherings and ceremonies), and the Sanctuary, at the far end of the West Kennet Avenue, where a succession of circular timber structures was eventually replaced by a compact arrangement of concentric stone circles, now destroyed.

As has been mentioned in passing earlier in this book, Avebury has been recognised as a significant ancient site ever since the days of the early antiquarians. John Aubrey, who rediscovered the stone circles in 1649, memorably declared that 'This old Monument... does as much exceed in bignes the so renowned Stoneheng as a Cathedral doeth a parish church'. From 1719–24, its partial destruction was admirably chronicled by William Stukeley, who lamented that 'within the space of twenty years, a few miserable farmers destroyed this, the noblest monument which is probably on the face of the earth; which has stood so many ages, and was made to stand so many more.' Stukeley's fieldwork was so meticulous that Aubrey Burl has commented that, 'Had it not been for Stukeley, it would be impossible today to write with any accuracy about Avebury.' (Aubrey 1980a; Stukeley 1743: 22; Burl 1979: 47)

The next great manifestations of interest in Avebury took place in the late nineteenth century and the early twentieth century. In the 1870s, the preservationist Sir John Lubbock (Lord Avebury) bought Silbury Hill and other parts of the temple complex. In 1883, the year after his Ancient Monuments Act was finally passed by Parliament, Silbury and the West Kennet Long Barrow became the first recipients of the new legislative protection. (Pitts 1996: 38)

190

In the 1930s many of the stones in Avebury's circles and its surviving avenue, which had fallen or been buried in the Middle Ages and the eighteenth century, were resurrected by its last private owner, the Scottish marmalade heir and archaeological enthusiast Alexander Keiller, whose bold restoration paved the way for a significant growth of interest in Avebury in the 1960s, when it was revived as a centre of profound mystical significance by John Michell, and its geometry and astronomy were investigated by Alexander Thom.

Michael Dames: the Goddess at Avebury

As has also been pointed out, Richard Atkinson's failure to inspire the public during the televised excavation of Silbury Hill in 1968–9 inspired Michael Dames, a graduate in geography and archaeology, and a lecturer in the history of art, to create a vision of Avebury in *The Silbury Treasure* (1976) and *The Avebury Cycle* (1977) that was the perfect sacred landscape for the new paganism, combining worship of the Great Goddess with the festivals of the Celtic year. Unaware of Peter Ucko's repudiation of the theory of the Goddess, Dames, in Ronald Hutton's words, 'looks up the great books of the fifties and sixties, finds Jacquetta Hawkes, Stuart Piggott, O.G.S. Crawford telling him the Neolithic was the time of the Great Goddess, finds that Silbury Hill was Neolithic, looks at it with an artist's eye and sees that, from above – from aerial photographs – it makes the figure of a Great Goddess.' (Hutton 1998: 184)

Dames' focus on the Celtic ritual year also began with Silbury. He took Atkinson's suggestion that flying ants found in the core of the mound during the excavations of 1968–9 were entombed during the mating season at the start of August, combined it with Maire MacNeill's study of gatherings on hill-tops in Ireland to celebrate the start of the potato harvest (which took place within living memory at the same time of the year), added an eighteenth century Scottish tradition of raising earthen mounds, again at the same time of year, and concluded triumphantly that Silbury was a harvest hill, used by the people of the Neolithic to celebrate the Goddess and the fertility of the land at Lughnasa. (Atkinson 1969: 4; Dames 1976: 88–97; MacNeill 1962)

In *The Avebury Cycle*, Dames extended his theory to include the rest of the Avebury complex, concocting a seasonal round that involved initiation rites at the Sanctuary at Imbolc, celebrations of fertility in the stone circles at Beltane, and ceremonies at the West Kennet Long Barrow at Samhain. Along the way, other landscape features were incorporated, in particular the source of the River Kennet, Swallowhead Springs, which regularly dries up at Samhain only to be reborn miraculously at Imbolc. (Dames 1977: 80–1, 150–6, 53–9, 35)

Throughout both books, Dames' inspiration came not only from those archaeologists who had embraced the goddess, but also from allied writers, whose works had been similarly influential but whose authority was now being increasingly questioned by rigorous, albeit specialised academic research. These included Robert Graves and the big names in post-war anthropology, psychology and the philosophy of religions – Gertrude Levy, Carl Gustav Jung and his disciple Erich Neumann, Mircea Eliade

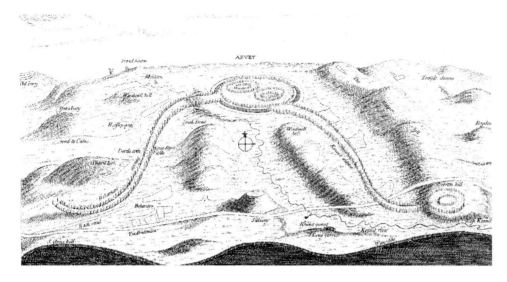

Stukeley's notorious serpent plan of the Avebury complex, in which he altered the distances between the monuments and changed the shape of the Sanctuary from circular to oval to resemble a serpent's head. From Abury *(1743).*

and Joseph Campbell – and it was in this unquestioning milieu of grand archetypes and sweeping generalizations that Dames was even able to resuscitate William Stukeley's theory, long reviled by archaeologists, that the monuments of Avebury were laid out in the form of a great serpent.

For those who were unaware of the discrepancies in Dames' methodology – and there were many, not least the assumption that long barrows and henges, for example, were in use during the same period – his vision was compelling. As Ronald Hutton pointed out, 'They were ceremonies which people could perform, and so, within a year, people were there. That's why women dance on Silbury Hill at the August full moon.' (Hutton 1998: 185)

The converts referred to by Hutton were spiritual feminists, whose contribution to the growth of paganism in general will be discussed at length below, but noticeably his theories fed just as effortlessly into the earth mysteries movement, as well as the spiritual reverberations of the landscape that were experienced by the more sensitive members of the travelling festival community.

The travellers at Avebury

Within a few years, the vanguard of the travellers' scene duly rolled up at Avebury. Recalling the events of that time, Del Richardson wrote, 'It was the summer of 1980 and we'd come a long road out of Wales. We were camped on downland, on the ancient greenway three miles above Avebury, on our way to the Summer Solstice Celebrations at Stonehenge.' Bev Richardson recalled riding out from the camp one morning on horseback to visit the stones, accompanied by his son and daughter, in a passage so seemingly removed from the modern world that it recalls Aubrey's initial discovery of the stones, when he 'galloped into the village and was 'wonderfully surprised at the sight of those vast stones of which I had never heard before': 'And whooping and hollering into the mist down away along that broad green rutted broken track they galloped... to a great hollow on the edge of the village. And like broken teeth disappearing into the mist, great stones and deep banks [stood]. Grown about with rabbit-cropped grass, these ancient stones, this place of power, hidden within its ruins amongst the mist, retained much of its ageless majesty. And sometimes the man led, and sometimes the girl led, and always the boy tumbled after, shouting and hollering at the tail of the other two. And in and out of the stones they wove a fairy pattern with their joyful shouts.' (Richardson 1997; Burl 1979: 42)

In 1981, some of the travellers even attempted to hold a free festival at Avebury, which was described by the Festival Zone website as 'a good example of the impromptu, authority-hassled and minuscule free festivals of the 1980s', with around a hundred people attending. After gathering close to the stones on 22 May, the travellers – who included members of the Tibetan Ukranian Mountain Troupe – were almost immediately moved on by the police, relocating to a lay-by on the A4 at Overton Hill, on the Ridgeway, beside the Sanctuary, where a free food kitchen was set up, and a great pink parachute was raised as a windbreak. The following day, when news arrived of a 'more sheltered and groovy site down the road in the shadow of Silbury Hill... England's Great Pyramid', they duly relocated, enjoying 'lots of good vibes and sunshine flying about.' The Tibetans' diary entry, from their 'Book of the Road', pointed out that 'although it's still quite a small gathering, from what we've been told it's the most that's ever happened at Avebury, and from little acorns and all that, who knows?' The following morning, however, shortly after they opened their free tea kitchen, 'in rolled the pigs and told everyone to fuck off or else!' (Shark 2003q)

Pagan gatherings

More prominent than the travellers were the increasingly diverse gatherings of pagan women who had been attracted to Avebury by Michael Dames. At Lughnasa, in August 1984, under the salacious headline 'Naked women moon worshippers who invaded Avebury at the weekend are gone', a newspaper reported that '40 hippy women, many with children, arrived in the stone-circled village on Friday for a weekend of open-air worship.' The report described how, on the Saturday and the Sunday, 'the women, some of them topless as they walked, made their way to the Ridgeway', where 'they danced naked in the sunshine and for moonlight rituals too.' Afterwards, the locals were reluctant to discuss the 'hippy invasion.' One woman told the reporter, 'We want to keep it low-key because we don't want this type of event becoming too well-known.' (Weird Wiltshire 2003)

It was a vain hope. At Beltane 1985, just a month before the dreadful events of the Beanfield, 200 women gathered on Silbury Hill for a three-day pilgrimage to Stonehenge. Most were connected with the peace camp at Greenham Common, and Linda Lee, who wrote an article about the walk for *Festival Eye*, declared optimistically that it was 'a revival of a long-standing tradition... performed hundreds

Silbury Hill.
Copyright Andy Worthington.

and possibly thousands of years ago by women to link up the energies between Avebury and Stonehenge.' The Beltane Walk was the pagan peace movement personified. The women chanted, sang and danced on the summit of Silbury and 'asked the Goddess to bless us with cosmic energy and through us to join it with the energy of the earth so that we might become cauldrons in an alchemical marriage.' (Lee 1986: 17)

On the first day they walked across the Vale of Pewsey, camping on the edge of the MoD land on Salisbury Plain, where they ran up against a wall of police on the following morning. Clearly disorientated by a mass of women singing, 'We are the flow and we are the earth, We are the weavers and we are the web, We are the flow and we are the earth, We are the witches back from the dead', the police escorted the women across the plain to within four miles of Stonehenge, where they finally decided to stop them for good. Three times, however, the women slipped through the police lines, reaching the monument unmolested, and on the final day they 'went into Stonehenge and performed an anarchic ritual', with many of them staying overnight, sleeping in the stone circle under the light of a full moon while 'the authorities made no attempt to stop them.' (Lee 1986: 17)

From separatism to Starhawk

Significantly, one of the women on 1985's Beltane Walk, 'the woman focalising our rituals', in Linda Lee's words, was the American witch Starhawk. Born Miriam Simos,

Starhawk was a Californian who had been trained in Gardnerian Wicca and initiated into one of its North American derivations. She came to prominence with *The Spiral Dance*, published in 1979, which became the best-selling book on witchcraft to date, replacing *Witchcraft Today* as 'the model text for would-be witches.' In many ways, *The Spiral Dance* represented the coming of age of modern paganism, a significant step forward from the developments at the start of the decade, when the United States had begun to dominate the growth of the new religion through the work of radical feminist writers like Mary Daly and Andrea Dworkin. Daly and Dworkin had used the potent mythology of the European witch-hunts and the matriarchal religion of the Neolithic to create a separatist feminist movement of such contemporary political urgency that for the most part, as Ronald Hutton described it, witchcraft was 'a symbol without a practice in most feminism.' (Hutton 1999: 344-5; Daly 1973; Dworkin 1974)

The first significant modification to the rhetoric of American paganism in the 1970s came with the emergence of Zsuzsanna Budapest, a Hungarian by birth, and 'the daughter of a psychic who had taught her how to work ritual magic', who reintroduced a vital spiritual dimension to the movement, albeit one that still excluded men. Her version of Gerald Gardner's creation, Dianic Wicca (named after the goddess who shunned men) included rituals and tools derived from its British predecessor, but with 'the crucial distinction that only a goddess was revered and only women were admitted.' For Budapest, the essence of spiritual liberation for women was 'to abide in an all-female energy environment, to read no male writers, to listen to no male voices, to pray to no male gods.' (Hutton 1999: 344–5; Budapest 1979: 168)

What Starhawk brought back to paganism was a renewed balance of female and male energies, an updated reinterpretation of the leaning towards the feminine (though not to the exclusion of the male) that had been one of Gardner's most radical bequests in the first place. For Starhawk, as Ronald Hutton described it, 'the coven could be turned into a training group in which women could be liberated, men re-educated, and new forms of human relationship explored which were free of the old gender stereotypes and power structures.' (Hutton 1999: 346)

To her credit, Starhawk managed to reintegrate men without compromising her position as a spiritual leader of women, caught up in the forefront of the peace movement against the proliferation of nuclear weapons. Her feelings about Stonehenge, published in 1987's *Truth or Dare* (a response to her involvement in the peace movement that brims over with apocalyptic rage) reveal the manner in which she achieved this, leading a women's pilgrimage but identifying the monument with the wider environmental concerns of humanity as a whole: 'I found myself crying with deep, deep sobs and saying to myself "It's been so long! It's been so long!" As if I could feel the earth was so hurt and damaged, and the spirit of the stones was there to help us and yet it felt weak and tired and overwhelmed by the magnitude of the destruction.' (Starhawk 1987: 252)

The British Druid Order (Emma Restall Orr, left) performs a
goddess ceremony at the portal stones, vernal equinox 2003.
Copyright Andy Worthington.

The development of paganism

With hindsight, the separatist tendencies of paganism and the peace movement in the 1970s and early 1980s were a crucial phase in the empowerment of women. However, the reintegration of female and male energies promoted by Starhawk enabled the new religion to expand at an unprecedented rate. A particularly influential development at this time was the Fellowship of Isis, 'an international, multi-faithed organization that is dedicated to honouring the Goddess in Her many forms.' First established in Ireland on the vernal equinox in 1976 by Olivia Robertson and her brother Lawrence (both of whom had long-established connections with other key figures in Druidry and Wicca, including Ross Nichols and Gerald Gardner), the Fellowship of Isis rapidly became 'the largest and most creative goddess-centred movement in the world.' It expanded throughout the following decades to include new societies – the Noble Order of Tara, which maintained an environmental focus, and the Druid Clan of Dana, which became most closely involved with Stonehenge. The Fellowship also joined the Council of British Druid Orders, remaining as a member after the schism that led to the departure of OBOD and the BDO. By 2002, when it had over 20,000 members in 96 countries, it was by far the largest member of the Council. (Robertson 2003; Carr-Gomm 1991: 32; Faery Faith Network 2003)

In addition to the expansion of Goddess movements and the various strands of Druidry introduced in the previous chapter, new traditions also arose that were drawn explicitly from Norse and Anglo-Saxon mythology. Generally known as heathenism, these Northern traditions include a number of belief systems – Odinism, Asatru and Vanatru, for example – that are drawn from ancient Norse sources, although, typically, the situation is complicated by the fact that no single term is acceptable to all the groups, and some Odinists, for example, refuse to refer to themselves as heathens. (For a more detailed analysis, see Harvey 2000: 49–64)

In the same way that the Druid groups came together to form COBDO, the many facets of the new paganism were represented by an umbrella organisation called the Pagan Federation, which arose from the ashes of an earlier organisation – the Pagan Front – in 1981, under the enthusiastic and capable leadership of Leonora James (better-known by her pseudonym, Prudence Jones), a high priestess of Gardnerian Wicca and a graduate of Cambridge University with a background in philosophy and the classics, who brought an 'intellectual rigour' to the field that was 'generally lacking in British pagan witchcraft at the time.' The Pagan Federation became particularly prominent in 1988, when it was 'refounded with a larger and more formal structure', and Vivienne Crowley, another Wiccan high priestess who was also 'an accomplished poetess' and 'a very proficient Jungian psychologist', became secretary. James and Crowley embarked on a campaign of 'bombarding national and local politicians, the mass media, and educational institutions, with objective information about British Paganism', adding enormously to the appeal of the new religion, as well as helping to fend off disturbing and unfounded allegations of child sexual abuse that were being spread by American Christian evangelists in an attempt to discredit paganism as a whole. The following year, the mainstream acceptance of paganism in the UK was signalled when Crowley was invited to conduct a pagan ceremony as part of a multi-faith festival in Canterbury Cathedral. (Hutton 1999: 371–4)

The Gorsedd of Bards of Caer Abiri

This coming together of different faiths continued at Avebury at the autumn equinox in 1993, when Tim Sebastian of the Secular Order of Druids organised a multi-faith conference at which the Gorsedd of Bards of Caer Abiri was established. Based in the stone circles, the Gorsedd centred on a ceremony composed and conducted by Philip Shallcrass of the British Druid Order, using parts of Edward William's Primrose Hill ceremony of 1792, and it soon became a regular occurrence, taking place on the festival days of the eight-fold year, with representatives from 'many different spiritual traditions including Druids, Witches, Christians, Buddhists, Hindus, Heathens, Baha'i and Shamans.' (Shallcrass and Orr 2000)

The egalitarianism of the gatherings was summed up in an article by Philip Shallcrass and Emma Restall Orr – who became Joint Chief of the BDO in 1995 after meeting Shallcrass at the first Avebury Gorsedd. 'The multiplicity of faiths are recognised as equal and offered the opportunity to express their own spirituality within the Gorsedd circle. Each gathering begins with a call for peace, after which representatives of the different traditions call to the four cardinal directions, each in

The Gorsedd of Bards of Caer Abiri.
The British Druid Order celebrates the vernal equinox, 2003.
Copyright Andy Worthington.

their own way. So we might have a Christian prayer offered at the east, a shamanic chant at the south, a Wiccan call to the west and a prayer to Odin and Freya in the north. Thus we express the essential unity that weaves together in one circle those who seek the spiritual in their lives.' (Shallcrass and Orr 2000)

From humble beginnings, with twenty-five Bards initiated at the first event, the Gorseddau grew at an astonishing rate. Within five years, they were regularly attracting a thousand participants, becoming what Ronald Hutton described as the 'central event' of the new Druidry. Clearly inspired, the BDO initiated Gorseddau at several other locations: the Long Man of Wilmington (Caer Garanhir, Beltane 1997), Dragon Hill below the Uffington White Horse (Caer Rhiannon, Midsummer 1997), Stonehenge (Cor Gawr, Lughnasa 1997), the Rollrights (Caer Rhigor, Midsummer 1998), as well as a few oddities that must have stretched the Celtic lexicon to breaking point: Volunteer Park, Seattle (Caer Pugetia, Earth Day, 20 April 1997), and Milton Keynes (Caer Troia, Imbolc 1998). (Shallcrass and Orr 2000)

The Dongas and Twyford Down

No discussion of the growing awareness of sacred sites would be complete without an analysis of another development that erupted spontaneously in 1992, but that clearly owed much of its impetus to the combination of paganism and political protest conceived by the travelling community and the women of Greenham Common in the 1980s. This was the road protest movement, and from the beginning

The Dongas at Twyford Down. Copyright Adrian Arbib.

it demonstrated a raw, untutored paganism that went further than any previous protest movement in embracing the concept of the whole of the earth as a sacred landscape.

The story began in February 1992, when two young travellers, a woman called Sam and a man called Steph, pitched camp on Twyford Down near Winchester, an expanse of rolling chalk downland that was both a haven for wildlife and a repository of thousands of years of human history, including ancient tracks and Celtic field systems. The travellers were pleased to discover that this idyllic landscape was 'the most protected landscape in southern England', officially designated an Area of Outstanding Natural Beauty and a Site of Special Scientific Interest, and they were dismayed when a local rambler told them that an extension to the M3 was shortly to be driven through it. As it turned out, local people had been campaigning against the proposed extension for twenty years, writing letters, submitting petitions, lobbying parliament, mounting legal challenges and contributing to a public inquiry. The road scheme had even been the subject of an official complaint by the European Union, but this too had been ignored by the Department of Transport. (Road Alert! 1995; Monbiot 1997)

Sam and Steph resolved to take matters into their own hands, setting up a protest camp that immediately began to draw other supporters: 'travellers, environmentalists, students, pagans, even businessmen and Tory councillors, from all over the country.' The Twyford Down protest was the first outing for the British off-shoot of Earth First!, an American direct action group, and support also came from Friends of the Earth, but it was the passion and ingenuity of the traveller-

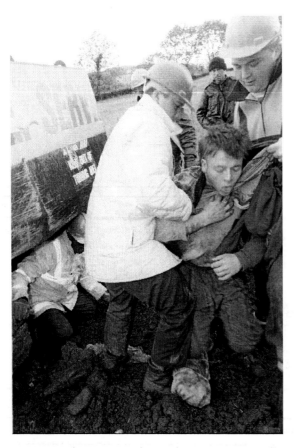

Violence at Solsbury Hill, 1994. A protestor is dragged from under plant machinery by private security guards. Copyright Adrian Arbib.

protestors that was to have the most resounding impact. In the early days, they contented themselves with digging defensive trenches, chaining themselves to earth-moving equipment and forming human chains across the landscape, but as the threat grew more severe, so too did their responses, and they were soon leaping onto moving machinery and hurling themselves into the path of the road-builders' giant trucks. It was these actions that finally drew the attention of the national press, who soon came up with an apposite name for them – the 'Dongas Tribe', derived from a South African word for a track, which had, ironically enough, been given to the ancient tracks that criss-crossed the landscape of Twyford Down by a teacher at the public school in Winchester that had sold the land to the DoT in the first place. (Monbiot 1997; Cryer 1993)

After ten months, the protestors were violently evicted from their camp by Group 4 Security on 9 December 1992, a day that became known as Yellow Wednesday. The naturalist David Bellamy, who had come to Twyford Down as a high profile political campaigner, witnessed the brutal events of that day, and his description echoed the shock experienced by Nick Davies at the Beanfield seven years before: 'I have been in many protests around the world in some very hairy countries and have never seen such unreasonable force used, especially on women. These boys were putting the boot and fist in and they didn't care if they were men or women. There were ministry people there but no one tried to call them off. The security men went completely

The desecration of nature at Solsbury Hill, 1994. Sally, a protestor, lies exhausted on the ravaged ground where trees once grew. Copyright Adrian Arbib.

over the top.' All that had changed in seven years, it seemed, was that a quasi-military police force had been replaced by a private security firm that was, if anything, even less accountable for its actions than its predecessors. (*The Guardian*, 15 December 1992)

Undeterred, the Dongas reformed their protest camp in February 1993, and direct action took place on a daily basis throughout the spring and summer, culminating in a site invasion by over 500 people on 4 July, two days after the DoT and Tarmac were granted a High Court injunction that led to the subsequent imprisonment of ten of the protestors. Significantly, however, their actions had already inspired other people, and throughout the country protest camps sprang up at the site of almost every road project proposed by the government.

The growth of the road protest movement

In June 1993, for example, protests against the construction of a toll bridge connecting the Isle of Skye to the Scottish mainland combined ecological issues (the destruction of Europe's second largest otter colony) with the first actions against the newly launched Private Finance Initiative (PFI), whereby the Bank of America bankrolled and profited from the bridge's construction. That same month, at Cradlewell, the site of a proposed bypass near Newcastle, a group calling themselves

'Kill the Bill', rally against the Criminal Justice Bill, summer 1993.
Photo provided by Chris Riley.

the Flowerpot Tribe began a sustained occupation of trees, a tactic that was to become increasingly influential as the protest movement grew. (Road Alert! 1995)

By September, the campaign had spread to London, where protests against the creation of a link road for the M11 through east London ran for two years, involving the occupation of entire streets of condemned houses and the creation of the 'Autonomous Area of Wanstonia' and 'Leytonstonia', independent mini-states complete with their own passports. In March 1994, after further large-scale protests at Twyford Down on 28–29 November 1993 and 3 January 1994, the Dongas turned their attention to Solsbury Hill on the outskirts of Bath, an Iron Age hill-fort that was to be cut into by a bypass that would also destroy miles of precious water-meadows and woodland, and in May the first protests against the M65 Blackburn bypass took place, at which tree-houses linked by high-level walkways were set up to protect the ancient woodland and bluebell dells of the Stanworth valley. (Road Alert! 1995)

In the months before the Criminal Justice Bill was passed, the protests intensified. As the journalist and activist George Monbiot noted, the legislation, which was 'crude, ill-drafted and repressive', had succeeded in creating 'the broadest, and oddest, counter-cultural coalition Britain has ever known', uniting 'Hunt saboteurs, peace protestors, football supporters, squatters, radical lawyers, gypsies, pensioners, ravers, disabled rights activists, even an assistant chief constable and a Tory ex-minister.' (Monbiot 1997)

On 2 July 1994, 5,000 people attended a mass trespass at Twyford Down, and another large demonstration took place on 18 July in Norfolk, where protestors calling themselves 'The Lizard Tribe' had been campaigning for a year against an expansion of the A11. In August, a protest camp was established on the Pollok Estate in Glasgow ('Pollok Free State') to protect a city amenity space from the development

Fusion of humanity and nature: a protestor and tree-houses in the Stanworth valley, 1994. Copyright Adrian Arbib.

of the M77, and in September protests began against a new stretch of the A30 in Devon, including, at the Fairmile camp, the first instance of elaborate underground tunnels that would collapse on the occupants if heavy machinery was deployed. In July and October, national demonstrations against the Bill in London drew crowds of over 100,000 people, and on 3 November, the day that it became law, numerous protests took place across the country, including an invasion of the M11 construction site by over 300 protestors. (Road Alert! 1995)

'The carving up of the Great Mother'

Although the Dongas provided inspiration for a grass-roots political movement of astonishing intensity that spread across the country in a matter of months, for the most part the political impulse arose as a result of a profound spiritual response to the agenda of the road builders. The majority of those who came to the road protest movement embraced the concept of the earth as sacred, opposing the government's road expansion plans as 'the carving up of the "Great Mother".' (Cryer 1993)

For some, this concept had undoubtedly filtered through from the ecological paganism of the anti-nuclear protests of the 1980s, but for others it was simply a visceral response to what they perceived as nothing short of the rape of the land. Gary, a former computer technician who took to the road at the end of 1992 and discovered the Dongas camp on Twyford Down shortly after, described his response to the bulldozers stripping the turf on Yellow Wednesday as 'like seeing a person having the skin pulled off alive', and lamented that 'in a matter of hours, what took our Great Mother Nature thousands of years to create was torn apart.' (Dongas 1995a)

If the earth as the Great Mother or Mother Nature was at the heart of the road protestors' pagan belief system, it was backed up by a range of other responses that reflected the majority of the influences that had been absorbed by paganism and the earth mysteries movement in the preceding decades. When the DoT began destroying the down in December 1992, Alex Plows 'experienced a vortex of energy ascend from the land and enter each of them', a force that she likened to 'the energy of the Dragon.' For Indra, the parallels were with indigenous people the world over: 'My mind has merged with the ancient tribes of the Americas, aboriginal and African peoples', and Niamh, who was part of the Solsbury Hill protest, focused on the Hopi prophesy that 'when the earth is sick, a tribe of people will come who will restore the earth to her beauty.' (Dongas 1995b, 1995c)

For others, the parallels were with England's mythical past. Gary recalled the camp on Twyford Down as 'a magic place – as if I had gone back in time to the Celts', and Kevin Jarvis, a resident of Solsbury Hill for whom the protest was a life-changing experience, described the arrival of the first protestors with 'their matted hair and earth-coloured clothing' as 'an ancient Celtic army warped forwards in time and preparing for battle.' Anna, who was 'awestruck' when she first met the Dongas in February 1993, found a different historical parallel, declaring, 'I imagine that a person would feel the same way if they met Robin Hood', and Geoff, who was part of the campaign for Solsbury Hill, was concerned to 'restore the balance of the sacred land of Albion.' (Dongas 1995a, 1995d, 1995b, 1995e)

The Dongas and the ritual year

The protestors also adopted the eight-fold ritual year developed by Ross Nichols and the Wiccans. Gary described 'following the old pagan calendar of pre-Christian England, which is very dear to me now, as with anyone who is close to Nature.' In 1992, a fortnight after the events of Yellow Wednesday, the Dongas held a winter solstice celebration at the Cerne Abbas Giant in Dorset, and in 1994 the protest camp on Solsbury Hill was convened immediately after a spring equinox party on Twyford Down, and was followed by a large Beltane gathering, which included a party in Worley Lodge, 'a rather fine country retreat' whose owners had been obliged to sell their property to the DoT, but who had given their keys to the Dongas instead. For this new wave of protestors, Stonehenge once more assumed a central symbolic position, partly through the post-Beanfield mythology of the martyred festival, but primarily because of the enduring attraction of the monument and its solar mechanism. Gary described Stonehenge as 'one big, stone calendar – one of the most historic places in the world', and added that 'travellers meet there because of the celebration of summer.' (Dongas 1995a; Cryer 1993; Dongas 1995f)

To be strictly accurate, what Gary should have said was that travellers would have met there had it not been for the exclusion zone. Alex Plows recalled how she and others were effectively forced to abandon Stonehenge, as they were unwilling to spend the solstice 'having a ruck with the police.' She added, 'It was hardly like we were depoliticised – most of us were having a break from protest camps for a couple of weeks... We needed down time, to recharge in a sacred landscape.' The alternative sacred landscape chosen by the Dongas was Avebury, where, unlike Stonehenge, people were 'having lovely times in a more amenable landscape every summer', and the Dongas in particular were 'hanging out... in this semi-permanent state of magic reality... in West Woods, near the whole Avebury/West Kennet/Silbury Hill arena... a whole bunch of us living in benders deep in the woods, wandering all over the landscape on moonlit nights.' (Plows 2003)

The Tan Hill Fair

At Lughnasa in 1995, on the Marlborough Downs to the south of Avebury, the Dongas attempted to revive the Tan Hill Fair, which had last taken place in 1932. They were clearly inspired by Michael Dames, who had devoted a chapter of *The Avebury Cycle* to the fair, noting that it had taken place on St Anne's Day (6 August) for over 500 years (beginning with its mention in a Charter Roll of 1499), and suggesting, by relating St Anne to the Celtic goddess Aine, that it was a survival from the Neolithic, and that it was originally dedicated to the Great Goddess. (Dames 1977: 210–18)

Thirty members of the Dongas Tribe duly set about establishing a vibrant modern-day revival. Accompanied by goats and donkeys, they dragged handcarts and bow-topped wagons to the top of the hill, where they were soon stopped by the police, who arrived with six riot vans, three dog vans and a helicopter. According to George Monbiot, 'As the revellers trooped back down the hill, the officer in charge said, "When will you realise that this is Wiltshire, and you don't belong here?"' Faced with a familiar animosity, the Dongas did as the travellers had for two decades, relocating in an old green lane two miles away, where 'For three days 200 people rode horses with painted flanks and plaited tails, drank mead, [and] danced to the music of fiddles and mandolins... before they were thrown off by the police again.' (Monbiot 1996a)

The Land Is Ours

The Dongas subsequently disappeared into the green lanes on a more or less permanent basis, but the movement they had inspired led to the government largely abandoning its £19 billion programme of road expansion, and the passion for land reform that they revived, which stretched back to Gerrard Winstanley via Sid Rawle and Stonehenge, was sustained through the activities of a number of campaigning groups, in particular a coalition of volunteers known as The Land Is Ours (TLIO), whose campaigns included two separate occupations of land near St George's Hill in Surrey, where Winstanley's Diggers had begun their short-lived but influential campaign in 1649, and the establishment of an eco-village on thirteen acres of derelict land in Wandsworth.

The occupations of St George's Hill, which took place in 1995 and 1999, were largely symbolic gestures of communal living and farming that were designed to

*The New Diggers commemorate Gerrard Winstanley,
St George's Hill, Surrey, 1999. Copyright Alan Lodge.*

stimulate publicity and debate. The first occupation, which was TLIO's first major outing, only lasted a week, but during that time 600 volunteers occupied a disused airfield and set-aside land and managed to raise a temporary village, dig gardens, perform a play and distribute information in the neighbouring towns. The media coverage was favourable, and in George Monbiot's opinion they 'succeeded in generating the first stirrings of a national debate about land.' 300 activists returned on the 350th anniversary of Winstanley's occupation, hoping to raise a stone marker commemorating his achievements, and once more occupying a small corner of the hill. This second occupation, which took place under the glare of a high-profile media spotlight, lasted a month, but on both occasions the campaigners' evictions were resonant with irony: the injunctions that were used to remove them were raised by the inhabitants of a luxury housing development that now occupies most of the common land where Gerrard Winstanley first began his bold experiment at land reform. (Monbiot 1996b; TLIO 2002)

The Wandsworth eco-village, on the other hand, was nothing less than a practical demonstration of a viable alternative community. Lasting for five and a half months in 1996 before its eviction, the village was established on land owned by Guinness that was earmarked for the development of 'the 9th major superstore within a radius of a mile and a half.' It was one of the last major outings for John Pendragon, whose energy and enthusiasm provided a thread uniting thirty years of activism. The campaigners' recycled homes, gardens reclaimed from the wasteland, and ritual landscaping – including a large stone spiral and a small reminder of Stonehenge

*John Pendragon at the
Wandsworth eco-village.
Copyright Adrian Arbib.*

made of bricks – drew thousands of visitors from home and abroad and admiring profiles in a wide variety of newspapers and magazines. (TLIO 2002)

In the meantime, the new coalitions of spiritual and political campaigners continued to be drawn to Avebury and Stonehenge. At Avebury, Ronald Hutton observed that 'more and more travellers were starting to camp in the Avebury area for the festivals. They weren't coming there because of the Druids or the Gorsedd, they were coming because of the spiritual impulse, the worship of the land.' At Stonehenge, where the exclusion zone ensured that the political remained inseparable from the spiritual for the majority of those seeking access, the pressure on English Heritage continued to grow. (Hutton 1998: 186)

*Brickhenge at Wandsworth.
Copyright Adrian Arbib.*

Chapter Twelve

Negotiation

VE Day Celebrations 1995

In the immediate aftermath of the passing of the Criminal Justice Act (CJA) in November 1994, the pattern of protest at Stonehenge continued uninterrupted. At the winter solstice in 1994 and the spring equinox in 1995, a coalition of familiar protestors – Druids, travellers and free festival agitators – gathered outside the perimeter fence to complain about their continued exclusion and to celebrate the turning points of the solar year, and on 8 May 1995, the fiftieth anniversary of VE Day, a well-planned dawn invasion by 400 people resulted in the first large gathering in the stones since the autumn equinox in 1990.

The occupation was conceived as a symbolically laden response to the CJA, with the organisers stressing their belief that 'the freedoms that our nation fought for during

'God Save the Queen': a celebrant flies a flag, VE Day Celebrations 1995.
Copyright Adrian Arbib.

'Lest we forget': VE Day Celebrations 1995.
Copyright Adrian Arbib.

the war' were being eroded by the Act. It was planned the summer before as a direct result of the mingling of the older campaigners with the new wave of protestors at the road protest camps, and on the day the established campaigners for access to Stonehenge were joined by members of the Dongas, including Theo, who sang his 'Motorway Song', which had become an anthem of the new movement at Twyford Down, and Kevin Jarvis, the Solsbury Hill resident whose meeting with the tribe the year before had been a life-changing experience. (Jarvis 1995)

The surprise for all present was that at 8 a.m., Clews Everard, English Heritage's Stonehenge Manager, agreed to the protestors' request to be allowed to stay in the stones until dusk. Clews made it clear that 'although the protestors were unwelcome, she wanted to avoid conflict at all costs', and she told the gathering that 'The long-term aim and vision of English Heritage is to open up the stones for everybody to enjoy. But this is a long-term vision and it will only work if people like yourselves work with us, rather than against us.' (Jarvis 1995)

The rest of the day duly passed without confrontation. Picnics were unpacked, people sang and played instruments, and other members of the public, allowed in for a reduced fee, seemed to be pleased with 'the entertainment provided by the colourful occupying throng.' As a naked woman walked by, one security guard was heard to exclaim, 'I know English Heritage must be having kittens, but I'm going to enjoy every minute', and by mid-afternoon, in Kevin Jarvis' words, 'everybody had settled into a series of concentric circles. At the epicentre was a group of musicians surrounded by a ring of exuberant dancers who were in turn encompassed by a sea of recumbent picnickers.' (Jarvis 1995; Goodwin 1995)

The Criminal Justice Act and the 'Stonehenge Two'

Despite the euphoria of the VE Day occupation and Kevin Jarvis' hope that 'the diplomacy and understanding of Monday the 8th indicates a way forward', it was a short-lived victory. On 1 June, the tenth anniversary of the Battle of the Beanfield, two people – Margaret Jones and Richard Lloyd, a lecturer and a student – were arrested at Stonehenge during a demonstration against the CJA at which banners declaring 'Free Stonehenge', 'Never Again' and 'Stonehenge Campaign 10 Years of Criminal Injustice' were displayed. Significantly, they were charged with 'trespassory assembly' under the first use of Section 70 of the CJA, which amended Section 14 of the 1986 Public Order Act so that 'police can ban groups of twenty or more meeting in a particular area if they fear 'serious disruption to the life of the community', even if the meeting is non-obstructive and non-violent.' (Irvine 1999: 1; *The Guardian*, 24 January 1997)

In the days prior to the demonstration, Salisbury District Council had made an order under the new amendments prohibiting 'trespassory assemblies' at Stonehenge for a four-day period from 29 May, and at 6.40 p.m. on 1 June, after Police Inspector Mackie counted twenty-one people and cautioned them that they constituted a 'trespassory assembly', the majority of those present moved away. Jones and Lloyd stayed, 'to put their rights to the test', as Derry Irvine, the Lord Chancellor, later described it, and were duly arrested. (Irvine 1999: 1)

Convicted by magistrates in Salisbury on 3 October 1995, Jones and Lloyd had their sentences dismissed on appeal on 4 January 1996. In its judgment, Salisbury Crown Court held that the protestors 'were not obstructing the freedom of movement of others on the verge nor were they causing a public nuisance' and concluded that, as they were not 'being destructive, violent, disorderly, threatening a breach of the peace or, on the evidence, doing anything other than reasonably using the highway', there was no case to answer. (Lord Hutton 1999: 38)

This time the police appealed, and the retrial, which concluded in January 1997, went their way. The implications were alarming. In *The Guardian*, Alex Bellos warned that 'People attending a wide range of peaceful gatherings, including environmental protestors and ramblers' groups, can be arrested for doing nothing more than walking down the road, following a High Court judgement yesterday.' John Wadham, the director of Liberty (formerly the National Council for Civil Liberties), was equally appalled, declaring that 'A peaceful, non-obstructive gathering is a reasonable use of a public highway. To say that it is a form of trespass seems extraordinary.' (*The Guardian*, 24 January 1997)

Twelve years before, there had been no effective legislation to stop a festival of 40,000 people occupying the fields across the road from Stonehenge; now, just two people on the verge of a road could be arrested for doing nothing.

Arthur Pendragon: road protests, new Druids and the exclusion zone

Three weeks after the arrest of Jones and Lloyd, on the eve of the summer solstice, Arthur Pendragon was the third person to be arrested under the terms of the new Act

Protestors at Newbury disabling a contractor's crane. Copyright Adrian Arbib.

– and the first to be acquitted when the case came before Salisbury Magistrates' Court in September. As in previous years, members of the Warband were sent on a simultaneous quest to highlight the ongoing injustice of the exclusion zone, and on this occasion they excelled themselves, chaining up the doors of Fortress House, English Heritage's London headquarters, and making the front page of *The Independent*, under the headline 'Druid's Stonehenge Revenge.' (Pendragon 1999a; Pendragon and Stone 2003: 108)

The next few years saw an extraordinary increase in Arthur's activities, both against the exclusion zone at Stonehenge and as part of the road protest movement, which he had first become involved in at Beltane 1993, when one of the members of the Dongas camp on Twyford Down had invited him to conduct a ceremony. On the basis that if anyone needed his help, they had only to shout, 'Oy mush, get your bum over here and give us a hand', Arthur duly turned up and held a ceremony at dawn, accompanied by Tim Sebastian, Rollo Maughfling and a black, dread-locked biker called Parsley, who had been the first person to join the Warband and who stayed on with the Dongas after the Beltane event. Later that morning, when the diggers arrived and the Dongas were busy diving in front of the equipment and chaining themselves to it, Arthur and the other Druids joined in, recognising kindred spirits. Arthur led a charge, throwing off the security guards who tried to restrain him, and the whole

*Arthur Pendragon on one of
the thirty-nine occasions that
he was arrested at Newbury as
part of the 'Camelot Pact', a
deliberate attempt to overload
the legal system by filling the
local jails with protestors.
Copyright Adrian Arbib.*

gathering held a wild party when the diggers withdrew for the day. (Russell 1996; Pendragon and Stone 2003: 127–9)

Arthur subsequently attended other road protests on an occasional basis. At Beltane 1994, he was at Solsbury Hill, accompanied by Tim, Rollo and Pixi, the Warband's chief Minstrel and Bard, and in 1995 he was arrested again under the terms of the CJA at a protest camp at Whatley Quarry (and acquitted again in April 1996). In early 1996 he embraced the struggle on a full-time basis, joining the largest action to date, the campaign against the A34 Newbury bypass, which became known as the Third Battle of Newbury (the first two having taken place during the Civil War). (Andrews 2003; Pendragon 1999a)

Pixie Camp, where Arthur and his companions set up resistance, was just one of thirty camps established along the nine-mile route, an irreplaceable expanse of woodland, wildlife and streams, whose diversity was reflected in the names of the camps – Mary Hare, Tot Hill, Snelsmore Common, Castle Wood, Middle Oak, Granny Ash, Rickety Bridge, Redding's Copse – and the roll-call of protestors, ranging from 'radical anarchist vegans to animal rights activists to drop-out losers to spaced-out mystics to free-party people [and] reincarnated Arthurian Knights', according to Arthur and C.J. Stone. (Pendragon and Stone 2003: 140)

Evicted from Pixie Camp after a fierce struggle in which Arthur found himself halfway up a tree resisting the blandishments of a chainsaw operative by knighting him in mid-air, Arthur and his companions set up a new camp, Camelot (a new kind of castle for a new kind of king) and when this too was evicted the whole troupe moved on to Gotan, an off-road site that had been planted as a garden. It was here that Arthur met Kreb Dragonrider (or Mog-Ur Kreb Dragonrider to give him his full name). Described by Arthur and C.J. Stone as 'one of life's eternal innocents, a lesson to us all', Kreb was possessed of 'a kind of holy seriousness, a reverence, an innocence and reserve.' Profoundly deaf in one ear and partially deaf in the other, he had attended a local school for the deaf and knew the area intimately. Initially drawn to the protest camps out of curiosity, he found his vocation – 'to fight for the earth' – in Arthur's company, and became a devoted member of the Warband, establishing his own order – the South Downs Dragon Order of Druids – in 1998. (Pendragon and Stone 2003: 156)

Kreb was the latest in a wave of converts to the new Druidry. At the end of 1995, Veronica Hammond, who had pursued a Bardic course with OBOD until she found it 'dry and hierarchical', founded the Cotswold Order (COD) in the presence of Arthur and Tim Sebastian, and in the early days of the Newbury protests Arthur also met Hengist McStone, who established the Ancient and Modern Order of Druids. Hengist informed me that 'at Newbury I had become a civil disobedient and had lost my inhibitions', and he brought a fierce passion to the struggle for Stonehenge. Angered that 'a generation were criminalized by the "Solstice Operation"', and concerned that 'as the assault on civil rights grew each year the media became less and less concerned until only a handful of people knew about it', he was determined to challenge what he saw a 'a civil state of emergency.' (Hammond 2003; McStone 2002)

At the solstice, Arthur led the most concerted assault on the exclusion zone to date, a multi-pronged barrage of intruders approaching the temple from all directions. Arthur memorably made a citizen's arrest on the superintendent who arrested him, declaring that 'this arrest, this road block, and this so-called exclusion zone is illegal under articles 9, 10, 11 and 14 of the European Convention on Human Rights. As a European citizen I am making a citizen's arrest. In other words... you're nicked son!' By the end of the night, thirteen fully-robed Druids – and fourteen other followers – had been arrested, including Rollo Maughfling, Tim Sebastian, Dylan Ap Thuin, Hengist McStone, Stephen King 'the Lone Druid', and three key members of the Warband – Galahad, Pixi and the Orc. (Pendragon and Stone 2003: 113; Pendragon 2000)

A schism in Avebury

This period, when Arthur was taking the Druid movement deeper into radical political territory, was the time that the gulf between the members of the Council of British Druid Orders and the other Druid organisations became an unbridgeable chasm. When the Newbury protests started, one of the Druids outside Arthur's immediate circle issued a statement to the press in which, according to Arthur and C.J. Stone, he 'said words to the effect that, 'We're Druids, we're not political, and

Arthur Pendragon addresses a Druid circle, Avebury, vernal equinox 2003.
Copyright Andy Worthington.

although we feel for the trees we have no views on whether the Newbury bypass should be built or not'.' In C.J.'s interpretation, 'the Druid movement is split between those who will consecrate trees, but never get up a tree to defend it, and those who will both consecrate and defend the trees.' (Pendragon and Stone 2003: 132, 118)

After the meltdown that led to OBOD and the BDO leaving the Council, the lingering conflict between the two camps came to a head at the Gorsedd of Caer Abiri at Beltane 1997, although it was precipitated, ironically, not by conflict between individual Druids but by pressure from the general public. As Ronald Hutton described it, 'The congregation shouted down the political Druids when they began giving speeches upon the progress of campaigns over Stonehenge and road building schemes. The vast majority of people at Avebury wanted to have a spiritual experience, they wanted the processions, the ceremonies of naming and blessing, the music – they didn't want orators and soap-boxers shouting at them.' (Hutton 1998: 186)

A fraught atmosphere prevailed over the rest of the weekend. Tempers flared, and the spectre of a Stonehenge-like exclusion zone was unexpectedly raised when Chris Gingell, the National Trust manager, became embroiled in the conflict, adding to the tension by making a public speech in which he expressed his concern about five youngsters he had discovered lighting a fire on the summit of Silbury Hill the night before, watched over – 'benevolently', as Ronald Hutton put it – by a certain Druid Chief. Unfortunately, according to Hutton, Gingell 'said the wrong things to the company, went on far too long, and gave an impression of blaming the Druids collectively', and it was only through furious back-tracking on Gingell's part and the intervention of Philip Shallcrass and Hutton himself that a 'Battle of Avebury' was averted, and separate days were agreed for future Gorseddau – Arthur and the 'political' Druids on the nearest Saturday to the festival days, and Philip Shallcrass and his company on the Sunday. (Hutton 1998: 186–7)

The Round Table and the Truth and Reconciliation Committee

Despite the conflict at Avebury, the struggle for free and unrestricted access to Stonehenge remained firmly focused on Arthur, and it was only through his persistence that progress began to be made on the quarter days that had been off-limits since 1990. At the winter solstice in 1996, he finally met with some success, when open access was granted to representatives of COBDO and other members of the general public, although the campaign for access at the summer solstice was still deadlocked, and as that most contentious time of year rolled around again, Arthur was duly arrested once more.

A breakthrough of sorts occurred later that year when the first Round Table meetings were held, instigated, as the name suggests, by Arthur himself. For the first time, representatives of all the major bodies – English Heritage, the National Trust, the Wiltshire police and local and district councils, along with local landowners and farmers – sat down with the Druids and other pagans, to begin the long overdue process of beginning to come to some sort of agreement on access. As Arthur and C.J. Stone described it, 'there were numerous heated exchanges, plus the occasional walk out for dramatic effect.' (Pendragon 2000; Pendragon and Stone 2003: 231)

Despite the wide cross-section of interested parties represented at the Round Table meetings, many travellers and festival-goers felt themselves excluded, primarily because of suspicions and frustrations that were understandably rooted in the breakdown of communication in the late 1980s. In addition, the Round Table was not an open forum, although in truth anyone with an interest in the access arrangements could apply to attend, and would almost certainly have been permitted to do so.

A solution of sorts occurred in 1998, when another regular forum – the Truth and Reconciliation Committee (TRC) – was established by George Firsoff (as part of the Stonehenge Peace Process) and Thomas Daffern, Director of the International Institute of Peace Studies and Global Philosophy. Based on 'the experience and vision that guided the builders of the new South Africa' (a rather lofty aspiration that nevertheless acknowledged the deep scars caused by the ongoing conflict), the TRC was open to all. Its meetings duly attracted a number of travellers and festival-goers, including Paul Aitken and Hilary Jones, as well as local councillor Tim Abbott, representatives of various pagan groups, and other faces familiar from the Round Table – Arthur, Rollo Maughfling and Kreb Dragonrider. The authorities' input was minimal, however, consisting only of sporadic visits from Clews Everard and Superintendent Andy Hollingshead, the head of the South Wiltshire Constabulary. So, despite creating rousing debates and providing a forum for viewpoints that were not being put across at the Round Table, many of those involved could easily feel the real decisions were being made elsewhere. (Firsoff 1998; TRC 2003)

The Druids and Special Access

In the meantime, however, some of the other Druids had already succeeded in negotiating their own access arrangements, and the BDO in particular was adamant

Emma Restall Orr (centre) and Philip Shallcrass (right) conduct a handfasting during a British Druid Order ceremony at Stonehenge, 2002. Photo by Nick Leverton; copyright Theo Tigger.

that its own involvement in discussions with the authorities had been central to the development of a meaningful dialogue. As Philip Shallcrass put it, 'For several years, negotiations between English Heritage and the Council of British Druid Orders were carried on by three officers of the Council from the smaller, more militant groups. They made little progress. At around the time the BDO resigned from the Council, Bobcat [Emma Restall Orr] and I were invited to join the access talks. We were subsequently able to bring representatives of OBOD and the Pagan Federation into the discussions and real progress began to be made.' (Shallcrass 1999: 10)

Emma Restall Orr brought her own particular viewpoint on Stonehenge to these meetings. A late-comer to Stonehenge, she had been working, in the late 1980s, in a solicitor's office that dealt with many of the arrests at the monument, where she had formed the opinion that the temple was 'desecrated ground.' When she joined the BDO she was reluctantly drawn into dealing with Stonehenge, so she wrote a letter to Clews Everard, and a long telephone conversation followed, which resulted in a 'clear and honest relationship.' Her leanings towards spiritual feminism were revealed in the ways she compared and contrasted Avebury with Stonehenge. At Avebury, where she lived for a while, walking in the circle every day at dawn, 'my relationship with the Gods and guardians of the place grew stronger as the cycles flowed. The energy was warm to me, feminine strength, curvaceous and nurturing.' At Stonehenge, however, when she first entered the temple, 'I sensed the energy to be tight, flinched, bitter. Translating my perception, it felt like a reclusive and angry young man.' (Orr 1996)

Although, rather disappointingly, this interpretation of Stonehenge represented a retreat to spiritual sectarianism less than a decade after Starhawk had advocated the temple as a kind of barometer of universal pain, the result of Emma Restall Orr's involvement was that by 1995 both OBOD and the BDO had carved their own niches over the solstice period, securing access – for a small fee – for ceremonies on the Sunday before the solstice and 24 June respectively. After six years of exclusive privilege on the disputed solstice, Loxley's Druids also accepted the compromise, conducting ceremonies on 24 June in 1996 and 1997, and settling for 22 June in 1998, 23 June in 1999, and 22 June from 2000 onwards. Miranda Green described the BDO's first private access as follows: 'on the evening of 24 June 1995, a party of six adult Druids (three men and three women) and two children entered the monument unopposed and proceeded to perform rituals in celebration of Midsummer Day. To the accompaniment of drums, prayers were addressed to the Ancestral Spirits, the Animal Powers and the Four Quarters of the Sacred Circle. Prayers were also said for the freedom of access to the stones.' (Loxley 2003; Green 1997: 175–6)

The circumstances surrounding the private access arrangements cut to the heart of the conflict between the militant Druids and their more sedate counterparts. Throughout this period, Philip Shallcrass and Emma Restall Orr consistently emphasised that free access was an end result that would only be achieved through politeness and patience. Commenting on the pre-arranged access arrangements in 1999, they wrote, 'And how did we secure this privilege? We asked. Simple as that.' Arthur, on the other hand, maintained just as consistently that securing special access and then praying for freedom for others was simply not enough. (Shallcrass and Orr 1999)

Solstice 1998: access and egos

Despite the Druidic concessions and the convening of the Round Table, the exclusion zone that had spread a desolate silence over the temple at the summer solstice for a decade remained firmly in place until 1998. That year, English Heritage finally came up with a partial compromise. They were prompted in particular by the experimental access arrangements introduced at the spring equinox, when '208 celebrants [were] granted access, all of whom left peacefully at the conclusion of the celebrations.' (Neville 1998)

Even so, the proposals put forward for the solstice were almost exactly the same as those that had last been attempted with disastrous results ten years before. 500 free tickets – for dates on and around the solstice – were offered in advance to a wide range of interested parties, 'local residents as well as astronomers, archaeologists, druids, pagans and travellers', according to Elizabeth Neville, the Chief Constable of Wiltshire. (Neville 1998)

Although around 250 people took up the offer, those who were committed to open access for all had no option but to turn it down yet again. The Stonehenge Campaign newsletter simply declared, 'Tickets exclude people and the Campaign wants to see free access for all.' One of their examples of exclusion – someone who 'simply got up that morning and decided to go to the stones' – was certainly excluded by English Heritage's access policy, which required all those who wished to attend the solstice to apply by the end of the May, with names and addresses provided for all attendees, a singularly insensitive policy in light of the legally dubious surveillance techniques to which travellers and former festival-goers had been subjected over the previous fifteen years. (Stonehenge Campaign 1998)

Compromised though the offer may have been, it was clearly not meant as a one-off gesture. That same year, English Heritage also introduced year-round 'Special Access' to Stonehenge for small groups of visitors paying in advance, finally allowing those for whom Stonehenge was more than just a pit-stop or a photo-opportunity the chance to acquaint – or reacquaint – themselves with the intimacies of the temple's inner space. Even this concession had its critics. Nora Morris, a pagan, wrote to UNESCO to complain about the British government's treatment of pagans, pointing out that 'English Heritage gives money to the established church for the upkeep of buildings' whereas 'We have to pay £12 each and to book well in advance for Stonehenge.' (Morris 1998)

At the solstice, the gulf between those with and without tickets was as pronounced as it had been ten years before. Arthur maintained his customary campaign for free access for all, getting himself arrested, 'which was odd', as C.J. Stone noted, 'as [he] actually had a ticket to get in. But that's Arthur for you.' In solidarity, Tim Sebastian also hurled himself at the police lines, joining Arthur in the cells, but elsewhere the police response to those without tickets was less restrained. At a roadblock on the edge of the exclusion zone, C.J., who had been rebuffed by the police in a civil manner, along with a group of nonplussed German tourists, watched helplessly as 'an old hippie turned up. He tried walking through the police cordon. We watched them beat him up. As we left he was on the floor. Several policemen had surrounded him and were giving him a good kicking before dragging him into a van.' (Stone 1999: 238, 236)

In the meantime, around a hundred people, including representatives of six different Druid groups, other pagans, local people, archaeologists and forty press reporters and photographers, all took advantage of the special access arrangements. Dylan Ap Thuin declared that he was 'blessed with ticket no.1 out of 100', although according to the majority of reports it was not an entirely satisfactory occasion. Emma Restall Orr complained that 'With as many press as there were Druids, Pagans and others, and with the ethical problems of those with access moving through the lines of the exclusion zone, the whole event was very difficult', and Philip Shallcrass lamented that 'What should have been a joyous event for all was marred for many by the antics of one eccentric individual who conducted what amounted to a loud one-man performance, effectively excluding everyone else from the centre of the monument throughout the access time. Several people left the stones in tears, others in anger.' (Ap Thuin 2001; Orr 2000; Shallcrass 1999: 11)

The eccentric individual was Rollo Maughfling, and others were less charitable about the performance of the self-styled Arch-Druid of Stonehenge and Britain. According to the website Dispatch Online, Matthew McCabe of OBOD, a tutor of

Summer solstice 1998: a group of Druids gather outside the stones to watch the sun. Copyright Malcolm Coe.

tree and herb lore, 'had a few choice – and unprintable – words for the Arch-Druid who, he said, had appointed himself without reference to any Druid Order', and Kevin Carlyon, the head of a group of white witches called the Covenant of Earth Magic, who practice white magic 'as a science', bluntly declared 'I can't stand the bloke.' His wife Sandy added, 'Nobody gets on at these things. We call it the festival of bicker and bitchcraft.' (Dispatch Online 1998)

At the conclusion of the ceremonies, Clews Everard declared the event a success, adding 'Stonehenge means different things to different people. What we want to try to do is allow people to enjoy Stonehenge for what it is to them', but Kevin Carlyon expressed a note of caution: 'There will definitely be trouble if they grant exclusive access to one group and not another. There are going to be 10,000 other worshippers turning up with just as much right to access as the Druids.' (BBC Online 1998; Trull 1998)

A momentous decision in the House of Lords

In the event, Kevin Carlyon's warning was prescient. On 4 March 1999, the House of Lords finally overturned the police conviction of January 1997 against Margaret Jones and Richard Lloyd, the 'Stonehenge Two.' Five senior Lords were consulted over the appeal. Two – Lord Slynn of Hadley and Lord Hope of Craighead – upheld the conviction, while the other three – the Lord Chancellor, Lord Clyde and Lord Hutton – allowed the appeal. Lord Hutton in particular put forward a considered and far-reaching defence of civil liberties, taking in the right of free speech, the right to demonstrate, the right to protest on matters of public concern and the right of assembly. He quoted Lord Denning: 'These are rights which it is in the public interest that individuals should possess; and indeed, that they should exercise without impediment so long as no wrongful act is done. It is often the only means by which grievances can be brought to the knowledge of those in authority – at any rate with such impact as to gain a remedy.' He also quoted Lord Scarman, who had observed that the right to demonstrate is 'subject only to limits required by the need for good order and the passage of traffic', and concluded, 'It is time for the courts to recognise this too. They should not interfere by interlocutory injunction with the right to demonstrate and protest any more than they interfere with the right of free speech, provided that everything is done peaceably and in good order.' (Lord Hutton 1999: 43–4)

When Derry Irvine, the Lord Chancellor, reviewed the legal precedents used to secure the conviction against Jones and Lloyd, he was in no doubt that the 'rigid approach' of the nineteenth century sources cited by the Divisional Court 'would have some surprising consequences' that were clearly intolerable: 'It would entail that two friends who meet in the street and stop to talk are committing a trespass; so too a group of children playing on the pavement outside their homes; so too charity workers collecting donations; or political activists handing out leaflets; and so too a group of members of the Salvation Army singing hymns and addressing those who gather to listen.' (Irvine 1999: 5)

Declaring his verdict, Lord Irvine was concerned to establish, as 'an issue of fundamental constitutional importance', that 'the public highway is a public place which the public may enjoy for any reasonable purpose, provided the activity in question does not amount to a public or private nuisance and does not obstruct the highway by unreasonably impeding the primary right of the public to pass and repass: within these qualifications there is a public right of peaceful assembly on the highway.' (Irvine 1999: 1, 8)

It may not sound much, but it was a truly momentous decision. It sounded the death knell for the exclusion zone, and effectively signalled the end of the prohibition at solstice, although the way that it was dealt with in 1999 was clearly inadequate.

Solstice 1999: 'a classic game of British Bulldog'

Ignoring the threat posed by several thousand people being allowed to congregate outside the perimeter fence instead of facing the handcuffing-and-arrest scenario that had been prevalent since 1989, English Heritage offered a thousand free tickets over the solstice period, and those committed to open access were again obliged to refuse.

On solstice night, several thousand people duly turned up. Cars were banned from the immediate vicinity and the would-be sun worshippers had to make their way on foot to the perimeter fence, but few seemed to mind. As the crowds grew, a gentle party atmosphere prevailed. According to the Festival Generation website, 'fire jugglers, guitar players and chatting crowds mingled with police officers' and 'A group of students from Brighton ate delicacies from a picnic hamper and toasted the beginning of a "glorious summer" with glasses of red wine. "I liked the fact that everybody had to walk here", said a duvet-wrapped woman as she munched on a cracker and paté. "It's really mellowed people out – got rid of all the driving stress".' In the field opposite the monument, Kreb Dragonrider prepared to conduct a ceremony on the line of the avenue, declaring 'this is a very important day because it has important implications for crop growth and fertility', and as the light dwindled and the temperature plummeted, fires were lit and the music-making and chatter continued. (Festival Generation 1999)

Police and celebrants at the summer solstice 1999.
Copyright Mogg Morgan.

Sometime around 2 a.m., the mood changed. A few hundred people broke down the perimeter fence and proceeded to occupy the stones, and the night ended in clashes with the police and twenty-three arrests. The 150 or so Druids, archaeologists and locals who had successfully applied for access were prevented from entering the temple. Diverted to Amesbury in their coach, they were finally given the option of approaching the monument on foot, although those who did so arrived after sunrise. To add to the frustrations of those who had applied for access in advance, all other special access visits for 21 and 22 June were cancelled, and it was only after 'advice from staff on the ground' that the Ancient Druid Order's ceremony on 23 June was allowed to proceed. (Firsoff 1999)

In the aftermath of the occupation, rumours spread amongst sections of the pagan community that it was planned by outside agitators, bringing a newly ferocious political angle to Stonehenge from the J18 anti-capitalist demonstrations that had taken place in London a few days before. George Firsoff noted reports of 'Class War supporters shouting violent slogans', and Philip Shallcrass and Emma Restall Orr declared, without producing evidence, that the invasion was 'incited by political activists.' Shallcrass in particular was appalled by the attitude of a number of angry, drunken individuals that he encountered on the road outside, who 'saw themselves as society's dispossessed and seemed intent on wreaking revenge on society by any means possible.' As he described it, 'few spoke of celebration, none in terms of spirituality, ritual or respect', but significantly none of those he spoke to had either occupied the stones or declared any specific political allegiance either. (Firsoff 1999; Shallcrass and Orr 1999)

Sunrise at the summer solstice 1999.
Copyright Mogg Morgan.

Certainly a handful of intransigent troublemakers were among those who occupied the stones, but it would be misleading to suggest that the majority of those who invaded the site were bent on destruction. Given that the exclusion zone had been lifted, but that the access restrictions on congregating at the monument had not, a more realistic conclusion is that the invasion was simply a spontaneous demonstration of frustration by those with a long history of exclusion from the stones. This was the verdict of the Festival Generation website, whose author noted that 'As darkness fell increasing calls for an invasion of the site were heard and the crowd was divided between those who were content to stay around the fire while others agitated to 'liberate' the stones.' (Festival Generation 1999)

According to Arthur Pendragon, who had again been offered a ticket but had this time refused, declaring his intention to hold a peaceful ceremony on the outside, the fence collapsed through the 'sheer weight of numbers' and 'a large number of pilgrims simply walked into the henge from which EH security had already withdrawn.' Accompanied by a former manager of English Heritage properties, Arthur noted that 'the assembled pilgrims were thoroughly well behaved and impressed on me (the only white frock) their wish to join in the ritual at dawn.' The mood only changed at 3.30 a.m., when 'Wiltshire Constabulary moved in on direct instructions from their Divisional Commander to "sweep and clear the area" – his words not mine.' (Pendragon 1999b)

In the ensuing onslaught, Arthur was arrested after having two ribs broken ('a classic game of British Bulldog – pity the police play with batons and shields', as he later described it), others climbed up on the stones, and pandemonium was widespread, although one visitor, Mogg Morgan of the Oxford Golden Dawn Occult Society, took a sanguine approach to the conflict, explaining, 'Sometimes I looked around and saw someone being tripped or roughed up by the riot police, but to be honest

The children's playground at the first Reclaim The Streets,
Camden High Street, May 1995.
Copyright Adrian Arbib.

it's not the worst I've seen.' He suggested that the police had been 'reined in a lot since the baton swinging days of the Miners' Strike, Greenham Common and the Poll Tax Riots', and for him the most poignant moment of the night came during a lull in the confrontation, 'a strange silence as a beautiful naked woman strode out of the crowd and lay down on one of the recumbent stones. It seemed the ultimate protest and reclaiming of the site, her body so vulnerable yet the riot police with all their body shields and armour powerless before her.' (Pendragon 1999a; Morgan 1999)

The rise of global protest: from Reclaim the Streets to Seattle

The accusations that 'political activists' had instigated the invasion were also mistaken for another pertinent reason. They failed to take into account the overwhelmingly positive developments that had occurred in the protest movement in the previous few years, and that took their inspiration – like the parallel developments in the land reform movement – from the template provided by the road protestors. Two events in particular signalled the way forward. Firstly, the occupation of Claremont Road on the route of the M11 link road, where a vision of a new, co-operative urban environment had arisen that was car-free and people-centred. Secondly, the first massive demonstration against the Criminal Justice Bill, when the bicycle-powered Rinky Dink sound system had got people dancing in Trafalgar Square and on the streets of central London.

The new phase of protest began on 14 May 1995, when the Reclaim the Streets project occupied Camden High Street, crashing two old cars into each other to

Protestor and police at the J18 carnival, June 1999.
Copyright Alan Lodge.

create a road block, and filling up the street with carpets, armchairs, sofas, and a kids' playground. A huge party was held, which lasted from noon until 7 p.m., when it was all cleared up again, leaving the police wondering, 'Was it a protest? A party? An art installation? Some kind of a joke?' (Pendragon and Stone 2003: 183–4)

Within a year, Reclaim the Streets had spread not only to every other major city in the country but to dozens of other countries besides. In Britain they united with the road protestors on 13 July 1996 to occupy the M41 in west London. While a giant sound system kept 7,000 people dancing all day, a human shield of dancers hid a man with a pneumatic drill, breaking through the tarmac of the inner-city motorway to plant trees.

From the (literal) roots of these movements – centred on the quest for political justice, the principles of people power, and the sanctity of the earth – an awareness began to dawn that the wider focus of all the protestors' complaints was a global process of 'neo-liberalisation', centred on the activities of the World Bank, the International Monetary Fund (IMF) and the World Trade Organisation (WTO), whose prescriptions for transforming the ailing economies of countries in the developing world – the privatisation of all publicly-owned companies and utilities, the lifting of tariffs on imports from the west, and the deliberate suppression of state spending, which was inevitably applied to health, education and welfare – were widely perceived as a new and particularly grotesque manifestation of western imperialism.

Aided and abetted by the unprecedented power of the Internet as a tool for the free and unfettered transfer of ideas and information (a notable example of which was the Zapatistas movement in Mexico), protestors around the world began to converge in a new mass movement – anti-globalisation – that was opposed to the iniquities of the new world order. This new wave of protestors came together in an unprecedented trans-national coalition of 70,000 people at a WTO summit in Seattle in November 1999, and its passion – and its persecution at the hands of the police – paved the way for similar actions in Europe: a demonstration against an IMF/World Bank summit in Prague in September 2000, and a protest against a G8 summit in Genoa in July 2001, which drew 300,000 people, one of whom was shot dead by Italian police. (Bircham and Charlton 2001: 340–1)

At the J18 demonstration, just five months before Seattle, the political impetus was just as sharp, and the intention was to follow the same subversive combination of politics and partying that had been developed in the days of Reclaim the Streets and the road protests. For the majority of those attending, it was clear that it was the police, rather than a minority of violent troublemakers, who had engineered the transformation of a carnival into a confrontation.

In the wake of 1999's occupation, Philip Shallcrass and Emma Restall Orr visited Stonehenge on the afternoon of the solstice and described the stones as 'somehow black, the spirit having flinched into a catatonic state of withdrawal.' Three days later, they held their regular Midsummer ritual, attended by forty-five people, at which they called on the 'crow people of Salisbury Plain' to 'return from the shadows into which the hostility of June 21st had driven them.' That same day, 'Clews Everard for English Heritage publicly re-affirmed their resolve to see the stones open to all who come in peace', and Andy Hollingshead confirmed the support of the Wiltshire police. As the accusations and counter-accusations began to subside, however, few could have suspected how swiftly and decisively both English Heritage and the police were to respond, over the next twelve months, to the full ramifications of the House of Lords' decision. (Shallcrass and Orr 1999)

Chapter Thirteen

Return to the stones

Solstice 2000: 'This is what it's all about'

In the months that followed the summer solstice in 1999, as English Heritage and the Wiltshire police came to terms with the Lords' decision that the exclusion zone was illegal, they reached the inevitable conclusion that the prohibition on access to the stones at the solstice was now effectively unworkable. After sixteen years of prohibition, punctuated only by the occasional ill-conceived attempt to hold gatherings restricted to a ticket-holding elite, a mixture of compromise, conciliation and common sense prevailed, and on 11 May 2000, under the bold heading 'Stonehenge to be open to the public for summer solstice 2000', the chairman of the quango, Sir Neil Cossons, announced in a press release that 'there will be managed open access to Stonehenge over the summer solstice 2000.'

The terms and conditions of entry reflected this new spirit of compromise. Celebrants were requested not to attempt to take in amplified music – 'Stonehenge is seen by many as a sacred site and amplified music is not appropriate', as the official handout put it – and there were other sensible restrictions: no bottles, no fires or fireworks, no dogs or other animals, and no camping or climbing on the stones. Perhaps the most noticeable indication that this was a situation that had only come about after a good deal of wrangling behind the scenes was the time limit imposed on the gathering – eight hours at the stones, from 11.30 p.m. on 20 June to 7.30 a.m. on the morning of the solstice, with a further few hours allowed in the car park afterwards. The underlying message was clear – all were welcome who came in peace for the night of the solstice itself, but there was to be no suggestion that anything resembling a free festival would ever take place at Stonehenge again.

On the morning of 21 June 2000, over 6,000 people duly turned up to take advantage of the new détente, crowding into the stones to celebrate the crucial dawn, even though it rained all night and the sunrise was invisible. From around the globe, the world's media were out in force, and the following morning good news was for once allowed to dominate the newspapers' front pages. 'Modern pagans reclaim Stonehenge', trumpeted *The Times*, and *The Independent* led with 'Thousands see the dawn of a peaceful party at Stonehenge.' Although most newspapers relied on a handful of news agencies for their stories, recycling the same quotes, *The Guardian*'s John Vidal turned up in person, filing a jaunty piece of frontline correspondence entitled 'The weird and wonderful return to get stoned at Stonehenge', in which he talked to Tim Sebastian, who called it 'a return to the spirit

Fire procession, summer solstice 2003.
Copyright Paul Gapper.

of the free festivals of the 1970s', noted obscure details – the man selling 'Skunk truffles, trunk scuffles... £1 a go... wibbly wobbly truffles anyone?' – and singled out, for particular praise, the Barking Bateria, a group of around a hundred drummers, made up of lecturers and students at various London universities, inspired by the communal spirit of the Reclaim the Streets gatherings, who had first come together for the J18 carnival in 1999: 'Led by flaming torches and gals in bikinis, they alternately drummed, danced and ritually sang the crowd through the shortest night. And crucially, as the official 7 a.m. deadline to leave the site approached, they led the crowd quietly back to the car park. "Happy solstice", said one, conferring a huge smacker on a policeman. "See you next year".' (*The Times*, 22 June 2000; *The Independent*, 22 June 2000; *The Guardian*, 22 June 2000)

Most of all though, this was a night of celebration for all those who had experienced the solstice at the stones in the years before the Battle of the Beanfield, and all those who had been unable to do so in the years since. It was clearly a particularly triumphant occasion for Arthur Pendragon. Emma Restall Orr, who described him as 'the big-hearted warrior-druid fellow who calls himself King Arthur', observed that, around midnight, he 'was making a circle beside the temple, gathering together any who'd join him, encouraging folk to share the Druid vow... determined that the night would be smooth and without trouble.' At dawn, as C.J. Stone and Arthur himself described it, he entered the circle 'to great applause... bawling above the noise of the crowd: 'This is your Henge. This is your Temple. Do not ever let anyone tell you otherwise. You have as much right to be here as anyone else'.' Later, he told a cameraman, 'This is what it's all about. The only thing that I believe in is that this is

*Arthur Pendragon at
Stonehenge, summer solstice
2003.
Copyright Paul Gapper.*

our Henge and that it's open to every fucker – not just Druids, not just pagans, but to everyone who wants to come here – and that's what I've been fighting for... It's the culmination of 14 years' work.' (Orr 2000; Pendragon and Stone 2003: 231–2)

If Arthur's words were a ringing vindication of the efforts of all those who had struggled for years to liberate the solstice celebration at the stones, it was left to festival veteran Margaret Greenfields to capture a more emotional side to the event: 'I was surprised, as I stumbled across those ruts in the field, clutching the hand of my 10 year-old daughter, that I had tears rolling down my face. We were back. And I tell you I wasn't the only person I saw that night in tears – a lot of old faces. Often we just nodded at each other, no need for words. It was one of the most emotional times of my life.' (Greenfields 2003)

Solstice 2001: 'the red sun rose in a clear sky'

In 2001, the numbers attending 'managed open access' to Stonehenge at the solstice swelled to 14,500, propelled by a number of factors including the largely favourable publicity of the year before, word of mouth and its global cousin the Internet, and, ironically for English Heritage, the everyday restrictions on approaching the stones

Horses and wagons at the summer solstice 2000.
Copyright Stuart Henderson.

that made the prospect of actually being able to touch them such a tantalising thrill for many who might otherwise not have been so interested in the solstice night itself.

Having been caught out by the speed with which access was reintroduced the year before, I belatedly became a part of this expanding congregation in 2001, visiting Stonehenge at the summer solstice for the first time in seventeen years. After driving down with a friend in the middle of the night and experiencing some initial residual paranoia – there were giant spotlights everywhere, and it looked like the familiar war zone of the bad old days – we were ushered politely into a huge field to the south of the Winterbourne Stoke barrow cemetery, on the edge of the great circle's immediate ritual landscape, where the floodlights were revealed as illumination for the car park, and stewards were directing hundreds of vehicles into neat rows. Mostly identical modern cars, there was also evidence of the last of the travellers – painted vans, the occasional rogue Routemaster bus, a few old army trucks, and some horses and wagons.

From the moment that we began to make our way towards the temple down a stretch of the slip-road that was closed to traffic and had suddenly become a pilgrims' path for the night, it was clear that we were largely being left to our own devices. The police disappeared after initial contact, and the rest of the security was discreet to the point of invisibility. Add to this the weather, a rare, balmy, summer night that lifted the spirits of almost everyone there, and the lack of outside distractions – no one

Waiting for dawn, summer solstice 2001.
Copyright Andy Worthington.

apart from two authorised catering vans selling anything – and it really was everyone's opportunity to engage with the great pre-Christian, pre-capitalist sun-temple, in as direct a way as possible, at the moment of its annual reaffirmation.

All around the stones, hundreds of groups of people – chatting, smoking, chilling – radiated from the central enclosure like rings around a giant planet, and in the horseshoe at the heart of the temple a dense congregation of revellers danced incessantly to the insistent rhythm of the night's only music – drums and voices. The drummers were caught up in the crowd on the fallen stones at the centre of the monument, which provided a podium for the writhing mass of all-night dancers. As dawn approached, other sun-watchers milled about the solstice-facing stones, and thousands more spilled out between them, down to the outlying Heel Stone, towards the hillside where the first light of dawn would appear.

As the sky warmed before dawn, there was no cloud, just a lake of mist lying in the dip between the celebrants and first light, and finally, at five to five, the red sun rose in a clear sky. The crowd roared, an almighty cheer – of release and reconciliation for some, a healing of the wounds caused by a long political battle, and of simple exultation for others, here for the first time, perhaps, marvelling at this radiant juncture of humanity and the cosmos. I wondered if some felt as I did, both vindicated and humbled, being here at this time, in this place, an experience that fuses human ingenuity with the eternal cycle of the seasons to such an extent that the passage of millennia can – however fleetingly – appear as nothing.

As in 2000, the publicity that followed the solstice in 2001 was largely favourable. *The Times* led with 'Magic of Stonehenge summons up the sun', and *The Independent* offered 'Druids, drugs and a very naked dawn. It was like the Sixties, man.' Pam Alexander, the chief executive of English Heritage, declared, 'It's been wonderful, watching the sunrise. I felt the atmosphere was very much more relaxed

The crowd during the daylight hours, summer solstice 2001.
Copyright Andy Worthington.

this year.' Superintendent Jerry Wickham, who ran the police operation, admitted, 'We've been very pleased with what has happened. Generally, the crowd have been supportive and have gone up to have a joke with officers', and Mark Chivers, a spokesman for the police, conceded that 'there was no reason the festival should not become a regular event.' (*The Times*, 22 June 2001; *The Independent*, 22 June 2001: *The Guardian*, 22 June 2001)

Solstice 2002: 'the symbolic importance of the dawning sun'

By 2002, the growing popularity of the solstice at Stonehenge was such that an estimated 23,500 people turned up, and although there were the usual bouts of stone-climbing and drunkenness, there seemed to be a widespread feeling that the success of the event involved both individual freedom and collective responsibility, an acknowledgement that its very existence had only come about through an ongoing dialogue about shared rights and shared privileges between those charged with looking after the monument and those who felt that their presence was some kind of birthright.

Those who climbed on the stones were met with a chorus of disapproval – 'Leave it out mate', 'Don't be so selfish', 'It's not just your solstice you know' – and although the drinking was exuberant and sometimes no doubt to excess, with the odd casualty seemingly washed up in the ditch or against the foot of one of the stones and the sad clowns who at one point broke into a slurred rendition of 'Three Lions', it was a

*Bedraggled revellers dwarfed
by a trilithon, summer
solstice 2002.
Copyright Andy Worthington.*

warm atmosphere, with complete strangers gabbing cheerily to one another, and steward volunteers and the odd well-intentioned visitor wandering around collecting the empties.

As in previous years, the prohibition on amplified music was applied with ruthless efficiency. Suspect vehicles were stopped and searched on arrival, and all those carrying rave-sized rigs were turned away. This was a contrast to the rest of the policing – virtually non-existent, with only eleven arrests in total – but had the desired effect, ensuring that the focus of the event remained firmly on the stones, and that the great sarsen circle and horseshoe did not end up providing an exotic backdrop to a DJ playing records very loudly.

Even so, music provided the main pulse of the night, in the patterns set up by spontaneous groups of drummers, accompanied by little more than whooping and the odd whistle, who moved about inside the stones. Fumbling patterns of call and response gave way to surging waves of sonic synchronicity that bounced off the inner walls of this unparalleled amphitheatre, providing a suitably reverent organic soundtrack to the night, and bringing the monument and its modern-day admirers into some kind of creative harmony. Occasionally, when the stones bent the frequencies of the drums into wild distortions, the monument and its musicians were producing full-on tribal house music, 'amplified' sounds conjured up only by hands, skin and stones.

Apart from the odd niggle about security, with various celebrants complaining about seemingly random bans on a variety of acoustic instruments (while two drunks with swords passed through unmolested), the main obstacle to people's enjoyment of the night was the sickly green light, which, for the third year running, washed down like a fog from a number of huge spotlights around the henge and circles. The Conditions of Entry described it as 'ambient lighting', but it had something of the sedative hue of hospital decor, and although it served an understandable purpose in the early part of the night, it became an almost unbearable intrusion as the hours passed and a waxing moon rose up through the sky to the south. English Heritage cited health and safety reasons for the lighting – 'Lights will be systematically turned off as dawn approaches and only as soon as it is operationally safe to do so' – but it was somehow perverse to deprive what was largely an urban crowd of the rare enchantment of a sacred landscape illuminated only by the moon, and it was significant that, when the lights were finally shut down on that long, slow prelude to dawn, their extinguishing raised one of the largest cheers of the night.

Dawn, when it arrived, was shrouded in a veil of rain, but it did nothing to dampen the collective spirits. While a few people glanced at their watches or stared balefully at a solid wall of cloud to the north-east, a sustained stampede of drums, shouts and cheers suggested that the majority of those in attendance had fully embraced the symbolic importance of the dawning sun, whether it was visible or not. Despite the rain and the lack of entertainment, the crowd demonstrated that, with only the stones, the dawn and other people to focus on, it was possible to hold a meaningful gathering in a context that didn't involve either making money or spending it, a rare occurrence in this increasingly commodified world.

Solstice 2003: the biggest free party since Castlemorton?

The success of the summer solstice in 2002 confirmed 'managed open access' as 'the high point of an alternative social calendar', according to Maev Kennedy, who wrote an astute commentary for *The Guardian*, recognizing the solstice celebrations as 'a one night truce between a cosmology of invented Stonehenges', and explaining that 'Because, despite centuries of academic argument, nobody knows what Stonehenge was for, it welcomes for one night the myriad true believers, convinced that it is a statement of bronze age power, a temple to the earth goddess, the moon or the stars, or merely a superb excuse for an all night party.' (*The Guardian*, 22 June 2002)

The solstice in 2003 was expected be the biggest gathering ever seen at the stones, partly because the numbers in attendance had been increasing by 8–9,000 a year since 2000, but also because, for the first time since 'managed open access' began, the solstice fell on a Saturday. To complicate matters further, only the 'traditional' solstice fell on the Saturday, as the true astronomical solstice (measurable only by scientists and indiscernible to the naked eye) occurred sometime after 8 p.m. on the Sunday. After much discussion, the Round Table and the Truth and Reconciliation Committee agreed with the authorities that access should take place, as usual, on 21 June, an eminently sensible suggestion, given that it would have been next to impossible to publicise a date change for an event that had no official publicity whatsoever, and also because access on 22 June was reserved for the private

The crowd at dawn, summer solstice 2003.
Copyright Andy Worthington.

ceremonies of the Ancient Druid Order and others. All parties also agreed that access would start and finish later, running from 2 a.m. to 12 noon, to allow for a more family friendly gathering in the daylight hours and also, it was hoped, to tame the night-time revelry that was likened by some commentators to a wild rave.

Complaints began almost immediately. Contributors to various email groups argued that access should take place on the Sunday. Others proposed that full weekend access should be permitted, with camping allowed on the Saturday night, a heretical proposal that veered dangerously close to suggesting that the free festival be revived. A few hard-line anarchists went so far as to suggest that they would mobilise the massed forces of latent English insurrection to resist eviction from the site on the Saturday afternoon, an empty boast that was, nevertheless, taken seriously by the authorities.

In the end, although the numbers did indeed swell to over 30,000, the atmosphere throughout the night and into the morning was the by-now familiar mixture of John Michell's Lord of Misrule, a stoned, libertarian tribal gathering and a spiritual free-for-all. Notably, a majority of those in attendance were young people. Many, no doubt, were at Stonehenge on the summer solstice for the first time, drawn by reports of the gathering or curious about the temple itself, mostly too young to have taken part in the long history of the struggle for access to the monument. Of these, a majority were local people, reclaiming, perhaps unwittingly, a right that was fought for in 1901 and 1921, and that – like the 'rights' of others from further afield – has been contested, in one way or another, since 1962.

The sheer numbers caused their own problems – there was gridlock on the A303 for several miles and for several hours, the queues from the car parking field to the stones resembled, on occasion, the queue for the main stage at the Glastonbury Festival when a particularly popular band was taking to the stage, and the numbers overwhelmed the security guards and stewards to such an extent that abuse of the terms and conditions of entry was widespread, and countless bottles and several dogs were smuggled into the *sanctum sanctorum*.

The reward for the dedication of pilgrims and punters alike was, however, insuperable. Around 3 a.m., a luminous sky was already smeared with a transcendent palette of yellows and purples, and, as the sunrise neared, the whole of the dawn horizon lit up with burning red and orange like a primal fire. So astonishing was the spectacle that the drums and voices fell silent, and an extraordinary hush fell over the assembled throng for several minutes, until the spell was broken and the party resumed with drums and whistles and cheers.

On such a radiant morning as this, the extension of access into the daylight hours proved a resounding success, a long, gentle comedown after the exuberance of the night and the threshold of dawn. A headline in *The Salisbury Journal* declared, 'Stones solstice celebration "best in memory".' Rosanne Bell, a white witch from Birmingham, told a *Journal* reporter, 'I have been for the last four years – I just love it. There are so many people here and everybody gets on together. This is how I wish the world were.' (*The Salisbury Journal*, 26 June 2003)

Issues of sustainability at Stonehenge and Avebury

Behind the rosy image presented in the national and international media, however, certain parties began expressing concerns over the sustainability of the event itself. From the moment that 'managed open access' began, various high-ranking local dignitaries had been vociferous in their opposition to the renewal of open access at the solstice. At a meeting of Amesbury town council in September 2002, the Mayor, Neil Morrison, who had visited the solstice celebrations that year, highlighted what he saw as widespread alcohol and drug abuse, suggesting that the crowd of 23,500 was 'far too many' and concluding that 'It was a desperately frightening situation and it reminded me of the problems of the 1980s.' Councillor John Turner, a retired Major, added, with an old-fashioned oratorical flourish that would not have been out of place at any time in the previous century, 'A little too much freedom under the law has been given to the ungodly and it is fast becoming a situation where the tail is wagging the dog.' (Batten 2002)

In July 2003, more moderate misgivings were also spelt out by Scott Green, the National Trust's Property Manager for the Stonehenge Historic Landscape, who pointed out, in a letter to Steve Bubble, a Stonehenge campaigner who had written to him to inquire whether the Trust would be interested in making some land available for an alternative gathering to ease the pressure on the stones themselves, that 'the Trust is not convinced that the Solstice observance as it is currently celebrated is sustainable in the long term.' (Green 2003)

More worrying than the odd dissenting voice at Stonehenge is the situation at Avebury, which has been receiving a noticeably larger influx of visitors on and around the solstice in the years since 'managed open access' began at Stonehenge. In the aftermath of the solstice in 2002, under the heading 'Solstice celebrations leave a sour taste', a newspaper report suggested that the villagers 'reflected on a

Pagan celebrations at Avebury, summer solstice 2003.
Copyright Pete Glastonbury.

weekend invasion by travellers and called for steps to be taken to prevent a repeat.' One unnamed villager said, 'It was all good-natured but it is not what Avebury is really about. If the authorities don't do something now to nip it in the bud then it will become as bad as the Stonehenge festivals used to be.' By the time the parish council met with the police in July, the tone was almost hysterical. Council chairman John Cronk raised the spectre of the Beanfield, commenting that 'I have always been concerned about the risk of confrontation in the village'. In reply, Superintendent Jerry Wickham pointed out to the council that the reason for the influx was that 'Many of those at Stonehenge wanted to go to the Glastonbury Festival eight days later, but as they were not permitted to remain at Stonehenge, headed to Avebury for the intervening period.' He indicated that 'They come to Avebury because it is seen as a soft option', and assured the council that 'next year the police will be in Avebury in much greater numbers than they were this year.' (Weird Wiltshire 2003)

In the meantime, the council embarked on a number of independent initiatives to restrict access on the solstice, putting pressure on the National Trust to end its long-standing tolerance of camping and overnight parking in the overflow car park, and, more contentiously, enraging everyone from pagans and travellers to the Council for the Protection of Rural England (CPRE) by painting double yellow lines on all the roadside verges in and around the village in the week before the solstice. At the solstice itself, while 30,000 people cavorted at Stonehenge, many of the thousands who had gathered at Avebury instead found that their enjoyment of the night was marred by a heavy-handed policy towards their vehicles that had arisen as a direct result of the council's determination to restrict parking, aided by the increased police presence that was promised by Jerry Wickham.

John Northam, a barrister, and Rachel Phelan, a graduate, who had 'visited [the] ancient site, on Midsummer's morning, in a spirit of curiosity', wrote to *The Guardian* to point out their concerns about 'a new and subtle approach taken by the Police, aimed at restricting peoples' rights of self-expression, assembly and worship.' With nowhere to park in the village itself, Northam and Phelan, along with many others, had followed police instructions to park half a mile away, on the verge of the Swindon road, which they duly did, noting that 'There were no signs or any other indication that we were parking illegally, nor was there a warning that cars would be towed away.' After an enjoyable night, in which they were 'taken by the fact that people from all walks of life were represented at the event', they returned to their car, only to find that it had been towed away, along with at least thirty others, and that the police 'were unable to provide us with the address of the garage it had been taken to.' Four hours later, a senior officer 'authorised the use of police vehicles to take those drivers that they believed to be respectable' to the garage at Swindon, where they were charged a towing fee of £105 and a statutory fine of £30. After wondering whether 'the high-handed and unnecessarily punitive approach taken by the Police was aimed at provoking a riot so that events of this kind can be banned', the indignant professionals reported that a senior officer told them, 'it has been a hard lesson but we hope you have learned it', and concluded, 'We certainly have, and we feel morally obliged to return to Avebury every year with as many people as we can muster.' (Northam and Phelan 2003)

Pagan misgivings

In addition to councillors and the National Trust, representatives of various pagan groups have also expressed doubts about the success of the new access arrangements at Stonehenge. Matthew McCabe of OBOD, who seemed happy enough at the solstice in 2000, when he was interviewed by a reporter from CNN, had changed his mind by the following year when he told BBC Online, 'There's a conflict between the need for a party and the need for a spiritual ceremony to mark the summer solstice at Stonehenge. The two seem to be incompatible, because the revellers aren't interested in co-operating with the Druids, so the Druids get slightly disillusioned. Who's going to stand up and ask 5,000 people to move out of the stones so the Druids can get in for dawn?' McCabe added that, of the 130 members of OBOD who attended the Order's private ceremony on 23 June, only six had also turned up for the public solstice, and he noted that 'Most seemed to be relieved that they didn't even have to think about going to rough it with the revellers.' (Stonehenge Campaign 2000, 2001)

Similar sentiments were echoed by Emma Restall Orr of the British Druid Order, who outlined her concerns after attending the reopening of the public solstice in 2000. After conceding that it was a 'wet, wild and happy party' with, for the most part, 'an exhilarating atmosphere', and that she didn't mind 'in the slightest that there was no space, quiet or respect for the rituals that we might have wished to do', she posed a

*Mark Graham (right) and Emma Restall Orr of the British Druid Order
conduct a handfasting, Avebury, vernal equinox 2003.
Copyright Andy Worthington.*

single question: 'whether Stonehenge was, on 21 June, open for the people of Britain
(and the world beyond)?' After discounting Druidic claims for exclusive access –
'because I believe that it is a place that everyone should be free to go' – and refuting
English Heritage's 'exclusive rights to close the place completely', she concluded
nevertheless that 'the group who claimed the temple were just another minority sub-
culture.' (Orr 2000)

Although Matthew McCabe and Emma Restall Orr were undoubtedly voicing
criticisms and concerns that were held by other groups of Druids and pagans, the
unavoidable conclusion is that their denigration of the open, communal solstice was
somewhat hypocritical. For at least six years before the first 'managed open access'
in 2000, as was noted in Chapters Ten and Twelve, both OBOD and the BDO had
negotiated their own access on days around the solstice, while maintaining a
secondary commitment to open access for all. These gatherings are by all accounts
exactly the sort of small, disciplined and reverent gatherings that Matthew McCabe
and Emma Restall Orr wish to see at Stonehenge, and I consider their existence
should be accepted as part of the trade-off for the larger public gatherings on the
solstice itself. Judging the majority of a crowd of 6,000 people as a 'minority sub-
culture' does little to foster the impression that 'managed open access' was really
what the BDO had in mind when, as Emma Restall Orr put it, describing her

The crowd in the daylight hours, summer solstice 2003 – an eclectic mix of pagans and political activists, party-goers and tourists. Copyright Andy Worthington.

involvement in the Access Committee, 'It was decided that we should try and remove all of the "fences".' (Orr 2000)

In the last few years some members of the BDO have turned to other sites to celebrate the solstice itself. In 2002 and 2003, for example, they held an open public ceremony at an arts centre in Dudley, centred on a forty-foot high organic statue of a Green Man and featuring music, theatre and circus performers. However, Mark Graham, who has largely taken over Philip Shallcrass' role as the most prominent male representative of the Order at public ceremonies, seems to have retained his own affection for the public gathering at Stonehenge. At the solstice in 2001, he told Chris Gray of *The Independent*, 'We carry out ceremonies here for all sorts of reasons, such as the winter solstice and weddings, but there is something about being here for the summer solstice which makes it really special. There's been no trouble. Everyone's been friendly. There's a very high energy here.' (*The Independent*, 22 June 2001)

A universal symbol

To their credit, English Heritage and the Wiltshire police have failed to raise sustainability as an issue at any point in the negotiations of the last few years, although there is no indication that anyone in either organisation suspected, back in

June 2000, that within three years of instigating the access arrangements over 30,000 people would be turning up.

The numbers of people now celebrating the solstice is somewhat ironic. Throughout the recorded history of the solstice at Stonehenge, the largest crowds – in 1891, 1896, 1908, 1914, 1925, 1931 and throughout the 1950s and the early 1960s – gathered at the weekend, when the weather was fine, and numbered 3,000 people at the most, rather than the 30,000 of 2003. Even during the festival years, the number of people actually visiting the stones on the solstice was rarely more than a few thousand, a situation that concerned Bev Richardson, who noted that, as the festival grew, the spiritual significance of the temple dwindled, so that two-thirds of those attending the festival in 1977 visited the stones at the solstice, but only a thousand out of 40,000 did so in 1984. (Richardson in Shark 2003d)

With all these precedents, a reasonable assumption would be that English Heritage and the police seriously underestimated the popularity of 'managed open access', and this may well be so. Although there is some truth in Bev's insinuation that politics had taken over from spirituality at the time of the last Stonehenge festival, the events of the last two decades clearly demonstrate that the numbers of people interested in the significance of Stonehenge at the summer solstice – for reasons that are not only political but also spiritual and social – have continued to grow. Moreover, all these proliferating groups – caught up in the boundless expansion of paganism, the myriad strands of the protest movement, from the road protests to anti-globalisation, or simply constituting the flocks of the new and curious – have been mingling relentlessly in their search for spiritual, political and social solutions, and will continue to locate Stonehenge as a living temple and a multi-faceted counter-cultural temple that fulfils these needs.

Pagan expansion

In the decade since the Dongas and the PR successes of the Pagan Federation, paganism has continued to flourish, and with its growth have come more potential converts to the charms of Stonehenge. Druidry, as we have seen, underwent an explosion of interest in the late 1980s and early 1990s, and Wicca too has continued to expand from its Gardnerian roots and its offshoots of the 1960s and 1970s – Alexandrian Wicca and Dianic Wicca – into new groups and individual practitioners: hedgerow witches, 'traditional' witches, and Kevin Carlyon and his white witches, many of whom have been drawn to Stonehenge at the solstice as part of the eight-fold year.

Outside the flexible and creative descendents of Druidry and Wicca, the range of pagan celebrants is no less broad. There are Goddess worshippers; those who continue to be inspired by the legacy of the Dongas; and those who have come to paganism through earth mysteries, its spiritual godfather, John Michell, and its latest high-flying ambassador, the musician Julian Cope. There are heathens, including Jenny Blain and Robert Wallis, respectively a pagan anthropologist and a pagan archaeologist, who, since 2001, have been investigating 'who Pagans are' and 'how and why they engage with archaeological monuments' through their *Sacred Sites,*

Arthur Pendragon conducts a ceremony at Stonehenge, winter solstice 2003.
Copyright Pete Glastonbury.

Contested Rites/Rights project, funded by Sheffield Hallam University's Centre for Human Rights. Then there is Round Table regular Cerridwen Connelly and her TechnoPagans, whose motto is 'Pagans who honour the past but love living in the present', and whose website includes an apposite quote from Arthur C. Clarke – 'Technology sufficiently advanced is indistinguishable from magick' – and an amusing list of qualifications under the heading 'You are a TechnoPagan': 'if you 'program events' rather than cast spells', for example, and 'if you 'download data from the Cosmic Search Engine' instead of divining the future.' (Cope 1998; Wallis and Blain 2001; Blain and Wallis 2001, 2002a, 2002b; Connelly 2003, 2001)

According to estimates made by Ronald Hutton, in the late 1990s there were about 10,000 initiated witches and about 6,000 initiated Druids in Britain, with a further few thousand drawn from other kinds of initiatory paganism – working with Germanic, Scandinavian or Egyptian deities, ceremonial magic (the Ordo Templi Orientis, for example), or shamanist traditions. To these, Hutton added between 90,000 and 120,000 non-initiated Pagans 'who have an active Pagan identity, honour Pagan deities and make an effort to attend Pagan ceremonies, but are not inducted into a particular Pagan tradition', and his findings have been backed up in independent studies by David Burnett, an evangelical Christian, and the academic Joanne Pearson. (Hutton 1999: 401)

Moreover, the numbers of those drawn to paganism continue to grow. In June 2003, in an article entitled 'Sabrina, Harry and the Web help Paganism grow', Ronald Hutton and Matthew McCabe explained to Reuters journalist Pete Harrison the roles that television, the Internet, environmentalism and feminism have played in the expansion of paganism. Harrison's article singled out for particular importance the popularity of the Harry Potter books and the television shows *Sabrina the Teenage Witch* and *Buffy the Vampire Slayer* (to which should be added Peter Jackson's films of J.R.R. Tolkien's *Lord of the Rings* trilogy, which have revived a counter-cultural interest in Tolkien's mythology, whose last great manifestation took place in the hippie era). Ronald Hutton not only explained to Harrison the reasons for the success of paganism, but also the debt that all its modern manifestations still owed to Gerald Gardner: 'It's a religion that meets modern needs. Traditional religions have so many prohibitions: Thou shalt not do this or that. But Paganism has a message of liberation combined with good citizenship', summed up in the Wiccan Rede – 'Do what ye will an ye harm none' – described by Hutton as 'the witch religion's great statement of ethics.' (Harrison 2003; Hutton 1999: 248)

In November 2003, thousands of Buffy-loving youngsters attended the Witchcraft UK 2003 conference at the Fairfield Halls in Croydon, and presumably, although Stonehenge never featured in an episode of *Buffy the Vampire Slayer*, its ubiquity in pagan circles ensures that many of these new pagans will also be drawn to the temple and the summer solstice in the years to come.

The persistence of protest

As well as appeasing pagans, the public reopening of Stonehenge at the summer solstice in 2000 was also clearly intended to defuse the radical political views that had adhered to the temple over several generations, and that had undoubtedly been sharpened after the martyrdom of the festival at the Battle of the Beanfield.

This policy has largely been successful, for the simple reason that eight, ten or twelve hours at the stones is preferable, for most people, to the desolate solstices before the renewal of access, and also because, in certain essential respects, 'managed open access' is the heart of the Stonehenge Free Festival reborn. It once more allows the public to visit Stonehenge at the summer solstice, thereby reviving the centre of an alternative social calendar at once both ancient and modern; it constitutes some sort of a festival, albeit an acoustic one; and it is also free. English Heritage, and by extension the crowd itself, composed largely of tax-payers, foots the bill, estimated at £100,000 a year, a mere fraction of the millions it cost to keep everyone out.

The monument's curators have also avoided further conflict by reinstating access at the equinoxes and the winter solstice, all of which were banned in 1990, although not all dissent has dissipated over the last few years. As I hope to have demonstrated throughout this book, Stonehenge has been a potent counter-cultural symbol since the 1960s, handed on and reinterpreted through numerous different movements – the London squat scene, the free festivals, biker groups, anarchists, travellers, the convoy, peace protestors, the free party scene, the road protest movement and the current coalitions of anti-globalisation protestors. Such is the evolution and cross-

'Violence doesn't pacify': protestors in Glasgow march against the proposed war in Iraq, February 2003. Copyright Dot Young.

pollination of all these different elements and the ways in which they have continued to be readopted and reinterpreted, that they are unlikely to be removed with the granting of a single wish.

Even amongst those closest to the decision-making process that facilitated the reopening of the temple there are some who still exhibit a subversive streak. Arthur, for example, who played a prominent role in this counter-cultural history, accepted the time limit as a compromise not only because the access arrangements, as negotiated, restored open access on the summer solstice, but also because they allowed the celebrants to police themselves. With no ban on drugs or alcohol and the opportunity to look after their own welfare, Arthur was attempting to give back to the gathering the autonomy that had allowed both the Stonehenge festival and his own beloved biker groups to police their own alternative states in the first place.

Arthur has also maintained his role as an ecological and political protestor, demonstrating that the renewal of access at Stonehenge won a battle against the authorities but not the whole war. From July 2003, he joined a protest camp close to Twyford Down on the outskirts of Winchester, where Hampshire County Council's verbal promise to protect the surrounding meadow land as compensation for the construction of the M3 extension was about to be broken because the council had decided to create a road joining the town's park and ride extension with an existing

243

car park. Media-savvy stunts that compared favourably with Arthur's past campaigns included protestors 'chaining themselves to the gates of Hampshire County Council's headquarters and a ceremonial burning of cakes beside the statue of King Alfred' in the centre of town. (*The Hampshire Chronicle*, 31 December 2003)

Given its modern history, Stonehenge is unlikely to cease being a radical political symbol in the imminent future, especially with such a wide array of complaints building up against the government – the war in Iraq, which provoked the largest political protest in British history, when two million people marched through London in February 2003, anti-terrorist legislation that places the whole of the capital under a permanent version of the reviled stop and search 'sus' laws of the Thatcher era, and plans for unbridled road expansion, new airports and the remorseless expansion of housing and retail developments into the heart of the 'sacred' countryside.

Travellers and the festival

For some involved in the free festivals and the travellers' scene, even the compromise of 'managed open access' is not enough, and what is on offer is either insufficient or fatally flawed. Neil Goodwin, who attended the solstice in 2003, felt that it lacked a context, and that, despite the lack of distractions, the solstice experience itself had become a commodity. For Alan Lodge, the event itself is tainted. Alan has pointed out that all sixteen years of prohibition has achieved is to replace the festival years, when the majority of the crowd stayed at the festival, while 'a couple of hundred of us [went] over the road for a celebration of a few hours', with a situation where everyone is now at the stones. The figures back him up: the numbers now attending 'managed open access' are equivalent to those attending the free festival at the solstice before its suppression. (Lodge 2002)

Although the 'F' word is rarely mentioned, the festival remains an outstanding issue for many people. Everyone who has ever been involved in the Stonehenge Campaign, for example, understands that the current access arrangements only fulfil one of the campaign's two long-standing aims: 'the reinstatement of the Stonehenge People's Free Festival and religious access to Stonehenge itself.' Aptly, Alan Lodge is at the forefront of those attempting to remind the authorities that the issue of the long-suppressed free festival is still on the agenda. While many commentators have tried to blunt the prevailing bitterness from the days of the Beanfield, pointing out that a regime change has taken place and that those responsible for the violence of the 1980s are no longer in charge of operations, Alan has pointed out that he is 'still an "injuncted person"' and can be 'arrested for being in an area "delineated on a map therein between dates around the solstice"', because 'this order by Lord Justice Morland has never been rescinded.' (Lodge 2002)

For travellers like Alan, who were committed to the Stonehenge Free Festival as a 'gathering of the tribes' rather than a 'temporary gathering in the middle of the night under rules', there was little reason to believe that a line could be drawn anywhere that would meaningfully separate the past from the present. No one has ever apologised for the Beanfield, which was, as we have seen, followed by the events of Stoney Cross and the passing of the Public Order Act. After the brief euphoria of the

The place to be: young party-goers at the summer solstice 2003.
Copyright Andy Worthington.

free party scene in the late 1980s and early 1990s, the clampdown on travellers and free gatherings has only increased in the decade following the passage of the Criminal Justice Act in 1994.

The CJA reduced the number of travellers' vehicles allowed to congregate in one place from twelve to six, and drove the free party scene deep underground, to small gatherings in private woods or other remote locations. Attempts at larger gestures have been hard-won successes. In May 2002, a number of sound systems briefly reoccupied Castlemorton Common on the tenth anniversary of the last great gathering, but they were swiftly evicted. The party that finally followed it, at Steart Beach in Devon, when 14,000 people and thirty-four sound systems gathered over the four-day Golden Jubilee weekend at the start of June, only took place after vehicles had been shunted from county to county, and the occupants of a mile-long roadblock all got out of their cars and walked to the site. Only later did they realise, as the media lambasted them for their insensitivity, that they'd been forced to occupy a nature reserve.

The bitterest legacy of the CJA, however, is that it effectively criminalised the entire way of life of gypsies and other travellers by revoking the clauses of the 1968 Caravan Sites Act that required local councils to provide them with legally secure sites. Measured against this level of persecution, the acceptance of half a day at Stonehenge can be regarded with some justification as nothing less than a betrayal of the integrity of the travelling community in the festival years, when the extended gathering was the centrepiece of an entire way of life, the nomads' solstice so stoutly defended by Peter Fowler and Chris Chippindale in *Who Owns Stonehenge?*

A hunger for alternatives

Despite the success of the Major and Blair governments in keeping a lid on large illegal gatherings, the hunger for alternatives to a corporate nanny state appears to be growing. In September 2002, the music monthly *Mixmag* focused on a resurgence of the free party scene under the headline, 'Freedom for Clubland! Free parties, car cruises, illegal raves. Get in on the new D.I.Y.' In the article 'Ten free parties that changed the world' – a list which included Woodstock and Castlemorton – the 2002 solstice at Stonehenge was featured, with Arthur credited as having managed 'to convince the authorities not to ban alcohol consumption.' Readers who failed to check their calendars would have been disappointed, however, if they'd turned up in 2003 on the date quoted in the magazine: 'Summer Solstice, Stonehenge, 28th June.' (*Mixmag* 136, September 2002)

Although there is undoubtedly something of the 'Fatboy Slim Effect' taking place at Stonehenge – throw a free party and 250,000 people turn up, as they did for Norman Cook in summer 2002 on Brighton beach – clearly, apart from on protest marches, the opportunities for people to express themselves in large gatherings under their own terms have almost entirely disappeared in the decade since the passing of the Criminal Justice Act.

There are noticeably good paid festivals that have absorbed some of the old community principles – WOMAD, for example, which draws about 30,000 people to the riverside in Reading for a family-friendly festival of world music at the end of July – and several smaller events, which successfully juggle the need to make money with the desire to foster a communal spirit. A particular source of both praise and hostility is Michael Eavis' Glastonbury Festival, regarded by some as retaining the spirit of the free festivals in many essential characteristics, but by others – including a number of free festival veterans – as a betrayal of the movement's principles from the moment that a commercial, licensed festival replaced the 'traditional' free festivals in 1979.

In all fairness, Eavis has had little opportunity to do anything other than to submit to the increasing demands that are placed on him by the authorities each year, and his commitment to a free festival at Stonehenge has been unwavering. In 1988, for example, he explained to Jeremy Sandford how he was 'negotiating to buy a thousand acres near Stonehenge, and then resell it in half acre lots to different pseudonymous people who [would] then vanish', making it impossible for the authorities to prosecute the owners of the site when they held a festival. Explaining his reasons, he echoed the sentiments of those who had organised the first free festivals: 'The current philosophy of the survival of the fittest leaves so many people out of its get-rich-quick world, millions of them, and it's a small price to ask of a relatively rich society to allow a space like that where these people can go for a couple of weeks.' Although nothing concrete has materialised in the following years,

Eavis continues to pledge support for the idea. Sadly, however, the raising of the super-fence at Glastonbury in 2002, which immediately excluded at least 50,000 people, has only contributed to the prevalent sense of exclusion over the solstice period. Add this number to the 30,000 at Stonehenge, making do with half a day, and the country in June is awash with people looking for a more expansive solstice experience. (Sandford 1988)

In recent years, attendees at meetings of the Round Table and the TRC have noted murmurings from representatives of English Heritage and the Wiltshire police to the effect that they would not necessarily raise any objections to an alternative gathering taking place somewhere in the Stonehenge area over the solstice period (Viziondanz 2002). While this is conceivable in the sense that an alternative gathering would relieve pressure on both Stonehenge and Avebury, it remains unclear how, in the present political climate, such a gathering would be allowed to proceed. The survivors of the days of the free festivals – community festivals like the Eastern Sun Fayre – which took place in Norwich in August 2003, are free at the point of entry only because their costs are covered by funding and sponsorship, and all the necessary bureaucracy (mountains of it, from licensing to stewarding to health and safety) is undertaken by teams of dedicated volunteers.

Looking back over the last thirty years, the spontaneous world of the free festivals has disappeared, as surely as the infrastructure that sustained it. For Alan Lodge, the arrival of rave music was welcome because it revived the ailing travellers' scene, but it lacked a sense of community and the ethics that had sustained the free festivals: 'Bring what you expect to find. If not you, who? If not here, where? If not now, when?' Alan noted that in the rave years, 'many folks just thanked you very much, while others did the work, thus missing the point.' In the years since, the community spirit of the free festivals has retreated still further, but the hunger remains. (Lodge 2002)

Archaeological resurgence

The last group to be considered in connection with the monument at the start of the twenty-first century are the archaeologists. Throughout this most recent period, the majority of the archaeological establishment has maintained a dignified silence regarding the renewal of open access to Stonehenge at the summer solstice, to such an extent that the mind boggles to consider what Glyn Daniel would have made of it all.

Studies of the monument itself, however, have been remarkably fruitful, centred on the publication of *Stonehenge in its Landscape* in 1995. Commissioned by English Heritage and produced by a team of archaeologists from Wessex Archaeology, *Stonehenge in its Landscape* was described as 'magisterial and monumental' by Aubrey Burl. The editors of the book, headed by Rosamund Cleal, were allowed unprecedented access to the unpublished papers of Stuart Piggott and Richard Atkinson, who, despite their high profiles, only published a small amount of their findings in their own lifetimes, mainly in successive editions of Atkinson's *Stonehenge*. With newly-commissioned radiocarbon dates accompanying their

*Leaving the summer solstice
celebrations, 2003.
Copyright Andy Worthington.*

research, Cleal and her colleagues produced by far the most comprehensive overview of the archaeology of Stonehenge to date, refining Atkinson's chronology for the phases of the monument's development, and confirming, once and for all, that the sarsen Stonehenge was raised in the late Neolithic rather than the early Bronze Age. This, incidentally, is an assumption that has underpinned the Romanticism of the free-festival/earth mysteries movement throughout the whole of the modern counter-cultural history of Stonehenge. (Burl 2000: 351; Cleal, Walker and Montague 1995)

The publication of *Stonehenge in its Landscape* consolidated investigations that had begun in the 1980s with Julian Richards' Stonehenge Environs Project. This combined comprehensive field-walking expeditions, new developments in statistics, geo-chemical and geophysical investigations and limited excavation. Richards and his team partly excavated the ploughed remains of the Coneybury henge, just under a mile to the south-east of Stonehenge, which had first been recognised from the air in 1970. They also discovered over 100,000 worked flints in 750 hectares of land around the monument, putting together details of settlement and industry throughout the Neolithic and into the Bronze Age that confirmed the wider landscape as more than strictly ritual in intent. (Richards 1990)

In the early 1990s Julian Thomas contributed to the growing picture of the wider landscape and those who inhabited it, analysing the finds at Woodhenge. Radiocarbon dating revealed this to be contemporary with the sarsen Stonehenge or dating to the centuries just after it, when users of a distinctive type of pottery known as Grooved Ware (associated with henges and stone circles from the Orkneys to southern England) were also inhabiting Durrington Walls. In his meticulous studies of deposits in the post-holes, Thomas found that the bones of domesticated animals – pigs and cattle – were deposited inside the monument, whereas those of wild animals were restricted to the outer ditch. Even inside the monument the differentiation continued, with pig bones dominating the outer holes and cattle the inner. The same process applied to flints, which were 'natural' and restricted to the outer rings, and pottery, which was 'cultural' and deposited in the centre of the monument, leading Thomas to conclude that the people of Woodhenge – and, by extension, Stonehenge – were attempting to bring 'the world into balance through the relationships between opposites': 'inside and out, tame and wild, culture and nature', as Aubrey Burl put it. (Thomas 1991: 71–2; Burl 1999; 92)

Other research into the excavations at Woodhenge has focussed on the small chalk sculptures – discs, axes, phalli, balls and cups – that were deliberately deposited in pits on cardinal points and along solar alignments at Woodhenge. Found at many Grooved Ware sites, including Stonehenge (where examples were discovered by Colonel Hawley in connection with several of the largest sarsens), these objects confirm a preoccupation with astronomy and ritual, and have suggested to archaeologists that the people who raised and used Stonehenge and Woodhenge were preoccupied by fertility and death. (Burl 1999: 94–7)

These glimpses of the world of the Stonehenge people have continued in the years since the publication of *Stonehenge in its Landscape*, which has given a new authority to archaeological commentators. In 2000, Mike Pitts' book *Hengeworld* combined archaeological detective stories with a detailed study of current radiocarbon dates to look in detail at both Stonehenge and Avebury, and to place them in a larger landscape of settlement and ritual. Throughout this recent period Aubrey Burl has maintained a particularly prominent position, reviving the theory, first proposed by the astronomer C.A. Newham in 1972, that the entrance to the bank and ditch may initially have had a lunar alignment, with the post-holes discovered by Colonel Hawley functioning as sighting devices for recording the most northerly risings of the moon. Burl has also put forward the possibility that the Heel Stone, by analogy with similar outlying stones at the Rollrights and at Long Meg and Her Daughters in the Lake District, was the first stone to be raised at Stonehenge, 'a territorial marker, or a megalithic "signpost" on a trackway, or a statement that the land was occupied', although his most controversial proposal has been the suggestion that various components of the complex – in particular the horseshoe shape formed by the central trilithons – reveal influences from Brittany. In March 1997, his theory even made the front page of *The Guardian*. Under the heading 'Proudest symbol of British antiquity "is a French import"', Burl explained how Stonehenge could have been 'the handiwork of a powerful and intrusive aristocracy somewhere in western France, perhaps Brittany', provoking a hilarious Little Englander response from an English Heritage spokesman, who declared that 'If it were proved to be French it would undermine the English people's pride in it.' (Pitts 2001; Newham 1972; Burl 1999: 132-4, 104–5; *The Guardian*, 1 March 1997)

A conclusion of sorts

While these recent developments continue to open up the debate about the meaning of Stonehenge both inside and outside the archaeological establishment, clearly no one is any closer to a definitive understanding of the beliefs of the people who raised the temple. As Aubrey Burl has noted, 'Stonehenge begrudges its secrets. Each one explained – the date, the sources of the stones, the builders – leads to greater amazements, a spiralling complexity that even now eludes our understanding so that our studies of Stonehenge remain two-dimensional and incomplete.' (Burl 2000: 350)

For those committed to the continuation of 'managed open access' at Stonehenge, the current situation compares favourably with the confrontational days of Glyn Daniel. The temple's counter-cultural congregation can take comfort in the confirmation that the monument today remains as intolerant of dogma and sectarianism as it has throughout the whole of its modern history. As a result, only the most inflexible of its defenders can claim that the majority of those who have been drawn to the summer solstice celebrations over the last few years – whether beckoned by the mystery of the temple itself or by their own interpretation of its mythology – have no justifiable reason for doing so.

Chapter Fourteen

The future of Stonehenge

A new battleground

As 'managed open access' becomes entrenched and the major source of conflict at the summer solstice shifts to Avebury instead, one particular battle for Stonehenge still remains to be fought. This battle promises to be the defining struggle for Stonehenge in the early twenty-first century. It is centred on the attempt by English Heritage and the government to fulfil the plans for the 'improvement' of the wider Stonehenge landscape that have been rumbling on for over a decade – the enclosure of the A303 in a tunnel, the removal of the A344 and the building of a new visitors' centre and car park further away from the stones.

Few people doubt the necessity of doing something to improve the presentation of Stonehenge, but the current plans, based on a 'Master Plan' that was first presented in 1998 and restructured in 2000 as 'The Stonehenge Project', have attracted ferocious opposition from an extraordinary coalition of environmentalists, archaeologists and pagans, including Friends of the Earth, the CPRE, Transport 2000, RESCUE (the British Archaeological Trust) and the Pagan Federation – campaigning collectively as the Stonehenge Alliance – as well as the National Trust, the Council for British Archaeology, the international pressure group Save Stonehenge, and ICOMOS-UK, the International Commission on Monuments and Sites, made up of archaeologists responsible for advising UNESCO (which made Stonehenge and Avebury a World Heritage Site in 1986) on the status of its sites in the UK. (For the most comprehensive collection of articles relating to the groups mentioned above and the background to the proposals, see Save Stonehenge 2003a.)

The opposition to the proposals is based on suspicions regarding the motives behind plans for a new visitors' centre and plans to enclose the part of the A303 that runs closest to the monument in a tunnel. All the protestors' complaints are underpinned by an understanding of the conflict between the Master Plan endorsed by English Heritage, the National Trust and the government, and the responsibility of those same bodies as a UNESCO World Heritage Site. For a site to qualify as a World Heritage Site, its owners or curators are obliged to 'ensure the protection, conservation and presentation of the site, to the utmost of its resources.' They are also obliged to ensure that a Management Plan is produced – the Stonehenge World Heritage Management Plan – which 'provides the over-arching framework within which the Stonehenge Master Plan will be implemented', as Lord McIntosh explained to the House of Lords in 1998. (Young and Kennet 2000)

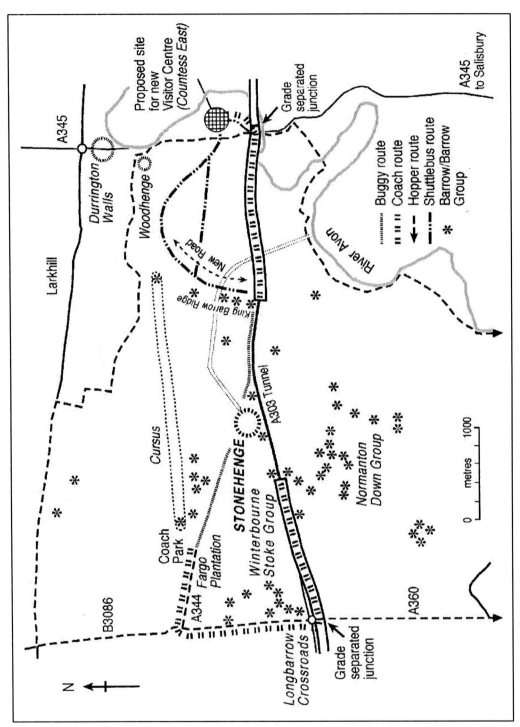

Map of the Stonehenge area, showing details of the proposed plans. The World Heritage Site comprises almost all of the area of the map to the west of the River Avon. Copyright Anne Tarver.

Despite these obligations, the Master Plan itself was announced by Heritage Secretary Chris Smith in September 1998, three months before the first working party for the Management Plan even took place. In an admirable résumé of the issues surrounding the project, the author Elizabeth Young and her husband Wayland Kennet, a Labour Lord and former minister, noted that 'The Master Plan was endorsed by officials from English Heritage and the National Trust', even though 'National Trust members were not consulted', and 'Public consultations are not known to have taken place.' Kennet and Young also noted of the first meeting of the working party for the Management Plan, that 'Despite requests, including formal written ones, no critical discussion of the Master Plan [was] permitted' by its chairperson, Lady Goss of English Heritage. (Young and Kennet 2000)

The central elements of the Master Plan – the A303 tunnel, the removal of the A344 and the creation of a new visitors' centre – were at the heart of the seductive image of 'a 6,000 acre prehistoric natural wilderness' that was proposed by English Heritage, the National Trust and the Tussaud Group in their bid for funding from the Millennium Commission for the 'Millennium Park' project that was introduced in Chapter Ten. The bid was announced in November 1996 and launched in May 1997, but collapsed almost immediately when funding was refused in June 1997. By the time a new appeal for business partners was launched in spring 1999, the lofty aspirations were toned down. Advertising for a new operator for the proposed visitors' centre, English Heritage described the project as a 'major international commercial opportunity', and in October, in a brief to Salisbury District Council, it was promised that the visitors' centre would include 'a range of catering outlets including fast food restaurants' and that a range of other retail outlets would be 'decided on [their] merits.' (CBA 2003; Young and Kennet 2000)

Opposition to the tunnel

At the heart of the protestors' complaints are the proposals for the tunnel, which are seen as a mixture of betrayed promises and naked hypocrisy. Chris Woodford of Save Stonehenge described the road proposals as 'a Trojan horse. They claim to be building it for the benefit of Stonehenge. Nothing could be further from the truth: it is part of a wider plan to create a massive new M303 motorway, by stealth, from London to the West Country.' (Save Stonehenge 2003b)

When the tunnel was first proposed in 1994 at the Great Debate, a major international conference on the future of Stonehenge, Sir Angus Young, the Director General of the National Trust, committed both the Trust and English Heritage to 'a long bored tunnel starting east of the New King Barrows and finishing to the west well past the monument', a tunnel that would be 2.5 miles (4 km) in length and that would cause minimal damage and disruption to the whole of the World Heritage Site. This commitment was reiterated in 1995 at a planning conference hosted by the Highways Agency (the government's road-building wing). But in September 1996 it was rejected as 'not an affordable solution' by the Major government, a position that was maintained at a ministerial meeting of the Blair government in November 1997, which described it as 'unaffordable and uneconomic.' The preferred option was a shorter, 'cut and cover' tunnel, 1.3 miles (2.1 km) in length, and this insistence first drew sustained hostility to the project. (Young and Kennet 2000; CBA 2003)

As was ably demonstrated in the Halcrow Report to the Highways Department in June 1998 that was largely ignored by those backing the project, an area ten times wider than the road enlargement would be disfigured by the building works (and would take place perilously close to the monument). In addition ten hectares of land inside the World Heritage Site but outside the 'cut and cover' tunnel would also be converted to dual carriageway, with approach cuttings, permanently lit and up to 500m in length, hacked out of the World Heritage Site landscape at either end of the tunnels. When David Part, the chairman of the Wiltshire Archaeology and Natural History Society, expressed misgivings about the project, he was assured by an official that, although five scheduled monuments would be lost as a result of the works, the rest of the damage could be overcome by 'sensitive implementation.' Young and Kennet noted the warped and surreal logic whereby 'dualling roads, altering the landscape and setting up permanently lit tunnel portals might, by 'sensitive implementation', somehow be transformed from vandalism to the acceptable.' (CBA 2003; Young and Kennet 2000)

Support for the tunnel outside the offices of the government, the Highways Agency and English Heritage was slim. Most noticeable was the unlikely endorsement of the British Druid Order, which urged pagans to 'have a little patience with the disruption and hold the image clear in our minds of how the temple will be, peaceful and free, in just a decade.' In 2001, Philip Shallcrass wrote, 'Each time I've walked the landscape around the henge for the past several years, I've connected with the spirits of the land and of our ancestors, partly to assess how they feel about the proposals for the roads. Bobcat has done the same. We have both found that the spirits are in no way opposed to the Stonehenge Master Plan as it stands.' Apparently, 'the spirits of the land are strong enough, tolerant enough, resilient and flexible enough to deal with it.' (Shallcrass and Orr 2002c)

From 1998, the campaigns against the tunnel increased in intensity. That year, the chairman of the Stonehenge Alliance, Lord Kennet, called the proposals 'barbaric', adding, 'No other country in the world would contemplate treating a site which is a world icon in such a way.' In December 1999, the government finally received the final draft of the Management Plan. As was expected, it stressed the integrity of the whole landscape of the World Heritage Site – not just 'the core' of the monument in its 'setting' – and suggested that all the tunnel options – including the long bored tunnel – 'be assessed in equal terms.' (*The Guardian*, 19 August 1998; Young and Kennet 2000; CBA 2003)

In July 2001, ICOMOS-UK reiterated the key concerns about the Master Plan that were expressed in the Management Plan, and in November 2002 the government finally attempted to reach a compromise, abandoning the 'cut and cover' tunnel and replacing it with a proposal for a bored tunnel of the same length. It was, however, a case of too little, too late, and the project's many critics made it clear that resistance would be maintained until the whole project was scrapped. At this point the

Willy X's anti-road sticker.
Image provided by Willy X.

National Trust, which, to the dismay of many of the scheme's opponents, was hitherto a partner in the Master Plan, finally opted out and joined the protestors. In a press release, the Trust insisted that it would 'press for the longest achievable tunnel past Stonehenge' and that it would be 'considering all the available evidence to assess why the Government believes that a 2.1km tunnel meets that description.' (CBA 2003)

The current deadlock

The protestors remain convinced that the only viable way forward is to resurrect the original proposal, endorsed by English Heritage and the National Trust in 1994, for a long bored tunnel, preferably one that starts and ends outside the confines of the World Heritage Site. They maintain that, although a shorter bored tunnel would side-step the desecration of the landscape around Stonehenge itself, there would still be 2.2 miles (3.5 km) of open dual carriageway and permanently lit tunnel cuttings within the larger confines of the World Heritage Site.

In June 2003, when all the opposing bodies produced press releases in response to the Highways Agency's draft orders and environmental statement on the proposed 'A303 Stonehenge Improvement Scheme', Chris Woodford of Save Stonehenge compared the current situation at Stonehenge with the road protest movement of the 1990s: 'Just like the controversial roads of the past – Twyford Down and the Newbury bypass – this road will be bulldozed through Stonehenge with no thought for public opposition.' In fact, there was a twelve-week consultation period after the publication of the Highways Agency's report, but Chris Woodford suggested that 'the pretence of a public consultation could backfire badly. If the Highways Agency thinks three days of tea and biscuits in an Amesbury hotel will deter three years of protest when the bulldozers start rolling, they've got another think coming.' (Save Stonehenge 2003b)

Save Stonehenge were not the only protestors making comparisons with the road protest movement. At a National Trust AGM in 2001, Dr Christopher Gillham attempted to persuade members that a 'warning to the Trust lies in the ruined landscape of another prehistoric site', pointing out that 'The Highways Agency and consultants Mott-Macdonald, with whom the Trust is now in consultation over Stonehenge, were the destroyers of the Iron Age site at Twyford Down as well as 14 archaeological sites at Newbury.' (Gillham 2001)

The vociferous resistance to the plans, which also includes Arthur Pendragon – ready if he is needed – and festival veteran Willy X, who is mounting his own independent campaign, printing and distributing thousands of stickers as he did in the heyday of the Stonehenge Free Festivals, suggests that an extraordinary coalition of protestors – as diverse as those opposed to the Criminal Justice Act, the occupation of Iraq and the inequalities of globalisation – is prepared, if necessary, to revive the spirit of the Dongas and the road protest movement at Stonehenge itself.

As the new century wears on, the great temple on Salisbury Plain may indeed have proved itself resistant to the claims of any one party, be they archaeologists, anarchists or pagans, but, as the conflict over the 'improvement' of the World Heritage Site reveals, its attraction as a symbol of celebration and subversion remains undimmed.

> Those who knew not of Stonehenge, who had never experienced its weird and lasting attraction, were astounded. What is this old pile of rocks which inspires such intensity of popular religious feeling and such vicious expressions of official jealousy?
>
> (John Michell 1986)

Bibliography

ABBOTT, Tim, 1990, 'Eye Witness', *Festival Eye* 1990.

AITKEN, Paul, 1998, 'Dialogue with Hilary, Wes and Paul' in Barbara Bender, *Stonehenge: Making Space*, Berg

ALLUM, Margaret, 2000, 'Greenham Common women inspired many', online at: www.greenleft.org.au/back/2000/423/423p14.htm

ANDREWS, Steve (The Bard of Ely), 2003, 'It Happened One Beltane', online at: ayla.brinkster.net/Bealtaine.asp

AP THUIN, Dylan, 2001, 'The Origins of the Insular Order of Druids', online at: www.neopagan.net/OriginsIOD.html

ATKINSON, R.J.C., 1956, *Stonehenge*, Hamish Hamilton

ATKINSON, R.J.C., 1967, 'Silbury Hill', *Antiquity* 41, 259-62

ATKINSON, R.J.C., 1969, *Silbury Hill*, BBC supplement

ATKINSON, R.J.C., 1979, *Stonehenge: Archaeology and Interpretation* (3rd edition), Penguin

ATKINSON, R.J.C., 1985, 'William Stukeley and the Stonehenge sunrise', *Archaeoastronomy* 8

AUBREY, John, 1980a, *Monumenta Britannica*, vol. 1, Dorset Publishing Co.

AUBREY, John, 1980b, *Monumenta Britannica*, vol. 2, Dorset Publishing Co.

AYERS, Nigel, 1996, 'Where's Wally?' *Transgressions*, 2/3, Salamander Press, online at: www.earthlydelights.co.uk/netnews/wally.html

BARNETT, Peter, 1998, 'The first quarter-century of the Green Party, 1973-1998', online at: www.greenparty.org.uk/information/silvergreen.htm

BARRETT, John, 1994, *Fragments from Antiquity: An Archaeology of Social Life in Britain, 2900–1200 BC*, Blackwell

BATTELEY, John, 1774, *The Antiquities of Richborough and Reculver.*

BATTEN, Roland, 2002, 'Solstice review reveals serious safety concerns', *The Salisbury Journal*, 12 September 2002

BBC ONLINE, 1998, 'Druids celebrate solstice', 21 June 1998, online at: news.bbc.co.uk/1/hi/uk/117024.stm

BECK, W., 1872, 'Sun-worshippers', *The Antiquary* 2, 29 June 1872, 158

BENDER, Barbara and Mark EDMONDS, 1992, 'De-romancing the stones', *The Guardian*, 15 June 1992

BENDER, Barbara, 1998, *Stonehenge: Making Space*, Berg

BENNETT, P. and T. WILSON, 1999, *The Old Stones of Rollright and District*, Cockley Press

BEY, Hakim, 1991, *T.A.Z.: The Temporary Autonomous Zone, Ontological Anarchy, Poetic Terrorism*

BIG STEVE, 1988, 'Freedom Festival', *Festival Eye*, Summer 88, online at: www.geocities.com/SoHo/9000/scfestiv.htm

BIRCHAM, Emma and John CHARLTON (eds.), 2001, *Anti-Capitalism: A Guide to the Movement*, Bookmarks Publications

BLAIN, J. and R.J. WALLIS, 2001, 'Stonehenge Solstice Access, 20–21 June 2001', a short report submitted to English Heritage, online at: www.sacredsites.org.uk/reports/StonehengeJune2001.html

BLAIN, J. and R.J. WALLIS, 2002a, 'Contemporary Paganism and Archaeology: Irreconcilable?', conference paper, Archaeology in the Public Domain, Sheffield, March 2002, online at: www.sacredsites.org.uk.papers/aypublic.html

BLAIN, J. and R.J. WALLIS, 2002b, 'A living landscape? Pagans, archaeology, and spirits in the land', *3rd Stone* 43, 20–7

BOLTON, Edmund, ('Philanactophil'), 1624, *Nero Caesar, or Monarchie Depraved*

BOMMES, M. and P. WRIGHT, 1982, 'Charms of residence, the public and the past', in R. Johnson et al. (eds.), *Making Histories: Studies in History Writing and Politics*, Hutchinson

BONEWITS, Isaac (ed.), 2002, The British Circle of the Universal Bond, 'The Ancient Druid Order', online at: www.neopagan.net/AODbooklet.html

BRADLEY, A.G., 1907, *Round About Wiltshire.*

BRITTON, John, 1845, *Memoir of John Aubrey.*

BROCK, E.F.L., 1891, *'Sunrise at Stonehenge on the longest day'*, *Journal of the British Archaeological Association* 47, 330–1

BUDAPEST, Zsuzsanna E., 1989, *The Grandmother of Time*, Harper and Row

BURCHARDT, Jeremy, 2002, *Paradise Lost: Rural Idyll and Social Change since 1800*, I.B. Tauris

BURNETT, Doug, 1998, 'Europe, 1970 – A Travelogue by Doug Burnett', online at: www.traveldoug.com/70europe.htm

BURL, Aubrey, 1976, *The Stone Circles of the British Isles*, Yale UP

BURL, Aubrey, 1979, *Prehistoric Avebury*, Yale UP

BURL, Aubrey, 1995, *A Guide to the Stone Circles of Britain, Ireland and Brittany*, Yale UP

BURL, Aubrey, 1999, *Great Stone Circles*, Yale UP

BURL, Aubrey, 2000a, *The Stone Circles of Britain, Ireland and Brittany*, Yale UP

BURL, Aubrey, 2000b, 'Myth-Conceptions', *3rd Stone* 37, 6–9

BUSSMAN, Jane, 1998, *Once in a Lifetime*, Virgin

CAMDEN, William, 1610, *Britannia.*

CAMPBELL, Thalia, 2003, personal communication, 28 August 2003

CAREY, Jim, 1997, 'A Criminal Culture?' *Squall*, online at: www.squall.co.uk/squall.cfm/ses/sq=2001061806/ct=2

CARNARVON, 4th Earl of, 1885, 'A vigil at Stonehenge', *National Review* 5, 540–6

CARNES, Mark C., 1989, *Secret Ritual and Manhood in Victorian America*, Yale UP

CARR-GOMM, Philip, 1991, *The Elements of the Druid Tradition*, Element

CARR-GOMM, Philip, 1992, Foreword to Ross Nichols, *The Book of Druidry*, Thorsons

CASTLEDEN, Rodney, 1987, *The Stonehenge People*, Routledge

CASTLEDEN, Rodney, 2000, 'The epic of the Stonehenge Bluestones: were they moved by ice, or by people?', *3rd Stone* 39, 12–25

CBA (Council for British Archaeology), 2003, 'The Stonehenge Saga. Stonehenge Conservation and Management: some recent developments', online at: www.britarch.ac.uk/stonehenge/

CHARLETON, Walter, 1663, *Chorea Gigantum, Or, The most Famous Antiquity of Great-Britan, Vulgarly called Stone-Heng, Standing on Salisbury Plain, Restored to the Danes*

CHILDE, V.G., 1954, *What Happened in History?* Penguin

CHIPPINDALE, Christopher, 1985, 'English Heritage and the future of Stonehenge', *Antiquity* 59, 132–7

CHIPPINDALE, Christopher, 1990, 'The Stonehenge Phenomenon' in *Who Owns Stonehenge?* Batsford

CHIPPINDALE, Christopher, 1994, *Stonehenge Complete* (2nd edition), Thames and Hudson

CLARKE, D., 2002, 'Beatles Ireland: John Lennon and Dorinish Island', online at: www.iol.ie/~beatlesireland/irish/irish1/dorinishisland.htm

CLARKE, Michael, 1982, *The Politics of Pop Festivals*, Junction Books

CLEAL, R., K. WALKER and R. MONTAGUE (eds.), 1995, *Stonehenge in its Landscape: Twentieth Century Excavations*, English Heritage

CONNELLY, Cerridwen, 2001, 'What is a TechnoPagan?' online at: www.technopagans.co.uk/TEKLIST.HTM

CONNELLY, Cerridwen, 2003, 'TechnoPagans Unlimited', online at: www.technopagans.co.uk/HOME.HTM

COPE, Julian, 1998, *The Modern Antiquarian: A Pre-Millennial Odyssey through Megalithic Britain*, Thorsons

CRAIG, Sheila (ed.), 1986, 'Stonehenge '85: A Collection of Material to Commemorate 'The Battle of the Beanfield', June 1st 1985', Unique Publications

CRAWFORD, O.G.S., 1953, editorial in *Antiquity* 27, 1

CRAWFORD, O.G.S., 1956, editorial in *Antiquity* 30, 131

CRAWFORD, O.G.S., 1957, *The Eye Goddess*, Phoenix House

CROWLEY, Aleister, 1929, *Moonchild*, reprinted 1970, Samuel Weiser

CRYER, Dominic, 1993, 'A visit with the Dongas Tribe', online at: www.tash.gn.apc.org/dongas.htm

CUNNINGTON, M.E., 1927, *Antiquity* 1, 92–100

CUNNINGTON, M.E., 1929, *Woodhenge. A Description of the Site as revealed by Excavations carried out there by Mr and Mrs B. Cunnington, 1926–7–8*

DALY, Mary, 1973, *Beyond God The Father*, Beacon

DAMES, Michael, 1976, *The Silbury Treasure: The Great Goddess Rediscovered*, Thames and Hudson

DAMES, Michael, 1977, *The Avebury Cycle*, Thames and Hudson

DANIEL, Glyn, 1958, *The Megalith Builders of Western Europe*, Hutchinson

DANIEL, Glyn, 1982, review in *Antiquity* 56, 164–6

DANIEL, Glyn, 1992, *Writing for Antiquity*, Thames and Hudson

DAYONIS, 1959, letter from Dayonis to Gerald Gardner, 28 June 1959, in the 'Toronto Collection' of Gardner's correspondence

DECHELETTE, Joseph, 1908, *Manual d'archaeologie prehistorique Celtique et Gallo-Romaine*, vol. 1, 594–6

DEVEREUX, Paul, 1990, 'Stonehenge as an Earth Mystery' in *Who Owns Stonehenge?* Batsford

DEVEREUX, Paul, 1991, *Earth Memory*, Quantum

DICE GEORGE (ed.), 2001, 'John Pendragon at Tribal Voices', tributes to John Pendragon, online at: www.phreak.co.uk/stonehenge/psb/johnpend.htm

DISPATCH ONLINE, 1998, 'Stonehenge solstice festival of bicker and bitchcraft', 24 June 1998, online at:
www.dispatch.co.za/1998/06/24/features/BITCHCRA.HTM

DIY, 1997a, 'So What Happened?' online at:
www.diydiscs.com/History/Party/systems.htm

DIY, 1997b, 'DiY Biography', online at: www.diydiscs.com/History/DIY/history.htm

DONGAS, 1995a, 'Gary's Story - From Printer to Donga', online at:
www.tash.gn.apc.org/gary.htm

DONGAS, 1995b, 'Anna's Story - Donga Tribe', online at:
www.tash.gn.apc.org/anna.htm

DONGAS, 1995c, 'Indra's Story - Twyford Down', online at:
www.tash.gn.apc.org/indra.htm

DONGAS, 1995d, 'Kevin's Story - Solsbury Hill', online at:
www.tash.gn.apc.org/kevin.htm

DONGAS, 1995e, 'Geoff's Story - Solsbury Hill', online at:
www.tash.gn.apc.org/geoff.htm

DONGAS, 1995f, 'Fluffy's Story - Solsbury Hill', online at:
www.tash.gn.apc.org/fluffy.htm

DOUGLAS, James, 1793, *Nenia Britannica*

DOUGLAS, Roger, 1977, 'Festival reports: Stonehenge Free Festival', online at:
www.festival-zone.0catch.com/fws-henge1-77-report.html

DUKE, Rev. E., 1846, *The Druidical Temples of the County of Wilts.*

DWORKIN, Andrea, 1974, *Woman Hating*, Dutton

EVANS, A.J., 1902, 'The Palace of Knossos', *Annual of the British School at Athens*, viii (1901-2), 1–124

EVERSLEY, Lord, 1910, 'How Stonehenge became desecrated and vulgarised by barbed-wire' in Rodney Legg (ed.), 1986, *Stonehenge Antiquaries*, Dorset Publishing Co.

FAERY FAITH NETWORK, 2003, 'About FOI', online at:
www.faeryfaith.org/foi/foiwelcome.html

FARREN, Mick and Edward BARKER, 1972, *Watch Out, Kids*, Open Gate Books

FARREN, Mick, 2001, *Give the Anarchist a Cigarette*, Jonathan Cape

FESTIVAL GENERATION, 1999, 'Groups divided over sunrise invasion', online at:
www.festival-generation.co.uk/festival_stonehenge_news.html

FIRSOFF, George, 1987, 'History of the Troubles: The Solstice Walkabout', online at: www.greenleaf.demon.co.uk/h870621.htm

FIRSOFF, George, 1988a, 'History of the Troubles: Biggest Stonehenge Gathering since 1984', online at: www.greenleaf.demon.co.uk/h880808.htm

FIRSOFF, George, 1988b, 'History of the Troubles: Policing the Stonehenge '88 Campaign', online at: www.greenleaf.demon.co.uk/h880914.htm

FIRSOFF, George, 1992, 'Why we need Stonehenge', leaflet

FIRSOFF, George, 1998, 'Truth & Reconciliation Commission for Stonehenge', Stonehenge Campaign Newsletter, Summer Solstice 1998, online at: www.geocities.com/soho/9000/scn9806.htm

FIRSOFF, George, 1999, 'History of the Troubles: Solstice Report 1999', online at: www.greenleaf.demon.co.uk/h990621.htm

FIRSOFF, George, 2002a, stonehengepeace email, 1 July 2002, online at: stonehengepeace@yahoogroups.com

FIRSOFF, George, 2002b, 'The Festival & the National Trust', online at: www.greenleaf.demon.co.uk/htrust.htm

FLEMING, Andrew, 1969, 'The Myth of the Mother Goddess', *World Archaeology* 1, 247–61

FOUNTAIN, Nigel, 1988, *Underground: The London Alternative Press 1966–74*, Routledge

FOWLER, Peter, 1990a, 'Stonehenge in a Democratic Society' in *Who Owns Stonehenge?* Batsford

FOWLER, Peter, 1990b, 'Stonehenge: Academic Claims and Responsibilities' in *Who Owns Stonehenge?* Batsford

GARDNER, Gerald B., 1954, *Witchcraft Today*, Rider

GARRARD, Bruce and Steve HIERONYMOUS (eds.), 1986, 'Stonehenge '86', Unique Publications

GILLHAM, Dr C., 2001, 'Motion to the National Trust on Stonehenge', October 2001, online at: www.savestonehenge.org.uk/ntmotion.html

GOODWIN, Neil, 1995, 'Operation Solstice', online at: www.cultureshop.org

GOODWIN, Neil, 2003, 'The Traveller's Tale', unpublished interview with Phil the Beer

GORSETH KERNOW, 2002, 'About Gorseth Kernow', online at: www.gorsethkernow.org.uk/english/about.htm

GOUGH, Richard, 1768, *Anecdotes of British Topography*

GOULSTONE, John, 1985a, 'Midsummer Observance at Stonehenge', *The Ley Hunter* 99, 7–8

GOULSTONE, John, 1985b, 'Folk Games at Silbury Hill and Stonehenge', *Antiquity* 59, 51–3

GOWLAND, William, 1902, 'Recent excavations at Stonehenge', *Archaeologia* 58, 37–105

GRANT, Kenneth, 1972, *The Magical Revival*, Muller

GRAVES, Robert, 1948, *The White Goddess*, Faber and Faber

GREEN, Miranda, 1997, *Exploring the World of the Druids*, Thames and Hudson

GREEN, Scott, 2003, letter to Steve Bubble, 18 July 2003, online at: stonehengeentertainmentsdiscussion@yahoogroups.com, Digest Number 157, 20 July 2003

GREEN ANARCHIST, 1984, 'London Stop the City', issue 3, Nov/Dec 1984, online at: www.greenanarchist.org.uk/Stc.htm

GREENFIELDS, Margaret, 2003, in 'Not only but also... some historical ramblings about the English festivals scene', compiled by Alan Dearling, online at: www.members.aol.com/adearling/enabler/nointro.htm

GRINSELL, Leslie, 1978, 'The Druids and Stonehenge', *West Country Folklore* 11, Toucan Press

HAMMOND, Veronica, 2003, personal communication, March 2003

HARPER, C.G., 1899, *The Exeter Road.*

HARRISON, Jane Ellen, 1903, *Prolegomena to the Study of Greek Religion.*

HARRISON, John, 1989, *The Stonehenge Conflict: Experiences and Opinions,* Monolith Publications

HARRISON, Pete, 2003, 'Sabrina, Harry and the Web help Paganism grow', Reuters, 19 June 2003.

HARVEY, Graham, 1997, *Listening People, Speaking Earth: Contemporary Paganism,* Hurst

HARVEY, Graham, 2000, 'Heathenism: a North European Pagan Tradition' in Graham Harvey and Charlotte Hardman (eds.), *Pagan Pathways: A Guide to the Ancient Earth Traditions,* Thorsons

HAWKES, Jacquetta, 1968, *Dawn of the Gods,* Chatto and Windus

HAWKES, Jacquetta, 1978, *A Land* (2nd edition), David and Charles

HAWKINS, Gerald, 1966, *Stonehenge Decoded,* Souvenir Press

HAYCOCK, David Boyd, 2003, 'The questionable reputation of Dr William Stukeley', *3rd Stone* 45, 16–21

HEMINGWAY, Andy, 2003, personal communication, 14 March 2003

HICKS, Arthur, 1988a, 'Search goes on for Stonehenge site', *Festival Eye,* Summer 88, 3

HICKS, Arthur, 1988b, 'Peace & Love?' *Festival Eye,* Summer 88, 5

HILL, Howard, 1980, *Freedom to Roam: the Struggle for Access to Britain's Moors and Mountains,* Moorland Publishing

'H.J.', 1875, 'Stonehenge', *Notes and Queries* 4, 83

HORNBLOWER, G.D., 1929, 'Predynastic figures of Women and their Successors', *Journal of Egyptian Archaeology* xv, 29–47

HOYLE, F., 1966, 'Speculations on Stonehenge', *Antiquity* 40, 261-76

HUDSON, Phil, 2002, 'Molesworth Free Festival', online at: www.festival-zone.0catch.com/molesworth-free-fest-1984.html

HUDSON, W.H., 1908, 'Stonehenge (June 21, 1908)', *The English Review,* December 1908, 60–8

HUGHES, Trevor, 1990, 'Spring Equinox 1990' in 'Stonehenge Decoded', Hawkfrendz Publications 15

HUNTER, Michael, 1975, *John Aubrey and the Realm of Learning,* Duckworth

HUTCHINSON, Horace G., 1914, *The Life of Sir John Lubbock*

HUTCHINSON, Roger, 'Stonehenge Free Festival 1977', poster, online at: www.festival-zone.0catch.com/Stonehenge-Poster-77.html

HUTTON, Lord, 1999, in House of Lords, 'Opinions of the Lords of Appeal for Judgment in the Cause Director of Public Prosecutions (Respondent) v. Jones and Another (Appelants) (On Appeal from a Divisional Court of the Queen's Bench Division)', 4 March 1999, online at: homepages.tcp.co.uk/~ait/judgment.html

HUTTON, Ronald, 1991, *The Pagan Religions of the Ancient British Isles*, Blackwell

HUTTON, Ronald, 1996, *The Stations of the Sun*, Oxford UP

HUTTON, Ronald, 1997, 'Witness statement prepared by Professor Ronald E Hutton for the trial of Arthur Pendragon at Southwark Crown Court, November 1997, regarding Arthur's right to carry the sword Excalibur', Appendix 3 in Arthur Pendragon and Christopher James Stone, 2003, *The Trials of Arthur*, Element

HUTTON, Ronald, 1998, 'Another Dialogue with Ronald Hutton' in Barbara Bender, *Stonehenge: Making Space*, Berg

HUTTON, Ronald, 1999, *The Triumph of the Moon*, Oxford UP

IRVINE, Lord, 1999, in House of Lords, 'Opinions of the Lords of Appeal for Judgment in the Cause Director of Public Prosecutions (Respondent) v. Jones and Another (Appelants) (On Appeal from a Divisional Court of the Queen's Bench Division)', 4 March 1999, online at: homepages.tcp.co.uk/~ait/judgment.html

JARVIS, Kevin, 1995, 'V.E. Day at Stonehenge', online at: www.tash.gn.apc.org/veday.htm

JONES, Hilary, 1998, 'Dialogue with Hilary, Wes and Paul' in Barbara Bender, *Stonehenge: Making Space*, Berg

JONES, Inigo and John WEBB, 1655, *The most notable Antiquity of Great Britain, vulgarly called Stone-Heng on Salisbury Plain, Restored*

JONES, Rhys, 1990, 'A British Aboriginal's land claim to Stonehenge' in *Who Owns Stonehenge?* Batsford

KEATS, John, 1818, *Endymion*

KIBBLEWHITE, Celia, 2003, personal communication, 5 September 2003

KING, Francis (ed.), 1973, *The Secret Rituals of the O.T.O.*, Daniel

KRYSTOF, 1989, 'Stonehenge Festival: Towards a New Beginning', *Festival Eye* 1989, online at: www.phreak.co.uk/stonehenge/psb/scfestiv.htm

LEE, Linda, 1986, 'Greenham Women revive Beltane Walk', *Festival Eye*, June 86

LEGG, Rodney, 1980, 'Stonehenge, public but untouchable' in Rodney Legg (ed.), 1986, *Stonehenge Antiquaries*, Dorset Publishing Co.

LEGG, Rodney (ed.), 1986, *Stonehenge Antiquaries*, Dorset Publishing Co.

LELAND, Charles, 1899, *Aradia*

LELAND, John, ed. Anthony Hall, 1709, *Commentarii de Scriptoribus Britannicis*

LOCKYER, Sir J.N., 1901, *Proceedings of the Royal Society* 69, 143

LOCKYER, Sir J.N., 1906, *Stonehenge and Other British Stone Monuments Astronomically Considered*

LODGE, Alan, 1998, 'John Pendragon remembered by Tash', *Stonehenge Campaign Newsletter*, Summer Solstice 1998, online at: www.geocities.com/soho/9000/scn9806.htm

LODGE, Alan, 2001, 'My Diary', online at: www.tash.gn.apc.org/diary.htm

LODGE, Alan, 2002, stonehengeentertainmentsdiscussion email, 5 October 2002,
    online at: stonehengeentertainmentsdiscussion@yahoogroups.com
LOXLEY, David, 2002, 'A Druid Version of Spirit', online at:
    www.yewgrove.demon.co.uk/dloxley.htm
LOXLEY, David, 2003, personal communication, February 2003
LUBBOCK, Sir John, 1865, *Prehistoric Times*
LUBBOCK, Sir John, 1866, 'Secret of the Druidical Stones' in *Athenaeum*

MACNEILL, Maire, 1962, *The Festival of Lughnasa*, Oxford UP
MALYON, Tim, 2003, personal communication, 20 December 2003
MARSH, Jan, 1982, *Back to the Land: The Pastoral Impulse in Victorian England
    from 1880–1914*, Quartet
MASSINGHAM, Harold, 1932, *Wold Without End*, Cobden-Sanderson
MAUGHFLING, Rollo, 1990, *Festival Eye* 1990, 39, reproduced in 'Druids and
    Stonehenge', online at: www.phreak.co.uk/stonehenge/psb/scdruids.htm
McKAY, George, 2000, *Glastonbury: A Very English Fair*, Victor Gollancz
McSTONE, Hengist, 2003, personal communication, 15 December 2002
MELLOR, Penny, 1980a, 'FWS Report: Cantlin Stone Free Festival July 4th +', online
    at: www.festival-zone.0catch.com/cantlin-stone-free-fest80.html
MELLOR, Penny, 1980b, 'FWS Report: Stonehenge Free Festival, Midsummer
    Solstice, 1980', online at:
    www.festival-zone.0catch.com/henge80-fws-report.html
MELLOR, Penny, 1980c, 'Festival Welfare Service report', online at:
    www.festival-zone.0catch.com/Psilocybin-Festival.html
MELLOR, Penny, 1983, FWS Report: Stonehenge Free Festival, Midsummer
    Solstice, 1983', online at:
    www.festival-zone.0catch.com/heng83-fws-report.html
MICHELET, Jules, 1866, *La Sorciere*
MICHELL, John, 1977, *A Little History of Astro-Archaeology: Stages in the
    Transformation of a Heresy*, Thames and Hudson
MICHELL, John, 1982, *Megalithomania*, Thames and Hudson
MICHELL, John, 1983, *The New View over Atlantis*, Thames and Hudson
MICHELL, John, 1986, 'Stonehenge, Its History, Meaning, Festival, Unlawful
    Management, Police Riot '85 & Future Prospects', Radical Traditionalist
    Papers No.6
MINNION, John and Philip BOLSOVER (eds.), 1983, *The CND Story: The First 25
    Years of CND in the Words of the People Involved*, Allison and Busby
MONBIOT, George, 1996a, 'Grubbing Out the Past', *The Guardian*, 10 January
    1996, online at: www.monbiot.com/dsp_article.cfm?article_id=205
MONBIOT, George, 1996b, 'The Land Is Ours', online at:
    www.mondodesigno.com/land.html
MONBIOT, George, 1997, 'Multi-issue politics', *The Times Literary Supplement*, 21
    February 1997, online at: ww.monbiot.com/dsp_article.cfm?article_id=275
MONBIOT, George, 2000, 'Digging Deeper', *BBC History*, June 2000, online at:
    www.monbiot.com/dsp_article.cfm?article_id=292
MOODY, Paul, 2002, 'All the fun of the fayre', *Time Out Carnival Guide 2002*

MORGAN, Mogg, 1999, 'Stonehenge Pilgrimage – Solstice 1999', online at: homepages.tesco.net/~mogg.morgan/solstice.htm

MORRIS, Nora, 1998, in Stonehenge Campaign Newsletter, Autumn Equinox 1998, online at: www.geocities.com/SoHo/9000/scn9809.htm

MURRAY, Margaret, 1921, *The Witch Cult in Western Europe*, Oxford UP

MURRAY, Margaret, 1931, *The God of the Witches*, Faber and Faber

NCCL (National Council for Civil Liberties), 1986, 'Stonehenge: A report into the civil liberties implications of the events relating to the convoys of summer 1985 and 1986', NCCL

NEVILLE, Elizabeth, 1998, letter from Elizabeth Neville, Chief Constable of Wiltshire to Richard Sheard, Chief Executive, Salisbury District Council, 24 March 1999, reproduced in Stonehenge Campaign News '99, online at: homepages.tcp.co.uk/~ait/stonehenge.html

NEVILLE, Richard, 1995, *Hippie Hippie Shake*, Bloomsbury

NEWHAM, C.A., 1972, *The Astronomical Significance of Stonehenge*, Moon Publications

NICHOLS, Ross, 1992, *The Book of Druidry*, Thorsons

NICHOLSON, J., 1987, 'The Times of the Sign' in L. Schreiber and J. Nicholson, *An English Figure: Two Essays on the work of John Michell*, Bozo

NIGHTINGALE, Robert, 1978, 'Release Report on Stonehenge Free Festival, June 16th–25th 1978', online at: www.festival-zone.0catch.com/fws-henge78report.html

NORTHAM, John and Rachel PHELAN, 2003, letter to *The Guardian*, June 2003, online at: stonehengepeace@yahoogroups.com, Digest Number 793, 26 June 2003

ORR, Emma Restall, 1996, 'Issues Facing Contemporary Druidry', online at: www.druidry.org/obod/druid-path/ero-issues.html

ORR, Emma Restall, 2000, 'Stonehenge: A View from the Moment', online at: www.druidry.org/obod/druid-path/ritual/summer_solstice2000.html

OUBRIDGE, Brig, 1986, 'Decommission "hippies"', *Green Line*, July 1986; reprinted in Bruce Garrard and Steve Hieronymous (eds.), 1986, *Stonehenge '86*, Unique Publications

PENDRAGON, Arthur, 1999a, 'The Loyal Arthurian Warband: Chronicles 86–98', online at: www.warband.org/warband_old/chronicles/chronicles_archive.htm

PENDRAGON, Arthur, 1999b, 'Summer Solstice 1999', online at: www.warband.org/sacred%20sites/stonehenge/summer_solstice 1999.htm

PENDRAGON, Arthur, 2000, 'The Loyal Arthurian Warband (1990-2000)', online at: www.warband.org/warband_old/sacred_sites/stonehenge/1990-2000.htm

PENDRAGON, Arthur and Christopher James STONE, 2003, *The Trials of Arthur: The Life and Times of a Modern-Day King*, Element

PENNICK, Nigel and Paul DEVEREUX, 1989, *Lines on the Landscape: Leys and Other Linear Enigmas*, Robert Hale

PETRIE, W.M.F., 1880, *Stonehenge: Plans, Descriptions, and Theories*

PHILLIPS, Megan, 1999, *'Liberty: A Brief History'*, online at:
www.liberty-human-rights.org.uk/about/history/pdfs/history-of-liberty.pdf

PIGGOTT, Stuart, 1938, 'The early bronze age in Wessex', *Proceedings of the Prehistoric Society*, vol. 4, 52–106

PIGGOTT, Stuart, 1950, *William Stukeley*, Oxford UP

PIGGOTT, Stuart, 1954, *The Neolithic Cultures of the British Isles*, Cambridge UP

PIGGOTT, Stuart, 1965, *Ancient Europe*, Edinburgh UP

PIGGOTT, Stuart, 1975, *The Druids*, Thames and Hudson

PIGGOTT, Stuart, 1985, *William Stukeley: An Eighteenth-Century Antiquary* (2nd edition), Thames and Hudson

PITTS, Mike, 1981, 'The Discovery of a New Stone at Stonehenge', *Archaeoastronomy* 4.2

PITTS, Mike, 1982, 'On the Road to Stonehenge: report on the investigations beside the A344 in 1968, 1979 and 1980', *Proceedings of the Prehistoric Society* 48, 75–132

PITTS, Mike, 1996, *Footprints through Avebury*, Digging Deeper

PITTS, Mike, 2000, *Hengeworld*, Arrow

PLOWS, Alex, 2003, in 'Not only but also...some historical ramblings about the English festivals scene', compiled by Alan Dearling, online at:
www.members.aol.com/adearling/enabler/nointro.htm

PONTING, Gerald, 2003, personal communication, 12 March 2003

PUBLIC RECORD OFFICE, 1962, PRO WORK/14/2789, letter from Gilpin to Cunliffe, 2 February 1962

REID, Douglas, 1996, letter to *The Salisbury Journal*, June 1996, reproduced in Stonehenge Campaign News '98, online at:
homepages.tcp.co.uk/~ait/news98.html

RENAUD, E.B., 1929, 'Prehistoric Female figurines from America and the Old World', *Scientific Monthly* 28, 507–13

RENFREW, Colin, 1971, 'Colin Renfrew describes Europe's creative barbarians', *The Listener* 7, January 1971, 12–14

RENFREW, Colin, 1973, 'Monuments, mobilization and social organisation in Neolithic Europe' in Renfrew, Colin (ed.), *The Explanation of Culture Change: Models in Prehistory*, Duckworth

RENTON, Alex, 1991, 'Seasoned players acting out ritual of the stones', *The Independent*, 22 June 1991

REYNOLDS, Simon, 1998, *Energy Flash: A Journey through Rave Music and Dance Culture*, Picador

RICHARDS, J., 1990, *Stonehenge Environs Project*, English Heritage

RICHARDSON, Bev, 1996, 'Bev and Del: Pagan Ireland – Bev's Gardnerian Roots', online at: www.synergy.ie/bevandel/gardiner.html

RICHARDSON, Bev and Del, 1997, 'Bev and Del: Pagan Ireland – The Pagan Page', online at: www.synergy.ie/bevandel/phantom.html

RICHARDSON, Bev and Del, 1998, 'Bev and Del: Pagan Ireland – About Us', online at: www.synergy.ie/bevandel/about.html

RICHARDSON, Bev, 2003, personal communication, 21 December 2003

RIMBAUD, Penny, 1981, 'The Last of the Hippies: An Hysterical Romance' in The Crass Collective, *A Series of Shock Slogans and Mindless Token Tantrums*, Exitstencil Press, online at: www.southern.com/southern/label/CRC/text/09438.html

ROAD ALERT! 1995, 'Synopsis of anti-road direct action campaigns; past and present', website no longer available. Details from: www.roadalert.org.uk

ROBERTSON, Olivia, 2003, 'Fellowship of Isis Homepage', online at: www.fellowshipofisis.com/intro.html

ROSENBERGER, Alex, 1986, 'Stonehenge '86: festival or fiasco?' *Festival Eye*, June 86

ROSENBERGER, Alex, 1989, 'Life on the Road', *Festival Eye*, Summer 89

RUGGLES, Clive, 1999, *Astronomy in Prehistoric Britain and Ireland*, Yale UP

RUSSELL, Chris, 1996, 'An Interview with The King', UK Online, online at: arthurpendragon.ukonline.co.uk/arthur.html

RUSSELL, Phil, 1973, 'The Windsor Free Festivals: Free press issues 1973–74', online at: tinpan.fortunecity.com/ebony/546/freep-30th-aug-73.html

RUSSELL, Phil, 1974, 'Free Stoned Henge Rocks Off Every Sun Day For Ever', leaflet, online at: www.festival-zone.0catch.com/Stoned-Henge-Leaflet-wa.html

SAMMES, Aylett, 1676, *Britannia Antiqua Illustrata*

SANDFORD, Jeremy and Ron REID, 1974, Tomorrow's *People*, Jerome Books

SANDFORD, Jeremy, 1982, 'Sing and Shout for Joy!' online at: www.festival-zone.0catch.com/henge-press-82.html

SANDFORD, Jeremy, 1988, 'Buying his way into Stonehenge', *The Guardian*, 2 June 1988

SAVE STONEHENGE, 2003a, Save Stonehenge home page, online at: www.savestonehenge.org.uk/homepage.html

SAVE STONEHENGE, 2003b, 'New Stonehenge plan is "Trojan Horse" for 4-lane motorway', press release, 5 June 2003, online at: www.savestonehenge.org.uk/ssnr050603.html

SCHNEWS, 2000, 'Diary of Adrian Molesworth', *Schnews* 246, 3 February 2000, online at: www.veggies.org.uk/calendar/moleswor.htm

SEBASTIAN, Tim, 1990, 'Triad: the Druid knowledge of Stonehenge' in *Who Owns Stonehenge?* Batsford

SHALLCRASS, Philip, 1999, 'Stonehenge and the Druids', online at: www.druidorder.demon.co.uk/druids_stonehenge.htm

SHALLCRASS, Philip, 2001, in Philip Shallcrass and Emma Restall Orr (eds.), *A Druid Directory: A Guide to Contemporary Druidry and Druid Orders*, online at: www.druidorder.demon.co.uk/Greywolf/Greywolf writings2.htm

SHALLCRASS, Philip, 2002, 'Greywolf: A Short Biography', online at: www.druidorder.demon.co.uk/Greywolf/Greywolf_biography.htm

SHALLCRASS, Philip and Emma Restall ORR, 1999, 'Solstice 1999', online at: www.druidorder.demon.co.uk/stonehenge1999.htm

SHALLCRASS, Philip and Emma Restall ORR, 2000, 'The Gorsedd of Bards of the Isles of Great Britain', online at: www.druidorder.demon.co.uk/gorsedd_bards.htm

SHALLCRASS, Philip and Emma Restall ORR, 2002a, 'Introducing the BDO', online at: www.druidorder.demon.co.uk/bdo_intro.htm

SHALLCRASS, Philip and Emma Restall ORR, 2002b, 'The British Druid Order', online at: www.druidorder.demon.co.uk/

SHALLCRASS, Philip and Emma Restall ORR, 2002c, 'Road Scheme Update, Feb 2001' in 'Stonehenge 2002', online at: www.druidorder.demon.co.uk/stonehenge2002.htm

SHARK, G.W., 2003a, 'The Hyde Park Free Concerts', online at: tinpan.fortunecity.com/ebony/546/hydepark-5-%2031-75.html

SHARK, G.W., 2003b, 'Bath Free Festivals', online at: www.festival-zone.0catch.com/bath-free-fest-72.html

SHARK, G.W., 2003c, 'The Trentishoe Whole Earth Fayres', online at: www.festival-zone.0catch.com/trentishoe-menu.html

SHARK, G.W., 2003d, 'The Stonehenge Free Festivals', online at: www.festival-zone.0catch.com/henge-menu.html

SHARK, G.W., 2003e, 'The Windsor Free Festivals', online at: tinpan.fortunecity.com/ebony/546/windsor-menu.html

SHARK, G.W., 2003f, 'The Watchfield Free Festival', online at: www.festival-zone.0catch.com/watchfieldfestival-menu.html

SHARK, G.W., 2003g, 'Meigan Fayre', online at: www.festival-zone.0catch.com/meigan-75-menu.html

SHARK, G.W., 2003h, 'Tangmere (Seasalter) Free Festival', online at: www.festival-zone.0catch.com/seasalter.html

SHARK, G.W., 2003i, 'Deeply Vale Free Festival', online at: www.festival-zone.0catch.com/deeply-vale-menu.html

SHARK, G.W., 2003j, 'Rivington Pike Free Festival', online at: www.festival-zone.0catch.com/rivington-pike-78.html

SHARK, G.W., 2003k, 'Psilocybin Festival', online at: www.festival-zone.0catch.com/Psilocybin-Festival.html

SHARK, G.W., 2003l, 'Greenham Common Peace Camp', online at: www.festival-zone.0catch.com/greenham-menu.html

SHARK, G.W., 2003m, 'Heathfield Free Festival', online at: www.festival-zone.0catch.com/heathfield.html

SHARK, G.W., 2003n, 'Cannabis Law Reform Rally', online at: www.festival-zone.0catch.com/law-reform.html

SHARK, G.W., 2003o, 'Pure Energy Fair', online at: www.festival-zone.0catch.com/pure-energy-fair.html

SHARK, G.W., 2003p, 'Cleeve Common Free Festival', online at: www.festival-zone.0catch.com/cleeve-common-1985.html

SHARK, G.W., 2003q, 'Avebury Free Festival', online at: www.festival-zone.0catch.com/avebury-free-festival.html

SHELLEY, Percy Bysshe, 1820, 'Song of Proserpine'

SMITH, Donald, 1986, letter from Donald Smith, Chief Constable of Wiltshire, to Mr B. Oubridge, Mr D. Aitken and others, 19 June 1986, Appendix 2 in NCCL, 'Stonehenge'

SMITH, John, 1771, *Choir Gaur: the Grand Orrery of the Ancient Druids Commonly Called Stonehenge*

SOUDEN, David, 1997, *Stonehenge: Mysteries of the Stones and Landscape*, Collins and Brown in association with English Heritage

STARHAWK, 1979, *The Spiral Dance: A Rebirth of the Religion of the Great Goddess*, Harper and Row

STARHAWK, 1987, *Truth or Dare*, Harper and Row

STONE, C.J., 1996, *Fierce Dancing*, Faber and Faber

STONE, C.J., 1999, *The Last of the Hippies*, Faber and Faber

STONEHENGE CAMPAIGN, 1998, Stonehenge Campaign News '98, online at: homepages.tcp.co.uk/~ait/news98.html

STONEHENGE CAMPAIGN, 2000, 'Media Reports: Summer Solstice 2000', online at: homepages.tcp.co.uk/~ait/news00.html

STONEHENGE CAMPAIGN, 2001, 'Media Reports: Summer Solstice 2001', online at: homepages.tcp.co.uk/~ait/news01.html

STONEHENGE CAMPAIGN, 2002, 'Media Reports: Summer Solstice 2002', online at: homepages.tcp.co.uk/~ait/news02.html

STOUT, Adam, 2001, 'Making the Past: The Politics of Prehistory', *3rd Stone* 40, 34–42

STOUT, Adam, 2003, 'The World Turned Upside Down', *3rd Stone* 46, 38–42

STUKELEY, William, 1723, 'The history of the temples and religion of the antient Celts', Cardiff Public Library, MS. 4.253

STUKELEY, William, 1740, *Stonehenge, A Temple Restor'd to the British Druids*

STUKELEY, William, 1743, *Abury Described*

SUBURBAN GUERILLAS, 1989, 'Stonehenge Solstice '89: The Suburban Guerilla Files', Hawkfrendz Publications 10

SUBURBAN GUERILLAS, 1990, 'Stonehenge Decoded', Hawkfrendz Publications 15

SUBURBAN GUERILLAS, 1991, 'The Trial of the Beanfield', Suburban Guerillas Publications 9

SUSTER, Gerald, 1988, *The Legacy of the Beast*, Allen

SYMONDS, John, 1971, *The Great Beast*, Macdonald

TAT (Travellers Aid Trust), 1988, 'TAT', booklet, included with TAT benefit LP

THOM, A., 1967, *Megalithic Sites in Britain*, Oxford UP

THOMAS, J., 1991, *Rethinking the Neolithic*, Cambridge UP

TIBETAN UKRANIAN MOUNTAIN TROUPE, 2003, 'Book of the Road 1980–82', online at: www.festival-zone.0catch.com/tibetans.html

TILLEY, Chris, 1994, *A Phenomenology of Landscape*, Berg

TLIO (The Land Is Ours), 2002, 'TLIO – Who & What?' online at: www.thelandisours.org/aims/who.html

TOLAND, John, 1726, *A Collection of Several Pieces of Mr John Toland*

TOLAND, John, 1747, 'A Specimen of the Critical History of the Celtic Religion and Learning: containing an Account of the Druids' in *Miscellaneous Works*

TRC (Truth and Reconciliation Committee), 2003, Reports of meetings, online at: www.greenleaf.demon.co.uk/trc.htm

TRENEMAN, Ann, 1998, 'Can Cornwall survive the solar eclipse?' *The Independent*, 29 December 1998

TRULL, D., 1998, 'Druids Go Home to Stonehenge', online at:
     www.noveltynet.org/content/paranormal/www.parascope.com/articles/slips/
     fs27_2.htm

UCKO, P.J., 1962, 'The Interpretation of Prehistoric Anthropomorphic figurines',
     Journal of the Royal Anthropological Institute 92, 38-54
UCKO, P.J., 1968, *Anthropomorphic figurines of Predynastic Egypt and Neolithic
     Crete with Comparative Material from the Prehistoric Near East and
     Mainland Greece*, Royal Anthropological Institute
UNDERWOOD, G., 1969, *The Pattern of the Past*, Museum Press

VIZIONDANZ, Brian, 2002, stonehengepeace email, 8 October 2002, online at:
     stonehengepeace@yahoogroups.com

WAINWRIGHT, Geoffrey, 1989, *The Henge Monuments: Ceremony and Society in
     Prehistoric Britain*, Thames and Hudson
WALKER, Helen, 1987, 'The Outdoor Movement in England & Wales 1900-1939',
     Sussex D.Phil. thesis
WALLIS, R.J. and J. BLAIN, 2001, 'Sacred Sites, Contested Rites/Rights:
     Contemporary Pagan Engagements with the Past', online at:
     www.sacredsites.org.uk
WARNER, Rex (trans.), 1960, *Julius Caesar: War Commentaries*, Collins
WEIRD WILTSHIRE, 2003, Stone Formation News Archive 1964-2003, online at:
     www.weirdwiltshire.co.uk/stones/archive.html
WELCH, Penny, 2003, 'Feminist Theory and the Contemporary Women's
     Movement: Selected campaigns of the 1980s', online at:
     pers-www.wlv.ac.uk/~le1810/1980s.htm
WILTSHIRE POLICE, 1981, an overview of policing Stonehenge from the 1950s to
     the 1980s, reproduced as 'The Police Viewpoint', online at:
     www.festival-zone.0catch.com/henge-police.html
WILTSHIRE RECORD OFFICE, 1966, WRO 2860/21, 'Report of meeting to discuss
     summer solstice arrangements at Stonehenge', 6 January 1966
WILTSHIRE RECORD OFFICE, 1970, WRO 2860/20, copy of letter from J.M.
     Melhuish to J.B. Score
WINWOOD, H.H., 1868, *Proceedings of the Bath Natural History and Antiquities
     Field Club* 2, 73–4
WOMEN'S LIBRARY, The, 2001, 'The Greenham Common Collection:
     Administrative/Biographical History', Archives Hub, online at:
     www.archiveshub.ac.uk/news/greenham.html
WOOD, John, 1747, *Choire Gaure, Vulgarly called Stonehenge, on Salisbury Plain*
WOOLLEY, Leonard and Jacquetta HAWKES, 1963, *Prehistory and The Beginnings
     of Civilization*, Harper and Row
WRIGHT, C.E. and Ruth C. (eds.), 1966, *The Diary of Humphrey Wanley*,
     Bibliographical Society
YOUNG, Elizabeth and Wayland KENNET, 2000, 'Stonehenge: the Saga
     Continues', *Journal of Architectural Conservation* 3, November 2000, 70–
     85, online at: www.savestonehenge.org.uk/saga.html

Index

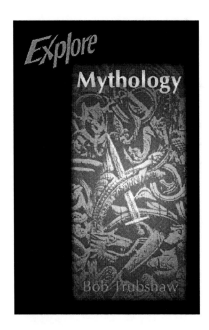

Explore Mythology

Bob Trubshaw

Myths are usually thought of as something to do with 'traditional cultures'. The study of such 'traditional' myths emphasises their importance in religion, national identity, hero-figures, understanding the origin of the universe, and predictions of an apocalyptic demise. The academic study of myths has done much to fit these ideas into the preconceived ideas of the relevant academics.

Only in recent years have such long-standing assumptions about myths begun to be questioned, opening up whole new ways of thinking about the way such myths define and structure how a society thinks about itself and the 'real world'.

These new approaches to the study of myth reveal that, to an astonishing extent, modern day thinking is every bit as 'mythological' as the world-views of, say, the Classical Greeks or obscure Polynesian tribes. Politics, religions, science, advertising and the mass media are all deeply implicated in the creation and use of myths.

Explore Mythology provides a lively introduction to the way myths have been studied, together with discussion of some of the most important 'mythic motifs' – such as heroes, national identity, and 'central places' – followed by a discussion of how these ideas permeate modern society. These sometimes contentious and profound ideas are presented in an easily readable style of writing.

ISBN 1 872883 62 1
Perfect bound. Demi 8vo (215 x 138 mm), 220 + xx pages, 17 line drawings. **£9.95**

Explore Folklore

Bob Trubshaw

**'A howling success, which plugs a
big and obvious gap'**
Professor Ronald Hutton

There have been fascinating
developments in the study of folklore
in the last twenty-or-so years, but few
books about British folklore and folk
customs reflect these exciting new
approaches. As a result there is a
huge gap between scholarly approaches to folklore studies and 'popular
beliefs' about the character and history of British folklore. *Explore Folklore*
is the first book to bridge that gap, and to show how much 'folklore' there is
in modern day Britain.

Explore Folklore shows there is much more to folklore than morris dancing
and fifty-something folksingers! The rituals of 'what we do on our holidays',
funerals, stag nights and 'lingerie parties' are all full of 'unselfconscious' folk
customs. Indeed, folklore is something that is integral to all our lives – it is so
intrinsic we do not think of it as being 'folklore'.

The implicit ideas underlying folk lore and customs are also explored.
There might appear to be little in common between people who touch wood
for luck (a 'tradition' invented in the last 200 years) and legends about
people who believe they have been abducted and subjected to intimate
body examinations by aliens. Yet, in their varying ways, these and other
'folk beliefs' reflect the wide spectrum of belief and disbelief in what is
easily dismissed as 'superstition'.

Explore Folklore provides a lively introduction to the study of most genres of
British folklore, presenting the more contentious and profound ideas in a
readily accessible manner.

ISBN 1 872883 60 5
Perfect bound, demi 8vo (215x138 mm), 200 pages, **£9.95**

Explore
Shamanism

Alby Stone

Shamanism is a complex and confusing subject. There are many different ideas about what shamanism is, who is a shaman, and what a shaman does. *Explore Shamanism* provides a much-needed up-to-date guide to the study of shamanism.

Focusing mainly on the shamans of Siberia and Central Asia, *Explore Shamanism* includes a historical survey of academic approaches to shamanism, an overview of the various theories about shamanism, and a discussion of the origins of shamanism based on the latest ideas. There are also more detailed explorations of the initiation of shamans; the costumes, drums and other tools of the shaman's trade; journeys to the spirit world; and the place of trance, spirit possession and ecstasy in shamanic performance.

Explore Shamanism also surveys revived and reconstructed shamanisms in the world today.

Alby Stone has been studying and writing about shamanism for twenty years.

ISBN 1 872883 68 0.
Perfect bound, Demi 8vo (215 x 138 mm), 184 + x pages, 2 photographs; 17 line drawings, **£9.95**

Explore Green Men

Mercia MacDermott
with photographs by
Ruth Wylie

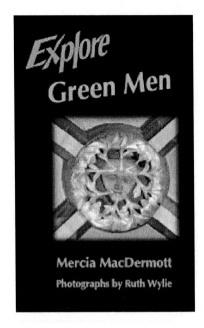

Explore Green Men is the first detailed study of the history of this motif for 25 years. Dr MacDermott's research follows the Green Man back from the previous earliest known examples into its hitherto unrecognised origins in India about 2,300 years ago.

The book starts by discussing the 'paganisation' of Green Men in recent decades, then follows backwards through the Victorian Gothic Revival, Baroque, Rococo and Italianate revivals, to their heyday in the Gothic and the supposed origins in the Romanesque. As part of this discussion there is background information on the cultural changes that affected how Green Men were regarded. The author also discusses the comparisons that have been made with Cernunnus, Robin Hood, Jack-in-the-Green, woodwoses, Baphomet, Al Khidr and Bulgarian *peperuda*. She also investigates which pagan god Green Men supposedly represent.

Explore Green Men is illustrated with 110 photographs and drawings, mostly of Green Men who have never before showed their faces in books.

This book will appeal to all with an interest in Green Men and to art historians looking for a reliable study of this fascinating decorative motif.

ISBN 1 872883 66 4

Perfect bound, demi 8vo (215 x 138 mm), 216 pages, 108 b&w photos, 2 line drawings **£9.95**

Heart of Albion

Publishing folklore, mythology and
local history since 1989

Further details of all Heart of Albion titles online at
www.hoap.co.uk

All titles available direct from Heart of Albion Press.

Heart of Albion Press
113 High Street, Avebury
Marlborough, SN8 1RF

Phone: 01672 539077
email: albion@indigogroup.co.uk
Web site: www.hoap.co.uk